Advance Praise for

Meditations on Creation in an Era of Extinction

"This is a stunning contribution to our understanding of extinction and its myriad challenges. It is a brilliant weaving of Christian theology, personal reflection, and environmental action. One of the most engaging books I have read in some time—destined to become a classic." —**Mary Evelyn Tucker, co-director, Yale Forum on Religion and Ecology**

"This book explores the evolution of humanity's environmental impact on creation and the colonial lens and cultural biases destroying our world. The ecological crisis in Australia and around the globe is of critical concern to the First Nations people. We consider ourselves the original conservationists, and our culture, law, ceremonies, and relationship with the Spirit Creator are founded on our connection and relationship with our Country. First Nations people have protested mining, pastoral destruction, and farming erosion on our lands for centuries and our protest has fallen on deaf ears. The Western empire, in its pursuit of power and wealth, stole lands, committed genocide, raped, and committed all manner of atrocities and, in so doing, separated themselves from the Spirit Creator and creation. Land has lost its spiritual and relational value and has been replaced as an economic commodity. History clearly records the growth of empires and the destruction of land, waterways, and seas. Empire's greed has disconnected them from the Spiritual life force of 'Mother Earth.' I highly recommend this book as it highlights the First Nations people's relationship to land, gives rise to their voices, and provides a soul-filling and life-giving perspective." —**Anne Pattel-Gray, professor and head of the School of Indigenous Studies, University of Divinity, Naarm (Melbourne)**

"In this brilliantly creative and lucid book, Rigby takes the ancient concept of the Hexameron found in early Church literature, and then brings it to life in dialogue with reflections on current eco-social issues. Rigby does not turn away from prophetic witness when considering the darker aspects of our earthly condition, and, step by step, walks the reader through scholarly material that is both profound and richly provocative. Woven into this narrative are moving stories arising from interviews of the author with those who have committed themselves to care for other creatures. There is a mystic quality to this book that is both ancient and deeply moving, since it draws its sources from contemplative practices, leading to a deep reflection on the demise of creatures that are being lost in our own lifetimes. This is a beautifully written and novel book that deserves wide readership." —**Celia Deane-Drummond, director, Laudato Si' Research Institute, and senior research fellow, Campion Hall, University of Oxford**

"Kate Rigby wraps the relentless reality of Earth's crisis in the gorgeous green forcefield of these Meditations. I know no other work that so brilliantly unfolds the mythic six days of Creation for our day: with delightfully fresh exegesis, graciously served natural science, and gripping narrative flow, her prophetic voice activates possibility right on the threshold of Too Late." —**Catherine Keller, George T. Cobb Professor of Constructive Theology, Drew University Theological School, and author,** *Facing Apocalypse: Climate, Democracy and Other Last Chances*

"We live in a time when the sacred body of the earth is marred by a multitude of extinctions. And each extinction is decreation. In a deeply lyrical and personal manner, Kate Rigby leads us on a spiritual meditation along the creaturely paths of conservation, loss, and hope. Voices and faces of animals, fragile humans, and hidden divinities intertwine in this spiritual hymn to the ecologies of the sacred, producing one of the most surprising and intimate works of contemporary environmentalism." —**Serenella Iovino, professor, University of North Carolina at Chapel Hill**

Meditations on Creation
in an Era of Extinction

ECOLOGY AND JUSTICE
An Orbis Series on Integral Ecology

ADVISORY BOARD MEMBERS

Mary Evelyn Tucker
John A. Grim
Leonardo Boff
Sean McDonagh

The Orbis Series on Integral Ecology publishes books seeking to integrate an understanding of Earth's interconnected life systems with sustainable social, political, and economic systems that enhance the Earth community. Books in the series concentrate on ways to:

- Reexamine human-Earth relations in light of contemporary cosmological and ecological science
- Develop visions of common life marked by ecological integrity and social justice
- Expand on the work of those exploring such fields as integral ecology, climate justice, Earth law, ecofeminism, and animal protection
- Promote inclusive participatory strategies that enhance the struggle of Earth's poor and oppressed for ecological justice
- Deepen appreciation for dialogue within and among religious traditions on issues of ecology and justice
- Encourage spiritual discipline, social engagement, and the transformation of religion and society toward these ends

Viewing the present moment as a time for fresh creativity and inspired by the encyclical *Laudato si'*, the series seeks authors who speak to ecojustice concerns and who bring into this dialogue perspectives from the Christian communities, from the world's religions, from secular and scientific circles, or from new paradigms of thought and action.

ECOLOGY & JUSTICE SERIES

Meditations on Creation in an Era of Extinction

KATE RIGBY

ORBIS BOOKS

Maryknoll, New York 10545

Founded in 1970, Orbis Books endeavors to publish works that enlighten the mind, nourish the spirit, and challenge the conscience. The publishing arm of the Maryknoll Fathers and Brothers, Orbis seeks to explore the global dimensions of the Christian faith and mission, to invite dialogue with diverse cultures and religious traditions, and to serve the cause of reconciliation and peace. The books published reflect the views of their authors and do not represent the official position of the Maryknoll Society. To learn more about Maryknoll and Orbis Books, please visit our website at www.orbisbooks.com.

Translations from Genesis and transliterations of key Hebrew terms, are taken from Robert Alter, *Genesis: Translation and Commentary* (New York: W. W. Norton, 1997). Unless otherwise indicated, all other biblical quotations are from *The New Oxford Annotated Bible* (*NRSV*), augmented 3rd ed., ed. Michael D. Coogan (Oxford: Oxford University Press, 2007).

"Galaxy Song," written by Eric Idle & John Du Prez, copyright © Python (Monty) Pictures Limited, reprinted with permission from Kay-Gee-Bee Music Ltd.

"Restoring Sabbath" by Diane Pacitti, reprinted with permission.

Cover image: Leonard French, *Seven Days of Creation: The Seventh Day—All the days became one and everything was alive on the earth*, 1962–65. Enamel on hessian covered board, 366cm diameter. Gifted, 1965. Australian National University Art Collection. Used with permission from the Leonard French Estate.

Cover photo: David Paterson, Dorian Photographics.

Manufactured in the United States of America

Library of Congress Cataloging-in-Publication Data

Names: Rigby, Catherine E., author.
Title: Meditations on creation in an era of extinction / Kate Rigby.
Description: Maryknoll, NY : Orbis Books, [2023] | Includes bibliographical references and index. | Summary: "A collection of theological meditations on creation and extinction guided by Genesis 1"— Provided by publisher.
Identifiers: LCCN 2023012398 (print) | LCCN 2023012399 (ebook) | ISBN 9781626985506 | ISBN 9798888660089 (epub)
Subjects: LCSH: Creation—Meditations. | Bible. Genesis, I—Meditations. | Extinction (Biology)—Miscellanea.
Classification: LCC BL227 .R54 2023 (print) | LCC BL227 (ebook) | DDC 231.7/65—dc23/eng20230722
LC record available at https://lccn.loc.gov/2023012398
LC ebook record available at https://lccn.loc.gov/2023012399

John Shelley Nurser (1929–2020)

Contents

Acknowledgments

These meditations on creation were a very long time in the making.

I was first introduced to Basil of Caesarea's *Hexamaeron* and the largely forgotten Christian literary genre of meditations on the six days of creation over twenty years ago by my then colleague at Monash University, Kevin Hart. We have exchanged notes on our respective explorations of the hexameron, and of the Christian contemplative tradition, sporadically ever since. It is to Kevin, then, that my first thanks are due.

It was only many years later, however, that I finally turned to this project in earnest. For this, I am indebted to the encouragement of the marvelously multidisciplinary team of writers and researchers called together at Duke University between 2018 and 2020 by Norman Wirzba and Jedediah Purdy, with the support of a grant from the Henry Luce Foundation. Among the contributors to our lively conversations around "Facing the Anthropocene," I am especially grateful to Norman, Janet Soskice, and Willie Jennings for theological guidance; Robin Wall Kimmerer for insights into ethnobotany; and Mari Joerstad, both for practical assistance and biblical expertise.

Further inspiration came from my participation in a UK Arts and Humanities Research Council network on "Extinction and Religion," led by Stefan Skrimshire and Jeremy Kidwell, during the same period. I am grateful for the opportunity to collaborate with them on this question and with other participants, especially James Hatley, Willis Jenkins, Timothy Leduc, and Lisa Sideris.

Among the many others whose conversations about matters theological, biblical, and eco-religious have nourished this work, I am indebted to Celia Deane-Drummond, Anne Elvey, Jacob Erickson, Norman Habel, Laurel Kearns, Catherine Keller, Russell Re Manning, and Maria Nita. For their special assistance with the "Third Day," I am also grateful to Fábio Py Murta de Almeida and José Augusto Pádua, and for translations, to Clarice Corfield and Rita Sousa-Silva. For his eager encouragement and expert assistance on the medieval period, I am particularly grateful to Constant Mews.

I was able to start writing this book—one that turned out to be not so much a scholarly book *about* the hexameral tradition, but a creative extension *of* it—with the assistance of a research fellowship from the Rachel Carson Center in Munich. I am immensely grateful to the RCC and to my fellow fellows, who provided welcome feedback on my work in progress: Antoine Acker, Jemma Dear, Stefan Dorondel, Tatiana Kasperski, Cherry Leonardi, Julia Leyda, Ute Hasenöhrl, Huiying Ng, Astrid Schrader, Nicole Seymour, and Tom Smith.

The book was completed only after my relocation to Germany from England early in 2022 to take up my current position as Alexander von Humboldt Professor of Environmental Humanities at the University of Cologne. My thanks are therefore due also to the Alexander von Humboldt Foundation, to all the team in our research hub for Multidisciplinary Environmental Studies in the Humanities, and, above all, to Saskia Maassen for her prodigious editorial assistance.

Special thanks are due to all those whom I interviewed for this project and to the organizations and initiatives with which they work in the defense of the living Earth and its diverse denizens, human and otherwise, at this time of planetary imperilment: Rabbi Jonathan Keren-Black and Thea Ormerod (GreenFaith

Australia-ARRCC); Marcia Maria de Oliveira (REPAM); Brooks Berndt (United Churches of Christ); Prof. Dr. Mathew Koshy Punnackadu (Church of South India); Dr. Robert Sluka and Queen Elizabeth Hare (A Rosha Kenya); Christina Nellist (POCA); and Rev. Lucy Winckett, Catherine Tidnam, Deborah Colvin, Sara Mark, and Diane Pacitti (St James's, Piccadilly).

As will become apparent, it is appropriate that I should also give thanks for my canine companions, especially the first, the motherly Lucy, who appears on the "Sixth Day," and the lovely Laska, who died right at the time that I embarked on writing this book.

As ever, I thank Robert Hartley, who has nourished and enlivened me in body, mind, and soul these past four decades and more.

For access to Leonard French's artwork "The Seventh Day," a photo of which graces the front cover, I am indebted to Linda Williams, Lisa and Sarah French, Oscar Capezio, Curator of the Australian National University's Art Collection, and the photographer, David Paterson.

I am also immensely grateful to Tom Hermans-Webster for his enthusiasm for this endeavor and his discerning editorial advice, together with all at Orbis Books for seeing it through to publication.

This book is dedicated to Canon John Shelley Nurser (1929–2020), who was among the first to raise the alarm about the plight of our planet within the Church of England.
As dean of St. Mark's Theological Centre in Canberra, Australia, he hosted the 1973 National Summer School on Religion, with a focus on this question, the proceeds of which were published in a volume called *Living with Nature*. Exactly four decades later, exasperated by the lack of meaningful action to arrest what he had long discerned was the ecocidal trajectory of fossil-fueled industrial modernity, he published an article in the *International Journal of Environmental Studies* titled, with his characteristic wry humor but also with deep anguish, "Global Suicide Is Unacceptable to Christians—And Very

Odd for Anyone." Here he argued that religious institutions should play a stronger role in persuading the nations of the world "to take the initiatives needed for avoiding global suicide."[1] John, a dear family friend, was excited when I told him about my endeavors to revivify the hexameral tradition to this end. It is my great sadness that he did not live to see it published. I am grateful to his family, and especially his widow, Elizabeth, for permitting me to dedicate it to his memory.

Kate Rigby, Cologne
March 2023

---

[1] John Nurser, "Global Suicide Is Unacceptable to Christians—And Very Odd for Anyone," *International Journal of Environmental Studies* 70, no. 6 (2013): 862–71.

Abbreviations of Hexamora

Hexamora frequently cited in this book are denoted, in parenthetical citations, by the following abbreviations:

AA   Theophilus Antiocheus. *Ad Autolycum* (*Theophilus to Autolycus*), translated by Marcus Dodds, in *The Ante-Nicene Fathers: Translations of the Writings of the Fathers down to 325AD*, edited by Rev. Alexander Roberts and James Donaldson, revised by A. Cleveland Coxe, vol. II, *Fathers of the Second Century: Hermas, Tatian, Athenagoras, Theophilus and Clement of Alexandria (entire)*, 135–96. Available online from Christian Classics Ethereal Library.

AeH   Aelfric. *The Anglo-Saxon Version of the Hexaemeron of St. Basil, or "Be Godes Six Daga Weorcum" and the Remains of St. Basil's "Admonitio ad filem spiritualem,"* translated by Rev. Henry W. Norman. 2nd ed. London: John Russell Smith, 1849.

AmH   Ambrose. *Hexameron, Paradise, and Cain and Abel*, translated by John J. Savage. New York: Fathers of the Church, 1961.

AnH   Anastasios. *Hexaemeron*, translated by Clement A. Kuehn. Rome: Pontifical Oriental Institute, 2008.

BaH   Basil of Caesarea. "Hexaëmeron," in *Saint Basil of Caesarea and Saint Gregory of Nyssa, Hexaëmeron*

	with *On the Making of Man*, translated by Rev. Blom-field Jackson, 15–153. Brooklyn, MA: Paterikon Publications, 2017.
BeH	Bede. *On Genesis*, translated with introduction and notes by Calvin B. Kendall. Liverpool: Liverpool University Press, 2008.
BoH	Bonaventure. *Hexaemeron: Conferences on the Six Days of Creation*, translated and notes by Jay M. Hammond. St. Bonaventure University: Franciscan Institute Publications, 2018.
CHoG	John Chrysostom. *Homilies on Genesis 1–17*, translated by Robert C. Hill. Washington, DC: Catholic University of America Press, 1986.
CW	Hugh of St. Victor. "On the Creation of the World," in *Trinity and Creation*, edited by Boyd Taylor Coolman and Dale M. Coulter, 130–39. Turnhout: Brepols, 2018.
DN	John the Scot (Joannus Scotus Eriugena). *Perephyseon: On the Division of Nature*, translated by Myra I. Uhlferler, with summaries by Jean A. Potter. Indianapolis: Bobbs-Merrill, 1979.
ESW	Abelard, Peter. *An Exposition of the Six-Day Work*, introduced, translated and notes by Wantda Zemler-Cizewski. Turnhout: Brepols, 2011.
LCG	Augustine. "Unfinished Literal Commentary on Genesis," in St. Augustine, *On Genesis*, edited by John E. Rotelle, introduction, translation, and notes by Edmund Hill. 111–55. New York: New City Press, 2020.
MoSDC	Traherne, Thomas. *Meditations on the Six Days of the Creation*, edited by George Robert Guffey. 1717; repr. New York: Augustan Reprint Society Press, 1966.

NoG   Hugh of St. Victor. "Notes on Genesis," in *Interpre-*
          tation of Scripture: Practice: A Selection of Works of
          Hugh, Andrew, Richard, and Leonius of St. Victor,
          and of Robert of Melun, Peter Comestor and Maurice
          of Sully, edited by Frans van Liere and Franklin T.
          Harkins, 63–68. Turnhout: Brepols, 2015.

OC   Philo. "On the Account of the World's Creation
          Given by Moses," in *Philo*, vol. 1, translated by F. H.
          Colson and G. H. Whitaker, 6–123. Cambridge,
          MA: Harvard University Press, 1929.

OHoG   Origen. *Homilies on Genesis and Exodus*, translated by
          Ronald E. Heine. Washington, DC: Catholic Univer-
          sity of America Press, 2002.

OMM   Gregory of Nyssa. "On the Making of Man," in
          Saint Basil of Caesarea and Saint Gregory of Nyssa,
          Hexaëmeron with On the Making of Man, translated
          by Rev. Blomfield Jackson, 161–258. Brooklyn, MA:
          Paterikon Publications, 2017.

SDC   Grosseteste, Robert. *On the Six Days of Creation,*
          a translation of the Hexaëmeron by F. C. J. Martin.
          Oxford University Press, 1996.

INTRODUCTION

"How long will the land mourn?"

Jer. 12:4

The Road to Kunming

In April 2020, villagers in the southern Chinese province of Yunan were amazed by the appearance of a herd of elephants in their midst. These itinerant elephants, it turns out, had ventured forth sometime the previous month from the Xishuangbanna National Nature Reserve around sixty miles farther south on the border with Laos and Myanmar, and they were still set on heading north. By the time they reached Yuanjiang County, over 250 miles from the reserve, a couple had turned back, but more had been born. Traveling night and day, nourishing themselves on pilfered crops, raided grain stores, and subsequently, gifted food put out to steer them away from human habitations, in early June 2021 they arrived, stressed and exhausted, on the edge of the provincial capital Kunming, a city of over eight million residents nearly four hundred miles from their home. There, they were finally intercepted and coaxed to turn around to retrace their weary steps to the reserve.

By the time they entered the final leg of their homeward trek in August, China's by now world-famous wandering elephants had consumed a whopping 180 tons of corn, bananas, and other food laid out for them; they had caused 150,000 people to be temporarily evacuated from their homes; and their damages bill was variously estimated at around $1 million.[1] They had also focused the world's attention on the precarious plight of Asian elephants and other endangered animals during the very year in which the UN's fifteenth conference of the Parties to the Convention on Biological Diversity (COP 15) was due to meet in China. As it happened, the conference had to be postponed, first for one year, and then another, and was eventually relocated to Montreal, where it finally took place in December 2022. But COP 15 was originally to have been held in Kunming, and at the inaugural session held in October 2021, a short-film made by the Yunnan government TV station was screened, which celebrated the trek of the Short-Trunk Clan as a successful instance of human-animal conflict resolution.[2]

While Asian elephants are known to roam, none from the Xishuangbanna Reserve had ever traveled so far out of their terrain into more densely populated areas and toward a cooler climatic zone for which they are ill-suited. It would surely be unduly anthropomorphic to assume that this herd, led by one or more matriarchs, as is the way with elephants, had a specific destination in mind. Looking on remotely from my own human perspective, however, and with an eye for symbolism, their trek struck me as something like a protest march, perhaps even a pilgrimage of sorts: one that cried out for our attention. It was as if these elephants had come to Kunming as emissaries of the wider communion of creatures: making their presence felt at the city gates in the lead-up to the

---

[1] Tessa Wong, "There and Back Again: The Epic Adventures of China's Wandering Elephants," *BBC News,* August 16, 2021; Vivian Wang, "15 Chinese Elephants Are on a Long March North. Why, No One Knows," *New York Times*, September 3, 2021.

[2] Dan Smyer Yü, "Collapsing Elephant Climes since the Little Ice Age: Climate Refugees, Animal Zomia, and Elephant Modernity in Yunnan," in Dan Smyer Yü and Jelle J. P. Wouters (eds), *Storying Multipolar Climes of the Himalaya, Andes and Artic: Anthropocenic Climate and Shapeshifting Watery Lifeworlds* (London: Routledge, 2023), 236–252; 236.

crucial conference at which the assembled delegates were to thrash out urgently needed measures to arrest the cascade of extinctions that is accelerating around the world as biomes are destroyed, the planet warms, and the abundance and diversity of Earth's free-living animals, plants, and fungi continue to dwindle.

Meanwhile, another entity was on the move. It too had set out from a location in China, probably the infamous Huanan Seafood Wholesale Market in Wuhan, Hubei Province. By the time the elephants from southern Yunan had started heading north, the novel coronavirus identified by Chinese medical authorities in January 2020 had gone global. And by the time they arrived back in the reserve, it had been decided to defer the major face-to-face meeting of COP 15 yet another year.

How are we to hear what Pope Francis has called the "cry of the earth" when we are enclosed within exclusively human worlds of concern, communication, and, all too often, conflict?[3] How are we to apprehend the Earth's cry when ever more of us live in proliferating cities that are remote from the places, people, and other beings who provide for our pressing daily needs? This is, to be sure, no easy feat for most of us. But once you have attuned your senses, opened your heart, and enlarged your mind, you will begin to hear this cry issuing ever more urgently from near and far, and in a variety of keys and media. The wandering elephants of Yunan might not have been intending to make their voices heard at COP 15: but their epic journey was, on one level, a cry of distress on the part of the elephants and a wake-up call for humans. Yet the story of their quest offers inspiration as well, for it also bears witness to the will to survive, the potential for ecological recovery, and the possibility of social reorientation.

Asian elephants have been doing it tough. Found across a variety of habitats, including grasslands, forests, and scrublands,

---

[3] Pope Francis, *Laudato si'* (Vatican City: Vatican Press, 2015).

from altitudes of nearly ten thousand feet down to sea level, they once ranged across about five million square miles, from the Middle East along the Iranian coast into the Indian subcontinent and China and beyond into Southeast Asia as far as Borneo. Thanks to the seeds that they distribute over large distances in their dung, they play an important role in maintaining plant diversity and shaping ecosystems. While the western populations in the Middle East had probably become extinct around 100 BCE, with those in China already largely eliminated some six hundred years ago, it is only in recent decades that increased human encroachment on their homeplaces and disruption of their lifeways—exacerbated by the illegal trade in their body parts—especially tusks and skin, has landed the Asian elephant on the Red List of Endangered Species of the International Union for Conservation of Nature (IUCN). Meanwhile, fragmentation of their habitat is bringing them into more frequent conflict with local communities, leading to human crop and property damage, injuries, and even deaths, in turn inciting revenge killing of elephants.[4]

Once widely distributed across southern China, by the mid-1990s fewer than two hundred Asian elephants survived there, principally in the Mengyang section of the Xishuangbanna Reserve. Within this refuge, their population has begun to recover, and although they still only constitute less than 1 percent of the global population, free-living Asian elephants are now thought to number nearly three hundred individuals in China. Thanks to strictly enforced legal protections, the growing Mengyang population has also been recolonizing neighboring areas. During this same period, however, their forested habitat has declined by some 15 percent, while conservation policies favoring a denser canopy

---

[4] C. Williams, S. K. Tiwari, V. R. Goswami, S. de Silva, A. Kumar, N. Baskaran, K. Yoganand, and V. Menon, *Elephas maximus, Asian Elephant*, IUCN Red List of Threatened Species 2020: e.T7140A45818198.

cover in that which remains have effectively reduced their food supply by shading out their preferred forage plants. Add to this a severe drought, almost certainly linked to climate change, and it appears likely that the troupe that headed to Kunming, like that which dispersed south from Mengyang around the same time, were in search of new territory to support their growing population. In a further twist to this tale, elephant experts surmise that it was the lull in human activity occasioned by the pandemic that initially lured them further afield.[5]

The case of the Kunming elephants, then, exemplifies many of the contradictions that currently beset human interrelationships with other living kinds. Their quest for new territory testifies, on the one hand, to a conservation success story, and, on the other, to ongoing pressure on wildlife habitat, not only from the expansion of agricultural, urban, and industrial land use, but also, increasingly, from human-caused global heating. Moreover, the expanding elephant population, not unlike that of wolves in parts of Europe and North America, in combination with habitat fragmentation, is leading to more frequent altercations with humans, with negative outcomes for all concerned. As a consequence of the global media attention garnered by their quest for new food sources, replete with endearing images of afternoon naps, mud baths, and play fights, the Kunming elephants made an engaging case for the need to make space for wildlife, while also ensuring protection for human communities who could be adversely affected by their potentially dangerous other-than-human neighbors: a case, that is, for protocols and practices for multispecies coexistence, entailing attitudinal changes as well as pragmatic measures.

---

[5] Ahimsa Campos-Arceiz et al., "The Return of the Elephants: How Two Groups of Dispersing Elephants Attracted the Attention of Billions and What Can We Learn from Their Behavior," *Conservation Letters* 14, no. 6 (2021): e12836.

Meanwhile, the fact that humans were holed up indoors to reduce the spread of COVID-19 evidently provided welcome affordances for these dispersing elephants, as it did for many free-living animals around the world. Yet the emergence of the virus itself, arising as it appears to have done from a situation in which trafficked wildlife and domesticated animals were being held in cruelly cramped conditions awaiting consumption, also testifies to the hazards that are occasioned by human exploitation of other creatures and their environs. For while many politicians have found it convenient to demonize the virus, if we trace it back to its source, we discover, Oedipus-like, that the true culprit is our own kind. From this perspective, the COVID-19 pandemic is another manifestation of Earth's cry—one that we ignore at our peril.

My goal in this book is to amplify Earth's cry, as well as disclosing its entwinement with what Pope Francis calls the "cry of the poor": the many ways, in other words, in which the diminishment of Earth's other-than-human kinds and wildlife population numbers, the degradation of our shared earthly environs, and the disordering of the climate are entangled with forms of social exclusion, domination, and inequity. At the same time I uphold the voices of those who are seeking to redress these ills, opening pathways toward more just, compassionate, and life-affirming patterns of coexistence with one another and our fellow earthlings within the wider communion of creatures.

Creation Stories:
Revisiting the "Six Days Work"

One of the peculiarities of human beings is that we evidently pose a problem to ourselves. I am not just talking about our tendency to make trouble for ourselves (along with many others besides)— although that is also part of the picture. What I am referring to here, rather, is our propensity to puzzle over our very existence. *Why are we here? What are we good for? What is our purpose? How should we relate to others?* We might not be alone in this. As far as we can tell, though, humans are the only earthlings who are inclined to try to answer these questions with stories that get passed down from generation to generation—whether in oral, pictorial, or written form, getting told in new media, accreting new meanings, and shaping the self-understanding of entire cultures until such time as they are felt to no longer ring true and so lose their grip as an explanatory framework.

These narratives commonly take the form of creation stories. Unlike scientific accounts, such stories are concerned not so much with the physical processes of cosmogenesis as with questions of meaning, value, and purpose—questions that properly lie outside the remit of the natural sciences. In that respect, they are not rendered redundant by advances in scientific knowledge; science on its own is no good substitute for these older tales, although it might well inform how we categorize and interpret them. Traditional creation stories are wondrously many and varied, but they share one crucial feature: they all imagine human beings being brought into a world that was not of our own making.

What are we to make of such creation narratives in an epoch when that is no longer entirely the case: an epoch that geologists—not unproblematically—have named the "Anthropocene," in which the consequences of human activities are likely to define Earth's geology for millennia into the future?

Now, lest we fall prey to hubris, it is important to note that children being born today still find themselves in a wider world that precedes and exceeds human fashioning: one in which a supervolcanic eruption, for instance, or a massive meteor strike could put all the changes that human societies have wrought on this one planet very much in the shade. Yet these human-made changes run deep: they are extremely wide-ranging and mind-bogglingly long-term. Among them are the proliferation of novel materials, such as aluminum, steel, plastic, and concrete, with a corresponding diminution of naturally occurring land cover; a massive increase in the prevalence of humans and their domesticated plants and animals, and a startling decrease in other-than-human free-living species; and the mushrooming circulation of sundry potentially pesky chemicals, notably radioactive plutonium from nuclear reactions, phosphorus and nitrogen from chemical fertilizers, and carbon dioxide and methane, primarily from the combustion of fossil fuels, but also, in the case of the latter, from the aforementioned livestock.[6]

For the most part, these industrial-era Earth system alterations, which began in England in the late eighteenth century but accelerated big-time from the 1950s, are also not good—at least not from the perspective of most living organisms, including ourselves. Just how bad they are shows up most clearly in two sets of statistics: extinction rates and economic disparity. The former charts the precipitous decline in the abundance and diversity of free-living animals, plants, and fungi. The extinction rate cannot be charted precisely, because most of the humbler kinds of critters, such as insects and soil microbiota, have been studied a lot less than more charismatic ones like birds and mammals. It is highly likely that many species are disappearing before they have even been identified by modern science. Nonetheless, the current estimate is that, in addition to those that have already been exterminated at human hands, albeit largely unintentionally, around 25 percent

---

[6] A good introduction to the basic science underlying the proposed Anthropocene epoch is Jan Zalasiewicz's *The Earth after Us: What Legacy Will Humans Leave in the Rocks?* (Oxford: Oxford University Press, 2008). For a more searching inquiry into the concept from the perspective of the humanities, and the various ways in which it is being used and contested, see Christophe Bonneuil and Jan-Baptiste Fressoz, *The Shock of the Anthropocene: The Earth, History, and Us*, trans. David Fernbach (London: Verso, 2016).

of Earth's living kinds (totaling at least one million species) are currently endangered, largely as a consequence of habitat destruction, pollution, and overexploitation, but increasingly also due to climate change. Shockingly, wildlife populations have evidently plummeted by nearly 70 percent since the 1970s.[7] While it is encouraging that the Montreal in the absence of effective policies to arrest climate change and redress unsustainable agriculture, fisheries, and forestry.[8]

The second set of statistics relating to economic disparity, which persists between regions of the Global South and the old industrial heartlands of the Global North and is actually growing in some of those nations (especially in the United States, Russia, and India),[9] shows clearly that the benefits and costs of the anthropogenic alteration of the planet are extremely unequally shared. Moreover, it is apparent that those who have contributed least to cause these changes are thus far suffering first and worst from their adverse consequences. This is dramatically so in the case of climate change, which, above 1.5 degrees of global temperature rise, is set to submerge several Pacific Island nations with some of the lowest per capita carbon emissions in the world. Meanwhile, the increase in the frequency and intensity of extreme weather events, which are now beginning to hit home in the old industrial heartlands

---

[7] S. Diaz et al., "Summary for Policymakers of the Global Assessment Report on Biodiversity and Ecosystem Services of the Intergovernmental Science–Policy Platform on Biodiversity and Ecosystem Services" (Bonn: IPBES Secretariat, 2019); World Wildlife Fund, *Living Planet Report 2022—Building a Nature Positive Society*, ed. R. E. A. Almond et al. (Gland, Switzerland: WWF, 2022).

[8] Convention on Biological Diversity 2022, "Kunming-Montreal Global Biodiversity Framework: Draft Decision Submitted by the President," December 18, 2022, 9.

[9] L. Chancel et al., *World Inequality Report 2022*, World Inequality Lab, wir2022.wid.world.

of the Global North, are causing carnage in many areas of the Global South, where people's existence is frequently precarious for other reasons as well.[10] Other forms of environmental adversity are also inequitably distributed, with those of lower socioeconomic standing, for example, more likely to be afflicted by various forms of pollution.[11] Nor are the impacts of biodiversity loss felt equally. Extinction is an inherently bio-cultural phenomenon that is "experienced, resisted, measured, enunciated, performed and narrated" in a variety of ways by different communities in different contexts.[12] For those who have strong affective ties, material dependence, or traditional kinship relations with specific species in decline, their dwindling and disappearance is bound to be particularly devastating.

For this reason I find the coinage "Anthropocene" misleading since it invokes an amorphous "humanity," masking salient differences among humans in terms of both culpability for, and vulnerability to, the earth system changes to which it refers. What is revealed in both of these sets of statistics, I believe, are the profound injustices inherent in a social order in which the efforts of a minority of humans to make the world more congenial to themselves (or so they imagined) has rendered it a whole lot less congenial for the majority of humans (including future generations), together with a significant proportion of our fellow earthlings of other kinds. The "cry of the Earth" and the "cry of the

[10] H.-O. Pörtner et al., "Summary for Policy Makers," in *Climate Change 2022: Impacts, Adaptation and Vulnerability. Contribution of Working Group II to the Sixth Assessment Report of the Intergovernmental Panel on Climate Change* (Cambridge: Cambridge University Press, 2022), 3–33.

[11] See "Fourth Day," later in this volume.

[12] D. B. Rose, T. van Dooren, and M. Chrulew, eds., *Extinction Studies: Stories of Time, Death, and Generations* (Durham, NC: Duke University Press, 2017), 2–3.

poor" are not one and the same, but they are intimately interlinked with one another.

From this perspective of unevenly shared planetary imperilment, then, I revisit in this book one of the historically most influential creation narratives: the account of the six days of creation from Genesis 1. This text was taken from the Hebrew sacred Scripture known as *Bereshit*, "In the beginning," in the Jewish Torah. However variously interpreted, it remains part of the religious inheritance of almost one-third of the world's human population today. Moreover, aspects of this creation story—notably, the exalted place that it accords humans in relation to our fellow creatures—continues to resonate in secular assumptions that privilege human knowledge, agency, and interests over those of other beings.

There are now two millennia of commentaries on this narrative within both the Jewish and Christian traditions. In this book I respond primarily to the latter, largely because I lack the expertise to do justice to the former, and also because it is the Christian take on creation that has had such a powerful influence on the dominant culture of the Western world.

In form, this book is inspired in particular by an ancient and, until recently, long-neglected genre of Christian literature that became known, in Greek, as the "hexameron." These were meditations on the biblical six (*hexa*) days (*hemera*) of creation, often in conversation with the natural philosophy of the time, and sometimes in the form of a sequence of homilies. The hexameral tradition took off in the fourth century with the remarkable homilies of Basil of Caesarea from 378 CE, although there were some important prior commentaries. The first recorded is "On the Account of the World's Creation Given by Moses" by the classically educated Jewish scholar Philo of Alexandria (c. 20 BCE–c. 50 CE). Early Christian commentators include Theophilus of Antioch (died c. 184), a pagan convert to Christianity, whose hexameron is incorporated into a series of books defending the new faith to a pagan friend (*Ad Autoctylus*), and Origen of Alexandria (c. 184–253 CE). Origen's unfinished *Hexapla*, a critical edition of the Hebrew Scriptures in the original with a transliteration, set alongside four different Greek translations, is regarded as the first work of Christian biblical scholarship. Following Basil's lead in the Eastern Church was John Chrysostom, whose homilies on Genesis 1–17 are believed to have been delivered in Antioch in 388.[13] The first Latin hexameron was composed by Ambrose, whose homilies on Genesis 1 were probably delivered during Holy Week in 387 in Milan, where he was then bishop. Ambrose's homilies are closely modeled on Basil's, as well as on the addendum written by Basil's younger brother, Gregory of Nyssa, who was concerned that Basil had broken off before completing his meditations on the creation of humankind, and therefore dedicated a whole book to the subject in 379.[14]

While Augustine did not write a hexameron as such, his *Unfinished Literal Commentary on Genesis* (written c. 393 and published with revisions in 426), among his other writings on the biblical creation narrative (notably, *On Creation: A Refutation of the Manichees* [389], and *Literal Meaning of Genesis* [416]), was highly influential among medieval writers, beginning with Bede's *On Genesis*

---

[13] The homilies on Genesis 1 in this series overlap with, but are not identical to, Chyrsostom's "Sermons on the Book of Genesis," evidently also written around this time. St. John Chrysostom, *Eight Sermons on the Book of Genesis*, translated with an introduction by Robert Charles Hill (Boston: Holy Cross Orthodox Press, 2004).

[14] For a more detailed discussion of ancient Christian readings of the biblical creation narrative, see Peter C. Bouteneff, *Beginnings: Ancient Christian Readings of the Biblical Creation Narratives* (Grand Rapids: Baker Academic, 2008), and Joseph Torchia, *Creation and Contingency in Early Patristic Thought: Beginnings of All Things* (London: Lexington, 2019). On Augustine, Philo, and Basil, see also Virginia Burrus, *Ancient Christian Ecopoetics: Cosmology, Saints, Things* (Philadelphia: University of Pennsylvania Press, 2019).

(c. 700) and continuing in a more philosophical and less orthodox vein in John the Scot's (also known as Eriugena's) *Perephysion: On the Division of Nature* (c. 867). Bede's commentary, together with Basil's, was taken up in turn by Aelfric (c. 955–c. 1010) in what is the first notable vernacular (Old English) hexameron. During the medieval period, the hexameron enjoyed a second heyday in the twelfth to thirteenth centuries. Among the major commentories of the High Middle Ages were those of Hugh of St. Victor (c. 1120), Thierry of Chartres (c. 1130–1140), Abelard (c. 1136/1137), Robert Grosse-teste (c. 1232–1235), and Bonaventure (1267).[15]

In the following centuries, the hexameral tradition was transposed into poetic form in such works as Guillaume de Salluste Du Bartas's *Le Semaine ou creation du Monde* (1594) and Torquato Tasso's *La sette giornata del mondo creatio* (1594), but it had petered out entirely by the late seventeenth century: not coincidentally, in the wake of the scientific revolution. Milton smuggled a hexameron into Book VII of *Paradise Lost* (1674) in the voice of the archangel Gabriel. But the last prose hexameron, at least in English, was Thomas Traherne's *Meditations on the Six Days of Creation*, probably penned for the wife of a friend in the mid-seventeenth century, and published erroneously under her name in 1717. Some modern poets subsequently picked it up, including Geoffrey Hill and James McAuley in the late twentieth century. And then, lo and behold, in early 2020, the archbishop of Canterbury recommended a book for use in Lenten reflections that takes the form of a hexameron: Ruth Valerio's powerful call to ecological transformation, *Saying Yes to Life*.[16] The time has clearly come for a renaissance of the hexameral tradition.

---

[15] Bibliographic details of the translations and editions of the hexamera referenced here can be found in the List of Abbreviations preceding this introduction.

[16] Ruth Valerio, *Saying Yes to Life* (London: SPCK Publishing, 2020).

Earlier hexameral writers commonly acknowledge that this narrative can be read through a variety of different interpretative lenses, and none can be claimed to be definitive or exhaustive. The line of interpretation that is most interesting from my perspective is what became known as the "literal" reading: not because it was literalistic in the modern sense, but rather because it was concerned with the work of creation as manifest in the natural world. Among those who take that approach, many acknowledge—and in the case of Grosseteste, for example, even contribute—to the science of the day. For most of these commentators, moreover, Genesis 1 afforded an opportunity for the celebration of the natural world. Basil was particularly effusive in this regard.

Addressing a congregation composed largely of artisans in the basilica of Cappadocia in 378, Basil exhorted his listeners to lift their gaze from things of merely human manufacture and behold instead the incomprehensible splendor and multitudinous marvels of earth, sea, and sky. Again and again, Basil remarked how his discourse had run away with him, yet also how far his words fell short of conveying the unspeakable wondrousness of the living world. Of the astonishing abundance and variety of living beings birthed by earth and sea in response to the divine call, he exclaimed, "What shall I say? What shall I leave unsaid? In the rich treasures of creation it is difficult to select what is most precious, the omission of which is most severe." (BaH, 78) Summoned forth by a loving creator and "the object of [his] continual care" (148), all things, he proclaimed, appeared to be "united in one universal sympathy" (34). Together, they composed a "harmonious symphony" (24), in which even the waters of "the deeps sing in their language a harmonious hymn to the glory of the Creator" within the "universal choir of creation" (62).

Rereading the hexameral tradition launched by Basil in the horizon of mass species extinction and the dwindling of wildlife is a gut-wrenching experience—for where these earlier commentators celebrate the incredible abundance and variety of living beings, each delighting in their existence after their own kind, we look out upon depletion, diminishment, and unspeakable suffering. And where they rejoice in the rhythm of the seasons and the fecundity of sea and land, we are faced with weather patterns that are becoming ever weirder and the disabling of Earth's capacity to sustain those complex connectivities that engender ecological flourishing.

Yet rereading this tradition is immensely painful for another reason as well. Basil was reluctant to speak of his own kind. He broke off his homilies after the making of the first humans, but prior to the verses that define their place in creation in terms of dominion and mastery. Other commentators, however, did not pull their punches on holding forth about humankind's exalted place in the scheme of things. Among those, as already mentioned, was Basil's younger brother, Gregory of Nyssa, who celebrated the making of man as the "king" for whom God had furnished on Earth a "royal lodging" (OMM, 168). Construing creation as culminating on day six with the making of our own kind, many are tempted to read all that went before as solely for the benefit of humanity. Even Traherne, who is second only to Basil in his evident delight in the natural world, felt drawn to declare that Man is the "Sum" and "End" of all Creatures: "the rest of the Creatures were without a Head.... They were worthless before, because they serv'd nothing, and were to no Purpose" (MoSDC, 84, 82).

Since Traherne's day, and at an accelerating rate over the past fifty years, ever more participants in the "universal choir of creation" have been silenced as a consequence of the industrial exploitation of the Earth that kicked off with the triumph of "fossil capitalism" in Britain in the late eighteenth century.[17] The mistreatment of Earth and its diverse denizens as a mere storehouse of "natural resources"

---

[17] Andreas Malm, *Fossil Capital: The Rise of Steam Power and the Roots of Global Warming* (Brooklyn, NY: Verso, 2016).

to be extracted, transformed, and set to work for exclusively human benefit, moreover, was initially (and in some quarters still is today) granted religious legitimacy with reference to our biblical calling to "Be fruitful and multiply and fill the earth and conquer it, and hold sway over the fish of the sea and the fowl of the heavens and every beast that crawls upon the earth" (Gen. 1.28). In my view, a hexameron for the era of extinction has to confront this toxic legacy and advance a more democratic and decolonial account of the human vocation. In endeavoring to do this myself, I have found great inspiration in the case studies of faith-based environmental action that inform my meditations in this book.

Your Kin(g)dom Come:
Pathways of Transformation

Inspired by the example set by Basil, Chrysostom, and Ambrose, each of the meditations on the six days of creation that follow is composed along the lines of a homily or sermon. Each opens with a personal recollection before proceeding to a close consideration of the passage for that "day." Here I bring my own response to the passage into conversation both with those of earlier commentators and with contemporary insights and understandings drawn from a range of sources, including modern sciences, ecological theologies, and Indigenous traditions. Turning my attention to today's world, I am then drawn toward darker reflections, in the tradition of prophetic witness, upon what has become of the earthly creation, said to have been so generously and gratuitously summoned forth in the biblical narrative, under the impact of fossil-fueled capitalist industrialization. At the time of writing, wracked by war and pestilence along with ongoing ecological unraveling and climate chaos, when all the horsemen of the apocalypse seem to be well and truly in our midst, the outlook looks pretty dire. Yet, in keeping with the role of the homily to offer words of comfort and encouragement along with warning and correction, each of these meditations ends with one or more examples of faith-based initiatives from around the world, mainly Christian but some interfaith, that are helping to resist the forces of destruction and injustice, advancing healing and regeneration.

These varied initiatives, ranging from contemplative practices to activist interventions, biodiversity conservation to consciousness raising, and artistic experimentation to political engagement, might be seen as responding in diverse ways to the human vocation that is referred to in the Jewish tradition as "repair of the world" (*tikkun olam*). Oriented toward safeguarding and restoring the potential for collective more-than-human flourishing, they are holding open the pathway toward a "kindom" yet to come. This kindom is not restricted to our own flesh and blood, fellow humans, but is inclusive of the wider communion of creatures in Basil's "universal choir of creation." As such, it resonates with the more-than-human, or multispecies, kinship ethics found among many Indigenous peoples. But it is also consistent, in my reading, with the sense of participation in the fate of the Earth and its diverse denizens invoked by those Hebrew prophets who refer to the land as "mourning," as its vegetation withers and animals dwindle, as a consequence of human wrongdoing. Using a verbal construction that can also mean "drying up" ('*ābal*), Jeremiah, for instance, cries out in desperation, "How long will the land mourn, / and the grass of every field wither? / For the wickedness of those who live in it / the animals and the birds are swept away" (Jer. 12:4). To this, the prophet discerns the Lord responding, "They [the people] made it a desolation; / desolate it mourns to me. / The whole land is made desolate, / but no one lays it to heart" (Jer. 12:11). Jeremiah was probably bearing witness to a regional environmental crisis, probably related to natural variability, but possibly compounded by agricultural intensification under the late Israelite monarchy, and linked, in his analysis, with an unjust social order that neglected to "protect the cause of the orphan" and "defend the rights of the needy" (Jer. 5:27–28), in which the ruling elite had grown "great and rich ... fat and sleek" (Jer. 5:23–24) at others' expense through treacherous trading practices.[18] Today, though, it is the entire Earth, the planet as a whole, that is "mourning"; and as its cries grow louder, mingling with those of the poor, ever more are laying it to heart.

To this end, my meditations end not with day six, as is conventional in the hexameral tradition, but with day seven—for the culmination of the biblical story is not, in fact, the making of humankind, but God's day of rest and enjoyment of all that had come forth, with the collaboration of sea and land, at the divine summons: the Sabbath day, in which we, too, are invited to join with the creator in celebrating the communion of all creatures—even now, even still, within an Earth for which we are being called ever more urgently to care and repair.

China's wandering elephants might not have made it to Kunming for COP 15. But what might it mean to consider that, as ambassadors of the diverse, more-than-human denizens of our common home, their eyes are upon us, not only at such crucial conventions, but in every hour of our everyday lives? How are we to truly hear and faithfully respond to the cry of the Earth and, comingled with it, the cry of the poor? And how might we reimagine our inherited creation narratives for a world in crisis?

Let us make a start, one day at a time.

---

[18] Michael Northcott, *A Moral Climate: The Ethics of Global Warming* (Maryknoll, NY: Orbis Books), 10–12.

First Day

When God began to create heaven and earth, and the earth then was welter and waste [tohu vabohu] *and darkness was over the face of the deep and God's breath hovering over the waters, God said, "Let there be light." And there was light. And God saw the light, that it was good, and God divided the light from the darkness. And god called the light Day, and the darkness He called Night. And it was evening and it was morning, first day.*

Genesis 1:1–5

❧

Have you ever known days when all the color has drained out of the world? Sleepless nights, devoid of hope, a yawning emptiness? Times when nothing seems to make sense anymore? When existence itself has lost all rhyme and reason: the very cosmos no more than a random accident, the burgeoning of life on this planet a mere freak of nature, its current unraveling at human hands an outcome that was always on the cards when an ape evolved that was too clever and too dexterous for its own, and everyone else's, good?

I know I have.

Yet even, or perhaps especially, in the midst of such bleak moments, have you not on occasion been startled by something that arrests your gaze with its unlikely loveliness? Unlikely, unanticipated, yet maybe perfectly ordinary—a flower, a smile, a glimpse of sky—in which you suddenly see something extra-ordinary: an inner radiance, perhaps, such as William Wordsworth once referred to in a peculiar turn of phrase as the "light of things." A light that appears only when we let go of grasping, relinquishing our urge to know and possess and command, and approach things instead with "a heart / that watches and receives"[1]—a light that intimates that you are not the sole maker of whatever random meanings you project onto an inherently meaningless world, but that others—the plant who produced that flower, the person who bore that smile, that gloriously sun- or moonlit sky—have their own meanings to impart ... so too, perhaps, does the very cosmos, of which, you now recall, you also are a part, with your own role to play, however humble, in its unfolding on this good Earth, not least by bearing witness, as did Gerard Manley Hopkins, to that indwelling, ongoing "dearest freshness deep down things."[2]

Or have you known other days and nights that are not bleak exactly, but deeply uncertain? Times of transition when a familiar pattern of meaning, set of relationships, or way of life no longer holds, and you cannot discern another emerging? Times when you feel unmoored, adrift, unable to plan or even prefigure more than a week, a day, an hour ahead? Times, perhaps, when you have lost a loved one, your job, your faith? Or times when, although little has altered in your own life, you sense that so much is changing, and so fast, and not for the better, in the wider world—beset as it is by madcap rulers, ruthless moneymakers, widening inequities, global heating, dwindling wildlife, novel pathogens, oceans of trash and trashed oceans ...—that you no

---

[1] William Wordsworth, "The Tables Turned," in *The Works of William Wordsworth: With an Introduction and Bibliography* (Ware, UK: Wordsworth Poetry Library, 1994), 481.

[2] Gerard Manley Hopkins, "God's Grandeur," in *Poems and Prose of Gerard Manley Hopkins*, ed. William Henry Gardner (Harmondsworth, UK: Penguin Classics, 1963), 27.

longer know how you should be living, what you ought to be doing, and from whence you might draw the strength and determination and wisdom to carry on? Times, perhaps, when you are at risk of becoming swamped by grief and rage and despair?

This also I have known all too well.

And yet, if you have allowed yourself to dwell for a while in this darkness, resisting the urge either to succumb to bitter cynicism or hurl yourself into frenetic action, have you ever sensed a kind of quivering in your depths, a hint of anticipation, a feeling that something was brewing, a change for the better, maybe, or at least an opening for meaningful engagement? In such moments, out of the blue, an opportunity might arise, a realization might crystallize, a relationship might form, that suddenly lights up your path, disclosing a way forward. At such times, you might even sense that, while it is entirely up to you how you respond, you are in some unfathomable yet undeniable manner being called forth along that path, regardless of whether you are game enough— or foolish enough, as some might suppose—to put a name to the source of that summons.

Enigmatic Beginnings

It is of such days and nights and times that I am reminded when I contemplate the strange opening of the first chapter of Genesis, with its gloomy wastes suddenly illuminated by a light that alternates with the abiding darkness; a tale the Christian Bible shares (albeit in a range of differing translations) with the Jewish Tanakh, where it is known by the first word of the Hebrew original, *Bereshit*, "In the beginning." And what a peculiar beginning this is. Having immersed myself in centuries of Christian commentaries on Genesis 1, I keep coming back to the laconic observation of the eleventh-century Jewish commentator of the Talmud and Tanakh,

Rabbi Shlomo Yitzchaki, known as Rashi, that "this text is nothing if not mysterious."[3]

The problems start right away with the question of temporality: Is this a moment in time, or the point from which time starts? Does this beginning precede time, and if so, what kind of a "beginning" could this be? Then there is the question of whether there was already something there for God to get to work on "at the beginning." Did that earthly *tohu vabohu*, a poetic elaboration on the word for "emptiness" or "futility" (*tohu*), of the watery "deep" (*tehom*), preexist the creation of heaven and earth? Or had they already been brought forth by the creator before the Most High subsequently summoned forth all those discrete spaces and entities and set them in order?

And what of the creator "himself"? All translations, beginning with the Greek of the Septuagint (c. third to first century BCE), sacrifice a subtle ambiguity in the Hebrew, which refers to the divine here, and throughout Genesis 1, with the plural noun *Elohim*, a plural that is picked up in later translations only in Genesis 1:26, where we read, "And God said, 'Let *us* make a human....'" Yet this always grammatically plural divinity, Elohim, is referred to by a singular masculine pronoun, such as in Genesis 1:10: "and the gathering of waters *He* called Seas." Is this divinity, then, singular or plural, or something else altogether, something both and neither, something perhaps best characterized as a "plurisingularity"?[4] Something is also striking about the syntax in that very first sentence: *Bereshit bara Elohim*. "*Bara*," created/creating, a verb used only of divine making in the Tanakh, is also in the masculine singular, and therefore jars with the plural of Elohim.

---

[3] Rashi, quoted in Avirah Gottlieb Zornberg, *The Beginning of Desire: Reflections on Genesis* (New York: Doubleday, 1996), 3.

[4] I take the term "plurisingularity" from Catherine Keller, who reinterprets the opening of Genesis 1 through a feminist process theological lens in *Face of the Deep: A Theology of Becoming* (New York: Routledge, 2003).

But might this word order not also open up the possibility that this beginning is, in some sense, also creating Elohim: *Bereshit ... bara Elohim*? That would not necessarily mean denying that the divine preexists the work of world-making; nor would it entail collapsing the creator, pantheistically, into the creation. But it would lend significance to something that is, in fact, fairly obvious, yet generally overlooked: namely, that the unnameable and ungraspable divine only becomes a *creator*, referred to here in the queer plurisingularity of Elohim, in and through the activity of creation. If so, this is from the start a story of pan*en*theistic co-becoming: a collaborative effort set in motion by a divine creator who is at once "above" and beyond, irreducible to the created, and yet, as Paul affirms, "through all and in all" (Eph. 4:6).

Among the earlier commentators on the hexameron, John the Scot, or Eriugena as he was also known, drew closest to this reading. In his remarkable ninth-century treatise *Perephyseon: On the Division of Nature*, he proposed that "creation subsists in God, and God is created in creation in a remarkable and ineffable way, manifesting himself, and, though invisible, making Himself visible ... though creating everything, making Himself created in everything" (DN, 197). This work was later viewed as heretical and committed to the flames by the Council of Paris in 1210, although some copies remained in circulation and possibly influenced medieval scholastic and mystical thought.[5]

Needless to say, this is not quite what the church fathers made of this narrative.

The early commentators on Genesis 1 from the first to fourth centuries CE, beginning with the Jewish scholar Philo of Alexandria (c. 20 BCE–c. 50 CE), whose treatise "On the Account

---

5 Jean A. Potter, "Introduction," in John the Scot, *Perephyseon: On the Division of Nature*, trans. Myra I. Uhlferler, with summaries by Jean A. Potter (Indianapolis: Bobbs-Merrill, 1979), xxiii–xxiv.

of the World's Creation Given by Moses" was highly influential among subsequent Christian writers, interpreted this strange story through the lens of the Hellenistic thought, generally Platonist with Stoic elements, in which they had been schooled. As a consequence, the earthiness of the ancient Hebrew worldview became partially eclipsed by a spirit-matter distinction entirely alien to the original wording. The term that gets translated into English as "heaven," *shemayim*, for example, also meant "sky," just as *erets*, generally translated as "earth," referred to "land." Drawn together in the phrase *et hashamayim v'et ha'aretz*, they form a figure of speech that could be used to invoke "all things," embracing the entire cosmos. However, *mayim* means waters, and since *dsham* is "there," some would say that *shamayim* is a contraction of *sham mayim*, thereby signaling the source of the waters that fall from above,[6] and hence referencing the more homely sky that we behold with our earthly eyes, rather than something as vast and abstract as the cosmos. This sky, *shemayim,* also figured as the dwelling place of the divine, a heavenly realm understood to be, in some sense, "on high"; but God might always choose to put in an appearance "down here" on Earth, as indeed the creator is said to have done in the beginning, hovering on the watery deep; and sundry angels too were in the habit of making surprise visitations.

Under the influence of Platonism, however, with its division between an immaterial, or "intelligible," realm of pure forms and their material, or "visible," copies, *shemayim* qua heaven tends to take leave of the sky that we see above our heads and becomes, as Philo put it, "incorporeal" (OC, 23). Similarly, that which is said to have been moving above the waters, *ruach* in Hebrew,

---

[6] I am indebted to Rabbi Jonathan Keren Black for this observation, as well as for other comments on this chapter. Any remaining errors are entirely my own.

increasingly became read as "spirit," leading some later Christian commentators to identify it as the third member of the Trinity, the "Holy Spirit," just as they would interpret God's Word, which "speaks" the world into being (following John 1), as Christ, thereby rendering the creation a thoroughly Trinitarian accomplishment (and neatly resolving the mystery of the plurisingularity of Elohim, which Jewish commentators had generally taken to refer to a divine court). Yet *ruach* originally meant "breath," as Alter has it in his translation, or "wind." Here, to be sure, it is associated with the divine: but it did not, as such, refer to anything immaterial, signaling rather a misty, moisty, animating emanation of the Most High moving within creation in the very process of its unfolding.

Notwithstanding Hellenistic influences, the spirit-matter distinction was generally not as hard and fast within ancient Jewish and Christian thought as it subsequently became in the modern period, above all under the influence of the dualistic philosophy of René Descartes (1596–1650). And on the matter of matter, there was one important point where Philo and his Christian successors parted company from the Platonists. In his *Timaeus* (c. 360 BCE), Plato had envisaged a creator god who fashions the world on the model of the ideal forms out of preexistent matter. From the first century onward, however, Jewish and Christian orthodoxy both settle around the doctrine that would later be known as *creatio ex nihilo* (creation out of nothing). The first Christian commentator on Genesis 1 to assert this explicitly was the pagan convert Theophilus of Antioch (c. 184), who stated, "All things God has made out of things that were not, into things that are, in order that through His works His greatness may be known and understood" (AA, 137). Together with the affirmation of divine supremacy, this view served the crucial purpose of countering other philosophies that were circulating at this time. Those philosophies argued that the material realm, sometimes thought to have been made by an inferior demiurge, was essentially evil, and radically opposed to, and separated from, the spiritual realm.

Yet if all things, including that originary *tohu vabohu* and watery deep, had been freely brought into existence out of nothing by a wise and good and loving God, who continues to care for them as their "Father and Maker" (OC, 11)—and indeed to sustain them, as Theophilus argued, through the "breath" "which God gave for animating creation" (AA, 155)—then nothing in creation is essentially evil and all might reveal the hand of its creator. In this way, the biblical story begins to be received as a narrative about the incalculable giftedness of our shared existence with other creatures and our ultimate dependence upon something beyond our ken. As such, it utters a call to gratitude and praise, contemplation and celebration, of and with what Basil of Caesarea (330–379) entitled the "universal choir of creation" (BaH, 62).

For the Jewish priests who were or had been held captive in exile in Babylon following the conquest of Judah by imperial Babylonian forces in the late sixth century BCE and who wrote or edited Genesis 1, the question of whether the creator made all things from scratch does not seem to have been a matter of pressing concern. It was more important, it seems, to give a distinctively Jewish, and, notwithstanding the plurisingularity of Elohim, expressly monotheistic account of the divine work of world-making emphatically pitched against the major creation narrative of their conquerors and captors. As recounted on the clay tablets of the *Enuma Elish* from the seventh century BCE, but possibly dating as far back as the Old Babylonian period (1900–1600 BCE), this major creation narrative was an extremely macho tale of violent intergenerational conflict between older and younger deities. It culminates in the murder of the great mother goddess of salt water, Tiamat, who had launched a reign of terror in response to the slaying of her first spouse, Apsu, god of fresh water, by one of their own sons, Marduk. Marduk proceeded to sever Tiamat's corpse in two, forming the heavens with one half and the earth with the other, turning her breasts into mountains, and causing the Tigris and Euphrates to flow from her eyes. While he was at this gory work of world-making, Marduk also fashioned the first humans out of the blood of Tiamat's second husband, Kingu, whom he had also slain, in order that they should serve the gods and relieve them of their labors.

There is, as some biblical scholars believe, a faint echo of this narrative in the figure of the watery deep: *tehom*, a feminine noun, which in the absence of a definite article might function as a proper noun, is a cognate of the Akkadian *tamtu* and Ugaritic *t-h-m*, both related to the earlier Sumerian *Tiamat*.[7] And not unlike Tiamat, the primal waters of Genesis 1 will also be separated, on day two, into an earthly and a heavenly portion. Yet this is no tale of violent conquest: while the earthly waters will be channeled in order to allow dry land to appear on day three, they hold their own; and on day five they will be invited to bring forth the myriad creatures who come to populate the aquatic and aerial realms. Although some of the more allegorizing Christian commentators, such as Origen of Alexandria (c. 184–c. 253) and Anastasios of Sinai (d. c. 700), associated the *tehom* with abyssal nether regions, into which "the devil and his angels" (OHoG, 47–48) will be exiled,[8] there is no suggestion in the text that it is a

---

[7] On connections and contrasts between the Babylonian and biblical creation narratives, as first noted by the biblical scholar Hermann Gunkel in *Schöpfung und Chaos in Urzeit und Endzeit* (1895), see also Ruth Valerio, *Saying Yes to Life* (London: SPCK, 2020), xii–xvii. For an English translation of Gunkel's books, see *Creation and Chaos in the Primeval Era and the Eschaton: A Religio-Historical Study of Genesis 1 and Revelation*, trans. K. William Whitney Jr. (Grand Rapids: Eerdmans, 2007).

[8] Anastasios posits that immediately after it had been created, earth was "handed over like a criminal to the abyss," to rise once more, in a foreshadowing of the resurrection of Christ, on the third day (AnH, 17).

locus of evil. Far from being vanquished, the watery deeps become an active participant in the divine work of world-making, and, as Basil affirmed, they continue to "sing in their language a harmonious hymn to the glory of the Creator" (BaH, 62).

Genesis 1 also departs from the violent machismo of the Babylonian creation narrative in the endearing connotations of the "hovering" action of the breath-wind-spirit over those deep and darkling waters. Elsewhere in the Hebrew Scriptures, this word, *mərahepet̲*, refers to an eagle fluttering over its young, suggesting "parturition or nurture as well as rapid back-and-forth movement."[9] Basil, delightfully, gives this parental connotation a maternal spin by recalling a Syriac translation that renders it as "cherishing," "as one sees a bird cover the eggs with her body and impart to them vital force from her own warmth" (BaH, 41–42). This is the meaning that Milton later ran with in *Paradise Lost*, where Adam is informed by the archangel Gabriel that "on the watery calm / His brooding wings the Spirit of God outspread" (Book VII, ll. 234–35).[10] Imaged as a brooding mother bird, Elohim, whose likeness will later be made manifest in both male and female guise in human form, appears not only oddly plurisingular but also queerly gender-bending: a far cry, indeed, from the matricidal warrior god of the Babylonian Empire.

Elsewhere in the Hebrew Scriptures, we learn of another expressly female member of the heavenly realm, who was, and remains, at work in creation. *Chochma*, Wisdom, better known from the Greek as Sophia, declares in Proverbs 8:22–31:

---

[9] Robert Alter, *Genesis: Translation and Commentary* (New York: W. W. Norton, 1997), 3.

[10] John Milton, "Paradise Lost," in *Paradise Lost and Selected Poetry and Prose*, ed. and with an intro. by Northrop Frye (New York: Holt, Rinehart and Winston, 1951), 166. References to this long poem hereafter are given in the text with book and line numbers.

The Lord created me at the beginning of his work,
the first of his acts of long ago.

Ages ago I was set up,
at the first, before the beginning of the earth.

When there were no depths I was brought forth,
when there were no springs abounding with water.

Before the mountains had been shaped,
before the hills, I was brought forth—

when he had not yet made earth and fields,
or the world's first bits of soil.

When he established the heavens, I was there,
when he drew a circle on the face of the deep,

when he made firm the skies above,
when he established the fountains of the deep,

when he assigned to the sea its limit,
so that the waters might not transgress his command,

when he marked out the foundations of the earth,
then I was beside him, like a master worker;

and I was daily his delight,
rejoicing before him always,

rejoicing in his inhabited wor
and delighting in the human race.

Similarly, in the Wisdom of Solomon, we are told that Chochma "pervades and penetrates" all things (7:24): "She embraces one end of the earth to the other, and She orders all things well" (8:1). As contemplative and interfaith teacher Rabbi Rami Shapiro reads this biblical testimony to the role of Sophia in creation, "Chochma was not simply the first of God's creations; she was the means through which all the others came forth.... She is the ordering principle of creation.... What you see when you see Her is analogous to seeing the grain in wood, the current of wind and oceans, and the laws of nature, both the macrocosmic and the microcosmic.... She is the Way things are."[11]

In consort with Chochma, then, while lovingly brooding on the watery deep, the first thing Elohim is said to have summoned forth in and through the divine Word was "light."

The Illumination of the Universe

What are we to make of this light, that is not yet the light of sun, moon, or stars, but some primordial other light? A light that does not conquer the darkness but comes graciously to alternate with it, pulsing rhythmically; each separated from, yet also linked with, the other through times of transition—the morning, as Philo puts it so beautifully, "gently restraining the darkness anticipates the sunrise with the glad tidings of its approach; while evening, supervening upon sunset, gives a gentle welcome to the oncoming mass of darkness" (OC, 27).

Philo, like most of the learned Christian commentators who followed him right through to the seventeenth century, did not mistake this narrative for science, or "natural philosophy," as the study of nature was known throughout that time. From their perspective, and mine, the efforts of modern biblical literalists to find empirical evidence in support of the biblical account of creation, together with the judgment of those who scoffingly dismiss it as unscientific, are founded on a fundamental category error. For however divinely inspired it might be considered by some, the truth of this mythopoetic work of Scripture principally concerns questions of meaning, value, and purpose. It does not stand or fall on its accordance with whatever is taken to be "the facts" within a

---

[11] Rami Shapiro, *The Divine Feminine in Biblical Wisdom Literature: Selections Annotated and Explained* (Woodstock, VT: SkyLight Paths, 2005), xxi–xxiii.

given order of empirical knowledge. Many of the hexameral authors did nonetheless take a lively interest in what was understood in their day about the natural world, and some entertain current observations and speculations regarding what became known as the "first Book of God"—the natural world—in their commentaries on the "second"—Scripture. This approach was referred to as "literal," not because it mistook the biblical narrative for a literal account, but because of its attention to the material world beyond the page. For Peter Abelard (1079–1142) and Thierry of Chartres (1100–1150), for example, that interest extended to the new insights about the physical nature of reality afforded by the reception of Islamic science, and enabled by experimentation as well as logical reasoning. Indeed, one of the last great medieval hexamera, written by Robert Grosseteste (1168–1253), a whopping 448-page compendium of natural philosophy, is no less significant as a contribution to the history of science as it is to theology.

Were we to take that tack today, we might turn to the utterly startling discoveries about the birth of the universe that have been facilitated by the crafting of ever more powerful tools that are giving us a growing, but still limited, understanding of the deep reaches of the time-space continuum. It all began, as astronomers currently believe, with a "big bang," or as physicist Brian Swimme and cultural historian Thomas Berry put it rather more poetically, the primordial "Flaring Forth."[12] Some 13.8 billion years ago, all the energy of the universe, which had been packed into a single point, is thought to have exploded outward, creating the matter that would eventually cohere into stars and planets, galaxies, and solar systems, including the one

---

[12] Brian Swimme and Thomas Berry, *The Universe Story: From the Primordial Flaring Forth to the Ecozoic Era—A Celebration of the Unfolding of the Cosmos* (London: Penguin, 1992).

of which our marvelously life-bearing Earth is a part, together with the still somewhat elusive physical principles that, for the time being, keep it all going.

Returning to that biblical first light, we might be tempted to discern a parallel here to the moment that astrophysicists describe as the time when the universe became "transparent." I was alerted to this by one of my interviewees for this project, Deborah Colvin, a former science teacher and sustainability champion at St. James's, Piccadilly. According to NASA, the James Webb Telescope has revealed that around 240,000 to 300,000 years after the big bang, the universe underwent its first major transformation, having been a murky and extremely hot soup of protons, neutrons, and electrons until that point. As it cooled, some of those protons and neutrons got together with one another, forming ionized atoms of hydrogen and deuterium, and the latter further fused with helium-4. Not to be left out, some of the electrons got attracted to the new kids on the block, those ionized atoms of hydrogen and helium, transforming them into stable neutral atoms, each of which emitted an ultraviolet photon. At this point the universe became transparent, because the passage of light was no longer being scattered off all of those freewheeling electrons. This "era of recombination" is the earliest point in the unfolding of the universe that can be looked back to with any kind of light, and it is the origin of the cosmic microwave background that has been disclosed by the satellites bringing more news of distant beginnings.

This moment of illumination—or at least of transparency to low-energy light—however, was followed by what is known as the cosmic "Dark Ages," during which these neutral atoms clumped together, forming molecular clouds, dust, and collections of gas that absorbed the light of the first stars. This gloomy period lasted another few hundred million years, until, for reasons that remain obscure, stars began to form and grow and multiply to the point when their tremendous energy precipitated a process of reionization, giving all those electrons the kick, and thereby rendering the universe transparent all over again, and irradiated by a whole new order of light.[13]

In Darkness and In Light: Called to Contemplation

In my meditations on the subsequent days of creation, I will be favoring ways of reading that focus on the natural world—in particular the living Earth, its present plight, and how we human creatures might be called to respond to her cry. Here, however, I would like to emulate those earlier commentators, for whom the biblical text also resonated on other, less literal levels. All agreed that its meanings were multivalent, unfolding, and not readily pinned down. Augustine (354–430), who warned repeatedly against rashly affirming any particular interpretation of certain points, distinguished four approaches: historical or "literal," allegorical or "figurative," analogical (i.e., with reference to the New Testament), and etiological (i.e., with reference to causal explanations), and he proceeded, very hesitantly, to attempt the first of these (an attempt that remained unfinished) (LCG, 113).

Most read the hexameron through at least two different lenses, but some treated it purely figuratively, such as Anastasios Sinaiti, who had no time for natural history in his sermons on the Hexaemeron from around 700, and viewed it exclusively as an allegory for the incarnation, crucifixion, and resurrection of Christ; the formation and ministry of the church; and the coming redemption. Far more interesting, in my view, is Bonaventure's incomplete, yet nonetheless monumental *Conferences on the Six Days of Creation*. First delivered as lectures at the University of Paris in 1267, it can be seen as an allegorical counterpart to Grosseteste's more literal

---

[13] James Webb Space Telescope, "First Light and Reionization," Goddard Space Flight Center, www.nasa.gov. For a more detailed account, see also Ethan Siegel, "When Did the Universe Become Transparent to Light?" *Forbes*, May 10, 2019.

reading. Bonaventure's hexameron, too, is very much in conversation with contemporary science, but his concerns are primarily epistemological, pondering ways of knowing rather than the nature of reality. He therefore interpreted each of the days of creation as a figure for different types and levels of understanding: namely, those "implanted by nature," "elevated by faith," "informed by Scripture," "suspended by contemplation," "elevated by the spirit of 'prophecy,'" "absorbed by rapture," and ultimately (and posthumously), "consummated in the state of glory" (BoH).

It is along these more figurative lines that I started my meditation on this opening passage, and it is to that way of reading that I now want to return. To begin with, let's go back to that question of temporality. Although Alter has this as "first day," he notes that the Hebrew, unusually, "uses a cardinal not an ordinal number here."[14] That is to say, this is not referred to as the *first* but as *one* day. Some of the hexameral commentators make much of this. Philo posited that this "one day" actually comprises the "whole" work of creation, which was accomplished all in one go, with each of the successive "days" simply a poetic device to bring to mind the different domains and inhabitants of the created order from a human perspective. Augustine, similarly, wondered whether the account of a sequential creation across six "days" was a narrative technique intended to "suggest sublime things to lowly people in a lowly manner by following the basic rule of storytelling, which requires the story teller's tale to have a beginning, a middle and an end?" (LCG, 115). Similarly, Abelard proposed that this "one day" included "all the works," and that the swiftness of their accomplishment is conveyed metaphorically in the figure of sudden illumination—"Be light" being a summons to all things, simply and miraculously, to be, or rather, to co-become (ESW, 46). Abelard indicated also that what was summoned into existence at the beginning did not remain static, but was subject to change through natural

---

[14] Alter, *Genesis*, 3.

causes over time, such that, for example, of the birds and fishes originally brought into being, "several species have at some point become obsolete, extinct" (ESW, 73).

Though I, too, am intrigued by the "oneness" and the wholeness of this "day," I interpret it somewhat differently: namely, as signalling a beginning that did not occur once and for all, but rather one that is, in some sense, always in process. This reading posits a continuing creation, *creatio continuo*, whereby discrete, albeit interconnected, entities are forever being drawn forth into actuality from the *tehomic* flux of undifferentiated potentiality, into which, sooner or later, they return: *creatio ex profundis*, "from the deep," as Catherine Keller puts it.[15] In conjunction with the belief that God's creation, whether or not *ex nihilo*, is always also fundamentally *ex amore*, from love, *creatio continuo* bears the reassurance of ongoing divine involvement in the often fraught processes of co-becoming.[16] It also conveys the promise of renewal, as a life-giving and life-loving Elohim holds open the possibility that surprisingly good things might be drawn out of the seemingly worst situations: including, just maybe, with sufficient human dedication to and collaboration with our fellow creatures of all kinds, a recovery of earthly flourishing on a planet that industrial "civilization" is fast returning to "welter and waste."

There are other figurative dimensions to this "one day" as well. It is not just a matter of what is or co-becomes, but how we and other creatures perceive it. On this reading, that "light" is not

---

[15] Keller, *Face of the Deep*. In my view, it is not necessary to oppose *creatio ex profundis* to *creatio ex nihilo*, if you take the view of some of the church fathers that the watery *tehom* was already part of Elohim's good creation.

[16] I take the term *creatio ex amore* from ecotheologian Norman Wirzba, for whom this is, in essence, the meaning of *ex nihilo*: "a teaching that declares divine love to be the sole reason for there being anything at all." *This Sacred Life: Humanity's Place in a Wounded World* (Cambridge: Cambridge University Press, 2021), 165.

just the *medium* but the *way* in which things become perceptible to one another, through whatever sensory, mental, technical, or other frameworks are peculiar to their manner of being in the world. John the Scot saw it somewhat along these lines too. In his profoundly immanental theology, according to which every creature was "an appearance of the divine" (DN, 199), the alternation of night and day, darkness and light, is an allegory for the dual dimensions of creation, which remains "obscure to us in its first state as cause in God's thoughts" and becomes "lucid and intelligible as effects when pronounced by his utterance" (200). To this, though, I would add that in disclosing themselves to others (and not only to human witnesses), all things nonetheless always also conceal some dimensions of their own being: neither we nor any other creature ever perceives another in its entirety.

The light of perception, then, is always accompanied by the dark of imperceptibility: we get a glimpse of things, each in our own way, but we can never fully grasp them. And if we think we have perceived and truly know them through and through, we run the risk of assuming that they are at our command, and potentially our disposal. Disrespecting their mystery, we are liable to do them damage. In the process, we—and here I am talking in particular about those of us who take themselves to be "human," since we are the ones who are most likely to go astray in this way—also diminish our own calling: the calling, that is, to coexist with care and consideration with other creatures in a world that is not of our making, yet on an Earth, for the future of which we have ended up acquiring significant responsibility.

At the risk of getting ahead of myself and broaching already the topic of the Sixth Day, this primordial First Day, which continues to resound across all our days, entails also the crucial question of reception: how we comport ourselves toward this wondrous *creatio continuo ex amore*. My suggestion is that we discern in the narrative of this "one day," which in some sense contains the whole, a call to contemplation—one that enjoins the cultivation of a way of being and becoming-with others, in which, to recall Wordsworth once again, we might glimpse that mysterious "light of things" that forever escapes our grasp, by encountering them in their ultimate unknowability with "a heart that watches/and receives."

Contemplative practices, frequently framed in terms of "mindfulness," have long been fostered in some quarters of the environmental movement. The Norwegian philosopher Arne Naess, who influentially distinguished "shallow environmentalism" from "deep long-range ecology," drew on Hindu approaches to self-transcendence as a pathway to participation in a vastly greater, transpersonal Self.[17] Within the deep ecology movement that he helped to seed, Buddhist meditative traditions, as mediated to the West by such marvelous teachers as Joanna Macy and Thich Nhat Hanh, have been widely embraced.

Such contemplative practices can be found in many other traditions as well. Among them are the swirling dances of Sufi dervishes; the oh-so-slow moves of Daoist Tai Chi practitioners; the joyous Gospel singing of Black American churches, with their roots in the rich soil of African spiritualities; and the deep listening to the land honed over the millennia by many Indigenous peoples around the world, such as, in Northern Australia, the practice named *dadirri* in the Ngan'gikurunggurr and Ngen'giwumirri languages of the Aboriginal peoples of the Daly River region, as explained by Ngangiwumirr elder Miriam Rose Ungenmerr-Baumann.[18]

Indeed, in the view of the famous nineteenth-century Lutheran theologian Friedrich Schleiermacher (1768–1834), who

---

[17] Arne Naess, "The Shallow and the Deep, Long-Range Ecology Movement: A Summary," *Inquiry* 16, no. 1–4 (1973): 95–100.

[18] Miriam Rose Foundation, "Dadirri," 1998, www.miriamrosefoundation.org.au. On Black American traditions of communal contemplative practice, see Barbara A. Holmes, *Joy Unspeakable: Contemplative Practices of the Black Church*, 2nd ed. (Minneapolis: Fortress Press, 2017).

founded both the modern historical-critical approach to the Bible and comparative religious studies, contemplative experience is the transcultural "essence" of all religions. In a series of talks published in 1798, and originally written in response to a request by his atheistic friends among the early German Romantics, to whom he referred in the subtitle as "cultured despisers" of religion, Schleiermacher proclaimed,

> The universe exists in uninterrupted activity and reveals itself to us in every moment. Every form that it brings forth, every being to which it gives a separate existence according to the fullness of life, every occurrence that spills forth from its rich, ever-fruitful womb, is an action of the same upon us. Thus to accept everything individual as a part of the whole and everything limited as a representation of the infinite is religion.[19]

For Schleiermacher, experiences of profound interconnectivity, of mystical participation in a sacred whole vastly exceeding human ken and control, afforded an awareness of radical dependence, fostering humility and gratitude. Contemplation, in this way, transforms our sense of space and place. But it also takes us out of our everyday sense of time: "To be one with the infinite in the midst of the finite and to be eternal in a moment, that is the immortality of religion."[20] To step aside from the busyness of the day and suspend for a while one's assumptions and intentions, recollections and prefigurations, hopes and desires, in order to attend to the present moment as it arises and passes, is, in a way, to participate in the time-out-of-time of *creatio continuo*, the ever-present coming-into-being of all things from the deep wellspring of undetermined possibility.

---

[19] Friedrich Schleiermacher, *On Religion: Speeches to Its Cultured Despisers*, intro., trans., and notes, R. Crouter (Cambridge: Cambridge University Press, 1988), 105.

[20] Schleiermacher, *On Religion*, 140.

Now, all of this is no easy matter. The first Christian contemplatives, the desert fathers and mothers of the late third and fourth centuries, felt that they needed to withdraw entirely from the social order and cultural norms of the troubled late Roman Empire and take themselves off into the wilds of Egypt, Syria, Asia Minor, and Palestine in order to dedicate themselves to the contemplative life: the inner work of self-transformation, devotion to God, and service to others. In our own troubled times, the spiritual practice inaugurated by these early Christian contemplatives is being reclaimed and reimagined in the guise of a "contemplative ecology."[21] And contemplative practices, whether Christian or otherwise, are also increasingly being recognized as a vehicle for the "inner transition" that is needed to reset our society along a sustainable path,[22] and (as they were long ago by Mahatma Gandhi) as a crucial foundation for eco-activism in the mode of nonviolent civil disobedience.

For the desert fathers and mothers, as Rev. Vanessa Elston explained in a talk for the United Kingdom's Christian Climate Action group in 2020, this tough inner work entailed a great deal of wrestling with sundry devious demons.[23] These manifested in particular in those pesky "thoughts" that would later be codified,

---

[21] Douglas E. Christie, *The Blue Sapphire of the Mind: Notes for a Contemplative Ecology* (Oxford: Oxford University Press, 2013). In my book *Reclaiming Romanticism: Toward an Ecopoetics of Decolonization* (London: Bloomsbury Academic, 2020), I explore what I call a "contemplative ecopoetics." On Christian contemplative traditions, see also Kevin Hart, "Contemplation of Creation," in *T&T Clark Companion to the Doctrine of Creation*, ed. Jason Goroncy (London: T&T Clark, forthcoming).

[22] See, e.g., the resources provided at Lund University's Centre for Sustainability Studies, "Contemplative Sustainable Futures," accessed March 30, 2023, www.contemplative-sustainable-futures.com. On the importance of contemplation to environmental action, see also Pope Francis's General Audience on "Care of the Common Home and Contemplative Dimension," September 16, 2020.

[23] Vanessa Elston, "Action and Contemplation in an Age of Apathy," Christian Climate Action, timdendy206, July 8, 2020, www.youtube.com.

minus one, as the "seven deadly sins": pride, lechery, anger, gluttony, avarice, envy or vanity, sloth or cynicism, and—the one that regrettably got lost off the list—despair. To these, as Reverend Elston notes, we might want to add pervasive anxiety, one of the most egregious "demons" of our age. And then there is our perennial distractedness: Bonaventure, as Franciscan Brother Samuel Double recalls, considered inattentiveness—to one another, and especially to the disadvantaged, to creation, and to the mystery of divine love at the heart of it all—to be a fundamental sin.[24]

Contemplation, understood in this Christian tradition as the prayerful opening to the divine and attention to others with a loving gaze, begins with the honest acknowledgment of all these troublesome tendencies. It entails forms of *apotaxis*, asceticism, and kenosis, self-emptying, in order to allow yourself to be so filled with divine love that you can loosen yourself away from whatever demons beset you, if not entirely and all at once, then over time, and to whatever degree might be vouchsafed to you. As in other meditative traditions, including the considerably more ancient ones of Buddhism, Hinduism, and Taoism, Christian contemplation requires being fully present to the here and now (*prosoche*) by emptying your mind of all those thoughts that are continuously buzzing around your head. Whenever they arise, you should avoid letting them grab your attention by looking away or "over their shoulder," and gently but firmly pushing them down beneath the "cloud of forgetting," as the anonymous author of a late-fourteenth-century classic of Christian mysticism, *The Cloud of Unknowing*, put it.[25] Ultimately, the Christian contemplative seeks to be fully present to, even united with, God, surrendering their separate selfhood in the unbounded ocean of divine love. Such an experience of

---

[24] Brother Double's reflection was also for Christian Climate Action.
[25] "The Cloud of Unknowing," in *The Cloud of Unknowing and other Works*, trans. with intro. and notes by A. C. Spearing (London: Penguin, 2001), 26–27.

self-transcendence might be "out of this world," if by "world" you understand prevailing and constraining societal structures, relations, and norms—but it can also allow you to enter more deeply and more often into the inner "light of things" within the more-than-human world with which your own existence is interwoven.

Yet contemplative experience can just as readily open onto absence as presence, unknowing as illumination. And it can deepen your anguished awareness of harm, suffering, and wrong. In fact, an entire strand of Christian mysticism is dedicated to this "negative path," or *via negativa*. This mode of contemplation is generally associated with apophatic theologies, premised on the transcendence and unknowability of the divine, as distinct from kataphatic theologies affirming divine immanence and attributes. It is along the via negativa that *The Cloud of Unknowing* takes us—although even here we are assured that God might "at times send out a beam of spiritual light, piercing this cloud of unknowing that is between you and him, and show you some of his mysteries, of which human beings are not permitted or able to speak."[26] Lost in the "cloud of unknowing," we might find ourselves bathed in a "bright darkness."[27]

In my experience, it is best not to overdraw this distinction: the practice of contemplation will take you through times that lean more to kataphasis and others that lean more to apophasis—times that fill you with the assurance of divine presence, full of hope that love and goodness and life abundant will win out in the end, and others that find you hollowed out, full of doubt, adrift in what St. John of the Cross (1542–1591) called the "dark night of the soul." Yet even at such times we might find glimmers of hope. Glossing John of the Cross, whose world was beset by war, famine, plague, and religious schism, contemporary Carmelite priest Iain Matthew writes, "Night signifies that which comes upon us and takes us out

---

[26] *Cloud of Unknowing*, 52.
[27] *Cloud of Unknowing*, 119.

of our own control; it announces that as the place of resurrection. A God who heals in darkness—this is John's word of hope in a destabilized world."[28]

Even in that dark night, then, we might get a taste of that peace that "passes all understanding" (Phil. 4:7). Precisely from that hard-won place of peace, within the cloud of unknowing, we can best contribute to the renewed flourishing of life on this hard-pressed planet, buoyed by a hope that is not premised on an optimistic assessment of likely outcomes (grounds for which are wearing thin), but rather derived precisely from uncertainty, trusting in possibility. Rebecca Solnit calls this "hope in the dark."[29] For some, it is fed by faith in that divine plurisingularity, who revels in abundant life and draws us, immemorially and unceasingly, toward loving-kindness and merciful justice.

As you may have already surmised, I am suggesting that these two modes of contemplative experience might offer a further way of understanding the alternation of light and dark that sets in on this "one day." Whether apophatic or kataphatic, and whether Christian or otherwise, contemplative practices provide an essential underpinning for the kinds of personal transformation and political engagement to which we are ever more urgently called in the face of deepening climate and environmental crises. In this connection, Reverend Elston recalls the words of Thomas Merton (1915–1968)—Trappist monk, scholar of Eastern religions, and advocate for interfaith understanding—whose writings laid the foundation for the renewal of Christian contemplation:

---

[28] Iain Matthew, *The Impact of God: Soundings from St. John of the Cross*, quoted in Richard Rohr, "John of the Cross: Poet, Pastor, Mystic," Daily Meditation, April 24, 2020, https://cac.org.

[29] Rebecca Solnit, *Untold Histories, Wild Possibilities*, 3rd ed. (Chicago: Haymarket Books, 2016).

What is the relation [of contemplation] to action? Simply this: He who attempts to act and do things for others and the world without deepening his own self-understanding, freedom, integrity, and capacity to love will not have anything to give others. He will communicate to them nothing but the contagion of his own obsessions, aggressiveness, ego-centered ambitions, delusions about ends and means, doctrinaire prejudices and ideas.[30]

Franciscan friar and founder of the Center for Action and Contemplation in New Mexico Richard Rohr (b. 1943) echoed this assessment in his reflections on the profound legacy of the co-originator of the practice of centering prayer, Cistercian Father Thomas Keating (1923–2018):

The only path forward for the survival of our species and perhaps even our planet [by which I think he means a vibrant diversity of other living kinds] is a path of nonviolence, of contemplation and action prioritizing justice and solidarity, an affirmation of Oneness and the interconnectedness of all things, which science confirms, and spirituality has always known on its deepest level.[31]

It is, then, from this place of quiet contemplation, both in darkness and in light, that will behold all that is said to have been summoned forth on the following days of creation. Lamenting what has become of the earthly creation within industrial modernity, we will nonetheless find inspiration in the prophetic witness and healing ministry of those who are responding to the commingled cries of the earth and the poor around the world today.

---

[30] Thomas Merton, *Thomas Merton: Spiritual Master: Essential Writings*, ed. Lawrence Cunningham (Mahwah, NJ: Paulist Press, 1992), 375.

[31] Richard Rohr, "The Freedom of Consent," Daily Meditation, October 30, 2020, https://cac.org.

It turns out I have tarried far longer than anticipated with this one day, about which so much more has and could be said. But perhaps that was inevitable: there was a lot of ground to cover, and deep waters to plumb.

Let me draw to a close, then, by trying to say where we have come thus far.

In this day that embraces the night, in this pulsing of darkness and light, we come to rest, poised to act, at ease with uncertainty, prepared for surprise. Alert yet at peace, we find hope in the gloom, faith without ground. We are lost in the moment, and wait to be found.

So, be still, take a breath, let it vibrate in your depths.

Be still, take another. Imagine it is your first: the breath that began to open up your world, the breath through which you partake in the primordial breath, hovering on the watery deep, that birthed the world in the beginning.

Can you sense something stirring?

For even here, even now, it is underway: a beginning that is forever becoming, unfolding in perpetuity: a beginning that is also renewing, unfurling the unforeseeable.

Second Day

*And God said, 'Let there be a vault in the midst of the waters,
and let it divide water from water. And God made the vault
and it divided the water beneath the vault from the water
above the vault, and so it was. And God called the vault
Heavens, and it was evening and it was morning, second day.*

Genesis 1:6–8

When I was growing up in Canberra, Australia's "bush capital,"
summer holidays brought the promise of a week or two on
the south coast of New South Wales during the long, hot lull
following the excitement of Christmas. For many years, those
family holidays took us to Tabourie Lake. Tucked away from
the Princes Highway that hugs the southeastern coastline of
Australia all the way from Sydney to Adelaide, this was a tiny
hamlet, seemingly remote from the major tourist hotspot of Bate-
man's Bay, forty-two kilometers to the south, and the smaller
township of Ulladulla, eleven kilometers to the north. We used
to stay in a little light-filled flat in a block of four, right alongside
the alluring lagoon that gives the place its misleading name, and
a short walk through coastal scrub to the powdery white sand,
intriguing rock pools, and busy waters of the beach.

It was there one year that I hit upon a very particular pleasure.
You had to find a spot in the surf where the swell was gentle and
flip over onto your back to gaze up at the vast blue dome of the

27

sky. Rocked by the pulsing waters in which, for the moment, you were suspended, your eyes were free to follow whatever puffs of cloud might be floating on high. You were aware that the next wave could well toss you over and suck you under. But what a comfort it was to trust that the heavens were quite definitely not going to fall—nor even, on those seemingly perpetually sunny days, to open.

Looking back from a time when even a clear blue sky carries the imprint of human industry and bears tidings of grave woe, what a luxury it was to believe that the watery earth below and the rain-bearing heavens above would go on forever, just as they were then—and that in between them was a fairly safe space within which the living world, to which you, too, belonged, had a good chance to thrive.

↬

Between the Waters, below the Firmament:
The Realm of Air

Something of that sense of security—a trust in the perdurance of the vital breathing space afforded to terrestrial creatures between the waters below and those above—is palpable in the odd word in Genesis 1:6 that has been variously translated into English as "firmament," "dome," and "vault." Robert Alter, who favors the latter, explains that the Hebrew *raki'a* suggests a hammered-out slab, not necessarily arched, but the English architectural term with its celestial associations created by poetic tradition is otherwise appropriate."[1] I agree that "vault" better captures the solidity connoted by the Hebrew word than does "dome." Yet I am especially fond of "firmament," not least for its reassuring connotation

---

[1] Robert Alter, *Genesis: Translation and Commentary* (New York: W. W. Norton, 1997), 3.

of, well, *firmness*. That this barrier should be conceived as holding firm must have been especially welcome for those who believed that it was holding back the celestial waters that would otherwise once more deluge the earth, as indeed they were said to have done in the biblical flood narrative, when "all the fountains of the great deep burst forth, and the windows of the heavens were opened" (Gen. 7:11) on account of the violence that a fallen humanity had unleashed within the terrestrial realm.

By contrast with the matricidal aggression by means of which the chaos monster of the watery deep was vanquished in the Babylonian creation narrative of Marduk and Tiamat, Genesis 1, as we have already seen, envisages a creator who graciously "lets be." An element of forcefulness nonetheless remains in the very solidity of the separation between the waters above and those below. While offering comfort to those who fear inundation, this firmament tears asunder what once had been one. In the Midrashic tradition, the element of sacrifice entailed in this sundering is registered in the story of the lower waters weeping over their separation from those above, and thereby also from "the presence of the King."[2] Yet just as the division of day and night is mediated by the transitional times of evening and dawning, so too, it seems, the earthly and heavenly waters remain in communication, as dew forms and vapor rises skyward from below and sweet rain pours down from on high. As the collaborative work of creation unfolds, it is by virtue of the opening afforded by this porous separation that new possibilities of co-becoming will be drawn forth.

Another reason I favor "firmament" is that this archaic term retains more of the strangeness of the original. Certainly, most of the hexameral commentators were puzzled by it. "Now, what would you say this means, the firmament? ... No sensible person

---

[2] Avirah Gottlieb Zornberg, *The Beginning of Desire: Reflections on Genesis* (New York: Doubleday, 1996), 5.

would be rash enough to make a decision on it," exclaimed John Chrysostom in his fourth Lenten homily on Genesis 1, delivered in Antioch in the late fourth century (CHoG, 55). Augustine, too, true to the "negative capability" that pervades his hesitantly "literal" commentary, insisted, "None of these things, however, should be rashly asserted, but they should all be discussed tentatively and with moderation" (LCG, 132). And at the height of the medieval revival of the hexameral tradition, Abelard, recalling Augustine, agreed that "it would be the height of arrogance for us to settle a question that so great a teacher abandoned as if unsure of himself" (ESW, 51).

In part, the problem pertained to developments within ancient cosmology. According to Hellenistic astronomy, the heavens encompassed and revolved around a spherical earth, rather than forming a lid above a flat one. How then could the waters remain suspended above this puzzling "firmament"? Surely, they would flow off and away as the heavens turned on their axis, acknowledges Ambrose, taking his cue from Basil in his Latin hexameron from 387 CE. He nonetheless proceeded to affirm that the biblical witness concerned matters beyond human ken, and could not be judged according to the reasoning of natural philosophy (AmH, 52–53).

While uncertainty was frequently acknowledged with respect to this mysterious "firmament," most commentators were reasonably confident in interpreting "heaven" or "heavens" in this passage as referring to the visible realm of the sky (as distinct from what most took to be the invisible Heaven of heavens, said to have been made, with the Earth, at the very beginning). For many, moreover, the "upper waters" were to be found there, in the sky. Suspended above the Earth, they were nonetheless engaged in a constant exchange with the "lower waters" in what looks very much like what we today would call the hydrological cycle. In Basil's reading, for example, the "aerial waters which veil the heavens,"

manifesting to us as clouds, are formed from "vapors that are sent
forth by rivers, fountains, marshes, lakes, and seas" (BaH, 57).
These "exhalations of the earth, gathered together in the heights
of the air … are condensed under the pressure of the wind," and
then fall back down once more in the guise of rain or snow (60).
Roundly rejecting the dualistic value judgments projected onto
these separate water bodies within allegorical readings such as
Origen's, whereby the upper waters signified holiness and the
lower wickedness, Basil held that all participated equally in God's
good creation. Recalling Psalm 148:7, in which "ye dragons and
all deeps" (57) are invited to join in praise for the Most High, he
affirms that "the deeps sing in their language a harmonious hymn
to the glory of the Creator" (60) within the "universal choir of
creation" (62).

Basil also had a particularly interesting take on the firmament,
suggesting that this was "not in reality a firm and solid substance,"
but something imperceptible to the senses; something less like a
hard barrier, and more like a "place" (BaH, 57). This suggestion
was taken up and taken further many centuries later by Thomas
Traherne (c. 1637–1674) in what was the first Protestant hexameron (at least in English), as well as one of the last works of this
kind until the present day.

Traherne shared with Basil a palpable delight in the natural
world, the workings of which were becoming better understood by
the mid-seventeenth century, thanks to advances in the empirical
sciences (including, of course, the initially hotly contested demo-
tion of Earth from the center of the universe to one planet among
others orbiting the sun). His effusive *Meditations on the Six Days
of Creation* appears to have been penned for the wife of a friend,
Susanna Hopton, and erroneously published under her name in
1717. Here, Traherne's concern was less with the mechanics of
nature than with questions of meaning, value, and purpose. To

this, he brought a whole new attention to how the physical world discloses itself to human sensory experience and poetic imagination. Affirming human corporeality, he celebrates, together with their divine creator, all those physical entities and processes to which humans (in company with other living beings) are indebted for our creaturely flourishing. Among those was the "firmament," which he describes as a "vast extended Space between the upper and the lower Waters" (MoSDC, 16). This space is graced by the presence of "*Air*, without which I cannot breath naturally in the least.... Not one *Sigh* in my Prayers, nor one *Tear* for my sins, can I have without this heavenly *Air* to refresh, enliven, and moisten me" (23). The opening up of this space, moreover, had brought forth Earth's thrillingly mutable weather-world: "*Vapours*, *Exhalations*, from whence come *Clouds* from the Ends of the Earth, *Storms*, *Dew*, *Hail*, *Snow* as *Wool*, *Hoar-Frosts* as *Ashes*, *Ice* as *Morsels*, *Lightnings*, *Thunders*, *Winds out of his Treasures* and *Tempests*" (24). And just as the speaker is enabled to offer up his prayers to heaven with each blessed breath and each tear of remorse, so, too, all these weathers, understood as manifestations of a living and breathing Earth, magnified their creator.

Traherne's older contemporary John Milton, in the verse hexameron that he smuggled into *Paradise Lost* (1667) in the voice of the archangel Gabriel, also parsed the "firmament" as an "expanse of liquid, pure, / Transparent elemental air diffused / In circuit to the uttermost convex / Of this great round" (VII, ll. 264–67). Yet he added that this is nonetheless "partition firm and sure / The waters underneath from those above / Dividing" (ll. 267–69), and proceeds to emphasize the orderliness of the "Chrystálline ocean" upon which the "World" was built, "the loud misrule / Of Chaos far removed" (ll. 271–72). Traherne's proto-romantically unruly yet nonetheless divinely graced weather-world, by contrast, seems to me more in sympathy with Gerard

Manley Hopkins (1844–1889) in his post-romantic celebration of "Wild air, world-mothering air, / Nestling me everywhere" in his rapturous "The Blessed Virgin compared to the Air we Breathe."[3]

Earth's Atmosphere and the Industrial Disordering of the Weather-World

Translating Traherne's line of interpretation into the language of contemporary science, we might liken the mysterious biblical firmament to Earth's precious atmosphere: the thin, permeable membrane composed of a medley of gases that surrounds the planet and is visible only from space. Held fast by the force of gravity, the atmosphere in which all earthlings move and live and have their being was co-created by volcanic eruptions and living organisms, beginning with the ancient photosynthesizing cyanobacteria that produced Earth's first oxygen, and continuing, among other things, with the cycling of oxygen and carbon dioxide between the diverse plants and animals that subsequently evolved. The resultant atmosphere has come to act rather like a shield, sustaining conditions congenial to the flourishing of life in a variety of ways: exerting sufficient pressure to keep water on the Earth's surface, absorbing some of the harmful radiation emitted by the sun, trapping some of the sun's warmth in what became known as the "greenhouse effect," and moderating diurnal and nocturnal temperature differentials. It is thanks to the light-scattering properties of gases and molecules in the atmosphere, moreover, that we see the sky as blue.

Basil believed that the aerial waters of the firmament were protecting the world from a fiery ether that would otherwise consume it. His cosmology might no longer hold good. Yet long in advance

---

[3] Gerard Manley Hopkins, "The Blessed Virgin Compared to the Air We Breathe," in *Poems and Prose of Gerard Manley Hopkins*, ed. William Henry Gardner (Harmondsworth, UK: Penguin Classics, 1963), 54.

of those solar end times, when the sun is expected to torch Earth in its death throes, it is clear that anthropogenic alterations to Earth's protective mantle are already endangering the life of this planet.

The first wake-up call came with the discovery that certain industrial chemicals were thinning the atmospheric ozone layer, allowing increased levels of ultraviolet solar radiation to blast parts of Earth's surface, thereby increasing the risk of cancer, cataracts, and immune and genetic damage. Who would have thought that our cooling systems and throwaway packaging could fray the sky? Prompt legislation to curtail the use of these troublesome substances showed almost immediate effects and promises to allow the ozone layer to fully repair itself over time. Far less successful so far have been efforts to rein in the combustion of the fossilized remains of ancient forests and sea creatures, which, in conjunction with ongoing deforestation and the expansion of animal husbandry, is elevating the quantity of greenhouse gases in the atmosphere, heating the planet up to an extent that is already proving perilous and is continuing to increase. The sky might not be falling, but industrial modernity has destabilized the firmament—unsettling the seasons and turning the weather ever wilder and weirder. Far from "conquering" the Earth, in accordance with the burdensome blessing accorded to humankind in Genesis 1:28, we are turning the planet into an even more unpredictable and perilous place than it was before, rendering it increasingly inhospitable to our own and many other kinds of life.

Earth's climate is a complex affair affected by numerous factors. These include fluctuations in solar activity, volcanic eruptions, and variations in Earth's orbit, in addition to levels of greenhouse gases. Global and regional climates have undergone substantial shifts many times in the course of planetary history, and humans have lived through several of these. Having evidently evolved on the African savannah during a planetary warm period around 300,000 years ago and subsequently fanning out into Europe, Asia,

and Oceania, our ancestors weathered the last Ice Age, which set
in some 33,000 years ago, not only surviving in those northern
climes that some of our kind had in the meantime colonized—in
company with our more hardy Neanderthal kin (some of whose
genes many of us are lucky enough to carry to this day)—but also
crossing over into the Americas. It is now thought that the easing of
the big chill around 11,500 years ago, ushering in a new era known
as the Holocene, afforded the comparatively mild and relatively
stable climatic conditions that proved suitable for the invention of
agriculture in those parts of the world graced with nutrient-rich
soils, reliable rainfall patterns, and potential beasts of burden.

Whether humankind, in company with countless other living
kinds, will survive the industrially altered conditions of the new era
that geologists believe the Earth has now entered (controversially
named the "Anthropocene"[4]) remains to be seen. Yet it is clear that
our collective more-than-human survival as earthlings will depend in
large part on how swiftly greenhouse gas emissions can be curtailed;
how effectively forests and other carbon sinks can be protected and
restored; and how well vulnerable populations, human and otherwise, can be enabled to adapt or migrate to new climes. We might not
have "dominion," and perhaps we should never have sought it, and
certainly not in the guise of ruthless domination and exploitation.
The adverse consequences of fossil-fueled industrialization—a project

---

[4] Scholars in the humanities and social sciences have come up with many
alternatives to "Anthropocene," primarily with a view to stressing, as I do also
in the Introduction, that it is not humanity at large who has altered the planet
in ways that will be legible in the fossil record millennia into the future, but a
particular human society (hence, e.g., the coinage "Capitolocene"). My own
variant is "Ploutocene": the era in which the realm of the dead, ruled by Plouton
in Greek mythology, in the guise of the fossilized remains of ancient forests,
invades the realm of the living, in the form of fossil fuel emissions, enriching
some (especially the "Ploutocrats" in the fossil fuel industry) but with disastrous
long-term consequences for the many. See Kate Rigby, *Reclaiming Romanticism:
Toward an Ecopoetics of Decolonization* (London: Bloomsbury, 2020), 11–12.

from which, hitherto, some have always benefited at the expense of many others—have nonetheless burdened contemporary societies with responsibilities that we cannot, at this critical moment, afford to shirk.

Global overheating is already assailing many creatures, human and otherwise, with a range of impacts that are affecting particular communities in varied ways in different parts of the world. Those that have cut closest to the bone for me personally are the catastrophic mega-fires in southeastern Australia. Coming thick and fast from the turn of the last century, each has been worse than the last: the tornado of flame that tore into Canberra in January 2003 (I was visiting: it was terrifying); the "Black Saturday" firestorm that blazed through much of Victoria in February 2009 (I was living in the densely forested Dandenong Ranges east of Melbourne: this was even more terrifying); and the fires that burned and burned and burned, in some places for up to two hundred days, through an area of eastern Australia the size of Great Britain, over the spring and summer of 2019–2020.[5] Among the areas incinerated along the south coast of New South Wales was the bushland around my childhood vacation destination of Tabourie Lake. I watched from afar, safe in rural Somerset, and my heart was broken.

Australian climates have long been quirky. From the northern tropics through the deserts of the center to the temperate regions of the south, they are influenced, to a greater or lesser degree, by irregular and nonannual cycles, largely driven by variations in sea temperatures in the Pacific and Indian Oceans (known as the La Niña / El Niño oscillation [ENSO] and the Indian Ocean Dipole).[6] With the

---

[5] Great Britain covers an area of 24.2495 million hectares, and the Royal Commission into National Natural Disaster Arrangements estimates that over 24 million hectares were burned during the "Black Summer" of 2019–2020, "Report," October 2020, p. 5, https://naturaldisaster.royalcommission.gov.au.

[6] Australian Bureau of Meteorology, "About Australian Climate," accessed March 30, 2023, http://www.bom.gov.au.

exception of Antarctica, this is the driest continent on the planet. But sometimes it rains in spades, and huge floods famously alternate with those long, dry, hot periods that European colonizers in the temperate zone called "droughts" and came to dread. Those droughts, in their experience, also brought "bushfires." What the oft hard-pressed settlers were not able to appreciate, though, was how the grasslands, wetlands, and forests of Australia had been shaped and cherished by millennia of highly skilled Aboriginal fire use, in conjunction with other forms of land care, at once ceremonial and practical.

When the British arrived in Botany Bay, they encountered one of the most biodiverse continents on Earth, whose vibrant collectives of plants, animals, and peoples were, in large part, sustained by the strategic deployment of cool fires on their ancestral lands (known as "Country" in Aboriginal English) by Australia's First Nations. The vitality of both the tropical savannah in the north and the grasslands of the south, onto which the invaders poured their hungry herds of hard-hoofed sheep and cattle, had been carefully cultivated by Aboriginal fire-stick farming. Patchwork burning ensured the protection of refugia, and frequent cool fires reduced the risk of big blazes, especially in the dry sclerophyll forests of the temperate zone, where the dominant tree species, eucalypts, rely upon fire to reproduce. The wet sclerophyll forests, where regular cool fires do not appear to have been set, also rely on fire and are believed to have regenerated themselves, phoenixlike, from their own ashes only in the wake of huge conflagrations occurring historically around every three hundred to four hundred years.[7]

The disruption of Aboriginal burning practices, in conjunction with other land-use changes, had already increased the incidence of big wildfires, especially in Victoria and South Australia, long

---

[7] Stephen Pyne, *Burning Bush: A Fire History of Australia* (Seattle: University of Washington Press, 1998); Tom Griffiths, *Forests of Ash: An Environmental History* (Cambridge: Cambridge University Press, 2002).

before the planet began to overheat. Now that it is doing so, with temperatures rising even more rapidly in Australia than the global average, extreme heat and uncontrollable fires threaten to make parts of the country unlivable, and not only for humans: at the height of the most recent drought, many koalas, who normally do not need to drink, died of thirst because the gum leaves they were eating had become too desiccated to rehydrate them, while entire colonies of flying foxes fell dead out of the trees by the thousands as temperatures peaked beyond their level of endurance. Then came the Black Summer of 2019–2020: although only thirty-three human lives were lost in the fires (with hundreds more dying as a consequence of smoke pollution), well over one billion animals, including countless insects, are believed to have perished. Survivors were left homeless and starving. Some entire species, already critically endangered by habitat loss and other environmental stressors, will probably be pushed over the brink of extinction. Others, not previously considered at risk, might well be so now.[8]

Global heating is afflicting Australia in other ways as well: floods are worsening, and cyclonic storms are getting bigger. According to a nationwide survey conducted in December 2022, 80 percent of respondents reported experiencing some form of climate-fueled disaster since 2019, with 38 percent of Queenslanders and 34 percent of people from New South Wales beset by more than one major flood event. All this is taking its toll on people's lives, livelihoods, and mental health.[9] It is also threatening entire ecosystems,

---

[8] Royal Commission into National Disaster Arrangements, "Report," 354–55. A report commissioned by the World Wildlife Fund found that up to three billion animals, excluding insects, were killed or displaced by the fires. Daniel Vernick, "Three Billion Animals Harmed by Australia's Fires," July 28, 2020, www.worldwildlife.org.

[9] Climate Council, "Summary of Results from National Survey of the Impact of Climate-Fuelled Disasters on the Mental Health of Australians," January 12, 2023, www.climatecouncil.org.au.

most dramatically so in the warming lower waters of the Pacific. There, off the coast of Queensland, that many-splendored thing, the Great Barrier Reef, is suffering repeated bleaching events, its color-burst of vibrant life fading to deathly white. Despite growing evidence that Australia is particularly vulnerable to the impacts of climate change, it continues to contribute disproportionately to greenhouse gas emissions. Because of the country's small population, Australia only generates a negligible percentage of total global emissions. Per capita emissions in Australia, however, are among the highest in the world: with only 0.3 percent of the world's population, Australia was estimated in 2019 to be releasing 1.3 percent of global carbon dioxide emissions. Australia also has one of the highest rates of land clearing in the world and an awful lot of methane-generating livestock. Moreover, Australia is one of the world's largest coal exporters, above all to China and increasingly also to India. Add those lucrative exports to the emissions ledger, and the tally of global carbon dioxide emissions looks more like 4 percent, making Australia the world's sixth-largest contributor to climate change.[10]

Pursuing Justice, Protecting Country, and Embracing Resistance: Initiatives from Australia and the Pacific

This point was highlighted in October 2014, when a flotilla of canoes from the South Pacific paddled out into the Port of Newcastle to confront the gigantic ships conveying the coal that is visiting disaster on low-lying islands.[11] The Pacific Climate Warriors

---

[10] Matt Macdonald, "How to Answer the Argument that Australia's Emissions are Too Small to Make a Difference," *The Conversation,* June 17, 2019, https://theconversation.com.

[11] Aaron Packard, "Coal Ships Stopped. The Warriors Have Risen," October 20, 2014, https://350.org.

proceeded to spread word of the injustice they were fighting elsewhere on the east coast of Australia. I heard them speak in Melbourne, where they had come to stage a sit-in at the headquarters of the Commonwealth Bank in protest against its investment in fossil fuel industries—in particular its support for the Indian-owned Adani Group, which was (and, at the time of writing, still is) planning to create the biggest coal mine in the world in Queensland's Galilee Basin. I had just come from the annual General Synod meeting of the Anglican Diocese of Melbourne, which, after vigorous debate, had finally passed a coauthored motion that I had presented, with beating heart, committing the diocese to disinvestment from fossil fuels. A few other synod members also joined the Climate Warriors event, including a priest, originally from Fiji, who had spoken movingly in favor of our divestment motion. The largely secular audience was nonetheless palpably startled when one of the Pacific Warriors told us that, where they came from, they were all "hard-core Christians" who took the Bible seriously. In their reading, he explained, God's promise to Noah and his descendants, along with all living things on Earth, that *God* would never again allow the waters to flood the world indicated that current sea-level rises were being caused by *humans*—some humans, that is, with others bearing the consequences—and that it was therefore up to us, all of us, whether as protesters or perpetrators or both, to rectify this calamitous and unjust situation.

I had a chance to learn more about the role of religion, predominantly Christianity, in Pacific Islander perceptions of climate change on a research visit to Kiribati (pronounced "Kiribas") the following year. Religion is an integral part of collective identity and everyday life in Kiribati. The tiny nation is spread across thirty-two coral atolls and one low-lying coral island just north and south of the equator, but nearly half of its 107,000 people live on the main island, Tarawa, where I conducted my research. Though estimates of religious affiliation vary, the 2010 census estimated that less than 1 percent of Kiribati islanders, or I-Kiribati, report no religious faith. Two percent are Baha'i, under 1 percent are Muslim, and the overwhelming majority are Christians of various denominations: around 56 percent Roman Catholic, 34 percent Kiribati Protestant (a Congregationalist denomination), 5 percent Mormon (Church of Latter-day Saints), 2 percent Seventh-day Adventist Church, with a smaller number of Jehovah's Witnesses and Assemblies of God adherents.[12] Certain traditional beliefs, values, and practices, largely pertaining to ancestral ties to place and duties to safeguard the remains of the dead in shrines on their home island, also remain strong, often coexisting with introduced faiths. This powerful sense of place-based belonging, embodied also in song, dance, and deep knowledge of the local seas and skies upon which people's subsistence has long depended, render the disordering and dislocation wrought by climate change especially traumatic.

Some of the very well-informed—and correspondingly desperately concerned—individuals I interviewed were frustrated by the lack of attention to, and in some quarters even skepticism toward, global heating that they encountered in their churches. This reticence now appears to have been overcome, with the Pacific Council of Churches, representing some 80 percent of the Pacific Islander population, already heavily involved with advocacy for climate change mitigation and building collective resilience in the face of its impacts.[13] Even back in 2015, though, my host, Pelenise Alofa, a leading climate change activist and Seventh-day Adventist, informed

---

[12] U.S. Department of State, "2016 Report on International Religious Freedom: Kiribati," accessed March 30, 2023, www.state.gov.

[13] The Secretary General of the Pacific Council of Churches, Rev. James Bhagwan, was one of the speakers at the Australia-Oceania online launch event of Greenfaith International, "Sacred People, Sacred Earth," November 18, 2021, and he is a signatory of Greenfaith's powerful Sacred People, Sacred Earth statement.

me that all the Christian denominations on the main island of Tarawa had representatives in the Kiribati Climate Action Network (KiriCAN), and she anticipated that the Baha'i community would also be sending a representative soon. Interestingly, participants included Evangelical denominations from the United States that have tended toward climate change denialism on their home turf (and elsewhere, including Australia). My first interview was with a very shy young representative from the Assemblies of God, whose small community had been badly affected by a recent mega king tide. At the time, Metaka Raeri was being briefed about his forthcoming trip to Australia as one of several young Pacific Islanders who would be receiving climate change advocacy training through the Pacific Calling Partnership (PCP), an Australian Catholic initiative that had been instrumental in the establishment of KiriCAN.[14]

Climate change had begun to catalyze conversations and collaborations among people of diverse religious traditions in Australia by then as well. In November 2009 I participated in a multifaith pilgrimage through townships devastated by the Black Saturday firestorm and bushland that was just beginning to regenerate. We traveled to unceded Yorta Yorta Country on the banks of the Murray River. Along the way, we stopped for a hearty lunch in the Sikh temple in Bairnsdale, which would later hit the international news on account of the thousands of meals they served to those displaced by the fires that raced through that area in January 2020. "Walking Humbly: Journey to the Murray" was organized by GreenFaith Australia, an initiative that had been founded in Melbourne right

---

[14] Another beneficiary of this program was the Seventh-day Adventist Tinaai Teaua, in whose gracious little vegetarian health retreat I was housed, and whom the PCP sponsored to attend the COP 21 Climate Convention later that year. I am indebted to Sara Penrhyn Jones for the opportunity to conduct this research in Kiribati as an International Partner Investigator in her UK Arts and Humanities Research Council-funded project, "Troubled Waters, Stormy Futures: Heritage in Times of Accelerated Climate Change."

around the time of the Black Saturday firestorm. This pilgrimage was timed for the lead-up to the Parliament of the World's Religions, which met in Melbourne in early December, bringing together some six thousand people from eighty countries and two hundred faith traditions, with a special focus on Indigenous spiritualities, and an intention to "make a world of difference" by "hearing each other" and "healing the earth."[15] Climate change loomed large at this convention, and many delegates took the opportunity to sign a petition urging concerted action from the delegates at the Copenhagen conference taking place at the same time.

The founding president of GreenFaith Australia is Jonathan Keren-Black. A Londoner by birth, Jonathan is a rabbi in the Progressive Jewish tradition, and he is as passionate about interfaith engagement as he is about environmental action. Having established the Jewish-Christian-Muslim Association of Australia, he and other members of this organization were keen to reach out to people belonging to some of the other two-hundred-plus faith traditions and subtraditions found in marvelously multicultural Melbourne, and they identified environmental concern as a common value around which they could gather. Inspired by groups such as GreenFaith in New Jersey, they established a grassroots multifaith group to form an Australian sister organization, comprising Sikhs, Buddhists, Hindus, and "spiritual seekers," as well as Jews, Christians, and Muslims.[16] Jonathan insists that no

---

[15] Kusamita Pederson, "The Parliament of the World's Religions 2009," *Interreligious Insight* 8, no. 1 (2010): 70–78. See also Graeme Sharrock's photo essay "'Hearing Each Other—Healing the Earth': Parliament of the World's Religions Meets," *Spectrum*, February 16, 2010, https://spectrummagazine.org.

[16] This collaboration was facilitated by my then–PhD student Elyse Rider, who had interviewed members of both groups as part of her action research project on Melbourne's growing interfaith ecology movement: Rider, "The Interfaith Ecology Movement," unpublished PhD thesis, Centre for Religious Studies, Monash University, 2011.

one religion has all the answers. His own environmentalism—which is expressed in his everyday life, his work as a rabbi, his experience of designing and building eco-homes, as well as in his activist engagement—is nonetheless founded in, and nourished by, his Jewish faith: in particular, his understanding that the human vocation is to be "caretakers of God's world," although he adds that he prefers to speak of the "spirit of the universe," since God-talk carries too much baggage (conjuring that "old man on a cloud with a beard").[17] Jonathan is exploring the language of a more atheist-humanist-leaning Judaism, centered on the inspiration and driver of our better inclinations, using the gender-neutral term *ruach* (or *ruack*, in his preferred transliteration). This could be analogous or related to the energizing breath-wind-spirit of Genesis 1 that hovered-vibrated-brooded on the watery deep "in the beginning." Reading the first part of Genesis, prior to the flood, as a "vegetarian charter" (while recalling that only "God" knows the ultimate meaning of the Torah, which discloses new facets with each rereading), Jonathan believes that we need to be far more mindful in our treatment of animals and their habitats, and he considers the escalating extinction rate to be a "terrible condemnation of humanity." He also describes the wealth of wisdom about care for the Earth within other Jewish texts and traditions, and he finds himself drawn back again and again to a roughly fourteen-hundred-year-old Midrash on the book of Ecclesiastes, according to which, "When God created Adam ... God told him: Everything has been created for your sake. Do not corrupt the world, for if you do, there will be no one to set it right after you."[18] From this

---

[17] All quotes from Rabbi Jonathan Keren-Black are shared with his permission from an interview conducted on November 9, 2020. I am also indebted to Jonathan for further editorial suggestions on this chapter.

[18] Midrash Ecclesiastes Rabbah. Jewish texts on ecology shared with the author by Rabbi Jonathan Keren-Black.

perspective, there are no second chances, and we cannot rely on any deus ex machina to clean up our mess.

Although he has met resistance in some quarters, Jonathan has done much to integrate ecological concerns into the praxis of Progressive Judaism, not only in Australia, but also internationally—notably as the author of a motion on taking care of the climate that has now been accepted by the World Union for Progressive Judaism. The 2010 edition of their prayer book, *Mishkan T'filah* (World Union Edition), of which he is a coeditor, includes Jonathan's poetic midrash on the flood narrative, which affirms, "Our task: to take care / Of God's world," while warning, "We have left it late to awaken."[19] At climate change rallies, as well as those in support of refugees, Jonathan can often be seen, and heard, deploying an ancient Jewish practice of "awakening": blowing the shofar, a horn traditionally used to announce the start of the new year and at other times of significance in the religious calendar, but also, biblically, to sound the alarm in response to an emergency. Jonathan is under no illusion about the powerful financial interests and their lobbying groups and political backers, who are trying to block this awakening. Though he is deeply concerned about Adani's poor pollution and human rights record, he is nonetheless wary of totalizing demonization. Recognizing that Adani is the leading manufacturer of high-end photovoltaics in India, his slogan at anti-Adani protests in Australia has not been "Stop Adani," but "Adani: Stop Coal, Start Solar."

---

[19] Yonatan ben Chayim (Jonathan Keren-Black), "The Rainbow," Australian Religious Response to Climate Change, from *Mishkan T'filah*, World Union Edition, ed. Elyse D. Frishman and the World Union Edition Editorial Team (New York: Central Conference of American Rabbis Press, 2010). This edition also includes a modified version of an older prayer for good weather in season, with a note that highlights "human dependence on the cycle of nature around the world," indicating that this is not about expecting God to intervene in the weather, but rather a reminder of the importance of taking care of the climate.

In 2013 GreenFaith joined forces with another interfaith initiative, the Sydney-based Australian Religious Response to Climate Change (ARRCC). This group was founded in 2008 with funding from an independent secular think-tank, the Climate Council, on the model of the USA's Interfaith Power and Light. The current ARRCC president is Thea Ormerod, an ardent Catholic and retired social worker, with decades of activist experience in the feminist, peace, and antipoverty movements, all within the framework of her faith. Her concern with social justice—in particular the grievous implications of global warming for those who had done least to cause it—first drew her into the climate movement. Additionally, Thea explained to me that she holds a sacramental view of creation, according to which "God imbues everything, holds everything in life," and that Jesus came to redeem the whole world, not just humans.[20]

Taking our cue from God's desire for the joyous collective flourishing of all life, Thea believes that we should be seeking to safeguard the goodness and beauty of creation, guided by the truth of science. Those old words about "having dominion" and "subduing the earth" belong to a historical context very different from our own, in her view. She adds that if "dominion" has any meaning today, it needs to be reframed in terms of "service," "in caring, in kindness, in benevolence, in a respectful relation with creation," as embodied in the self-giving love of Christ. Thea is very forthright in naming climate change a "great evil," and she identifies the attitudes and actions of those who are hindering meaningful action, including some members of the dominant political parties in the federal Parliament, with the worldly "powers and principalities" of darkness referred to by St. Paul. Standing up to these destructive forces is integral to her calling as a Christian, and she

---

[20] All quotes from Thea Ormerod are shared with her permission from an interview conducted on October 8, 2020.

is disappointed that more people of faith are not helping with the activist "heavy lifting." In her understanding, "Spirituality is not somehow different from activism": it encompasses how you live, involving service and being outspoken, prepared to fight for what is right ("nonviolently," she stresses), and ready to be pilloried for it.

ARRCC is engaged in a range of activities, such as lobbying, writing submissions, facilitating transformative lifestyle changes, and leading or participating in protests, sometimes incorporating interfaith liturgies and symbolic actions such as the "Funeral for Coal" vigils that Greenfaith/ARRCC held in various locations, including outside the offices of Labor opposition leader Bill Shorten and Liberal MP Josh Frydenberg in 2019. A primary focus has been trying to keep fossil fuels in the ground, including by means of nonviolent direct action. This has led to arrests for Thea and other ARRCC members (including clergy), first, at the site of the massive Whitehaven Coal mining lease in Laird Forest in New South Wales in 2014, and more recently at the site of the even bigger Adani Carmichael Mine site in Queensland's Galilee Basin.[21] The Laird Forest fight was lost, but the campaign against Adani is ongoing, and at this point appears to be gaining traction, as more and more investors pull out—among them, all four of Australia's big banks, including the Commonwealth.

Meanwhile, ARRCC is helping to build the network of GreenFaith International, which launched with a powerful statement in November 2020, "Sacred People, Sacred Earth," calling for transformative change to address the climate emergency. This was followed by a big year of action beginning on March 11, 2021, in the lead-up to the UN Climate Change Conference (COP 26),

---

[21] Front Line Action on Coal, "Faith Leaders from the Australian Religious Response to Climate Change Join the Blockade," March 12, 2014, https://leard. frontlineaction.org; Chris Shearer, "Faith Group Members Arrested in Anti-Adani Mine Protest," *Melbourne Anglican*, November 22, 2017.

which convened in Glasgow between October 31 and November 13 that year. In her End of Year reflection, Thea notes that the Australian government had finally agreed to join others around the world, along with many nonstate actors, in adopting a net-zero-by-2050 policy, and that with the "burgeoning growth of the climate movement, and the accelerating transition toward renewable energy," the chances of averting climate catastrophe seemed slightly better. Yet she concludes with the words of Rev. Fletcher Harper, cofounder of GreenFaith International: "It's time for people of faith to give up on hope as a strategy for climate justice, and instead to embrace resistance."[22]

Back in 2014 Rabbi Jonathan and Thea were part of a three-day ARRCC delegation to meet with MPs, senators, and advisers in Canberra. This visit also included an interfaith service and delivery of a letter to the Minerals Council of Australia, which, not coincidentally, is a five-minute walk from Australia's Parliament. The coal and other mineral "resources" that are being dug up around Australia and, for the most part, shipped abroad are all found on the unceded country of Australia's First Nations. At Maules Creek, ARRCC activists led an interfaith liturgy of lament with Gomeroi people, who had been protesting since 2010 against a planned coal mine on their Country. In their endeavors to block the Adani mine, they are standing with the Wangan and Jagalingou Traditional Custodians, as Torres Strait Islander elder Aunty Rose Elu affirmed at the launch of ARRCC Queensland's Climate Statement in November 2017.[23] While some Aboriginal communities have welcomed the training, employment, and financial opportunities that mining on their land might afford, others

---

[22] Thea Ormerod, End of Year Reflection, ARRCC newsletter, December 21, 2021, www.arrcc.org.au; citation from Rev. Harper from GreenFaith e-newsletter, November 17, 2021, https://greenfaith.org.

[23] Australian Religious Response to Climate Change, "Join-ARRCC in Stopping the Carmichael Coal Mine," accessed March 30, 2023, www.arrcc.org.au.

have been strongly opposed, and many communities have been split.[24] Increasingly, however, Indigenous Australians are beginning to realize that the impacts of global heating are likely to become so disruptive that some communities, especially in central and northern Australia, are likely to face another wave of forced removals, quite apart from the direct damage caused by mining operations on their Country.

This realization galvanized one remarkable young woman from the Widjabul clan of the Bundjalung nation, Larissa Baldwin, into climate activism. As she explained at a forum on "Creation, Country and Climate: Listening to Aboriginal and Torres Strait Island Christian Leaders," addressing the climate emergency is about "protecting Country": its people, place, and law.[25] Larissa works as First Nations campaign director with GetUp and is the founder of SEED, Australia's first youth-led climate network. She is helping to ensure that Indigenous knowledge, values, and land rights are no longer marginalized in climate change discussions and that traditional custodians are empowered to play a leadership role in the fight to keep fossil fuels in the ground. Although she was brought to the brink of despair during the 2019–2020 fires, during which a women's sacred site on her Country that had never been known to burn was ravaged by flame, Larissa finds hope in the new momentum for racial justice. In Australia and elsewhere, this includes seeking to ensure that the lands of First Nations remain livable.

---

[24] This appears to have been the case for the Gomoroi in connection with the Maules Creek mine. Oliver Laughland, "Maules Creek Coalmine Divides Local Families and Communities," *Guardian Australia,* April 9, 2014.

[25] The event took place in St. John's Cathedral in Brisbane and online in November 2020. The video of this gathering, at which Aunty Rose Elu also spoke about the grievous impacts of climate change that are already beginning to be felt by Torres Strait Islanders, is available at doingjustice2855, "Creation, Country & Climate: Listening to Aboriginal & Torres Strait Islands Christian Leaders," November 4, 2020, www.youtube.com.

In May 2022, Australians elected a new government with a far stronger commitment both to ensuring a voice for the continent's First Peoples and to addressing climate change, in its drivers as well as its impacts. Neither there, though, nor on an international level is there cause for complacency. Another two COP meetings have come and gone, and while the last-minute agreement at COP 27 to establish a fund for responding to "loss and damage" wrought by Earth's warming atmosphere was a significant achievement, there is still no credible plan for restricting global heating to below the guardrail of 1.5 degrees Celsius above preindustrial levels. In particular, as Thea observed in her evaluation of this crucial conference for ARRCC, "There was no real progress on the 'phasedown' of coal, oil and gas, building on a call to phasedown coal at COP 26 in Glasgow. Without a more rapid phasing out of fossil fuels, humanity is on track to far exceed 1.5°C of global heating."[26]

This is no time, then, for climate activists—however weary, worn, and sad—to lay aside their work of prophetic witness and political resistance. Accepting that they are in for what could be an even longer haul, in October 2022 ARRCC initiated a weekly online contemplative space titled "Weaving a Silence: Contemplating Earth and All the Stars." Interweaving poetry and prayer, spirituality and science, music and silence, these sessions invite ecospiritual activists of all faiths to "choose Earth as we transition from human-centeredness to 'Earth community' and in light of Evolutionary wisdom to discover our place in the story of the Universe."[27] Recalling the invitation to contemplation issued, in my reading, by the alternation of light and dark summoned into being on that primordial "one day" of creation, such spaces of stillness

---

[26] Thea Ormerod, "Advocacy and Outcomes at COP27," Australian Religious Response to Climate Change, www.arrcc.org.au.

[27] Australian Religious Response to Climate Change, "Weekly Online Contemplative Space," accessed March 30, 2023, www.arrcc.org.au.

afford refreshment, reinvigoration, and inspiration: a draft of living water to sustain the efforts of those fighting concertedly, yet peacefully, to hold open the potential for collective flourishing beneath the firmament that shields our hard-pressed Earth.

Here we are then, at a critical juncture in the wake of that "Second Day."

So be still once again. Take a breath. Feel it vibrate in your depths.

Enjoying still the breathing space that opened up with the separation of the waters, recall how you are the beneficiary of Earth's protective atmosphere, an inheritor of the benign climatic conditions that enabled new kinds of risky co-becoming—and collective unraveling—over the past 11,500 years or so.

But if you rest on the swell and look up to the sky, remember that there is a breach in the firmament. Whatever we do now, "a hard rain's a-gonna fall." Yet there is still much that can be done to reduce the damage and adjust to its consequences.

So, as they were around the world on GreenFaith's inspired Day of Action, March 11, 2021, let the shofars and conches be blown, the bells toll, cymbals clash, gongs be struck, drums be beaten, and the breath-borne sound of human voices be raised in every tongue between the waters above and, latterly, those below, for the sake of Earth's precious atmosphere and all that depend upon it.

"We have left it late to awaken."

Third Day

And God said, "Let the waters under the heavens be gathered
in one place so that the dry land will appear," and so it was.
And God called the dry land Earth and the gathering of waters
he called Seas, and God saw that it was good. And God said,
"Let the earth grow grass, plants yielding seed of each kind
and trees bearing fruit that has its seed within it of each kind,
and God saw that it was good. And it was evening and it was
morning, third day.

Genesis 1:9–13

⟡

As my husband will attest, I do not have a green thumb. The seed
I sow frequently fails to sprout. Yet when last summer I impul-
sively scattered the contents of an old packet of wildflower seeds,
long past their "use by" date, on the patch where he had just sown
sundry vegetable seeds, the resultant floral glory, while much
appreciated by bees and butterflies, left us with not a lettuce in
sight. Indoor plants, unless they prove particularly hardy, rarely
last long in my care. And when, in a fit of enthusiasm, I unearth
my bulbs to store them away during their dormant phase, in
accordance with online instructions, I am likely to completely
forget in which dark corner I have stashed them.

For all that, I am utterly enamored of plants, along with those
other earth-borne beings that we always took to be plants but

that biologists have now placed in a category all their own: those oddballs, the fungi. I love to eat them, for one thing: all manner of fruits, vegetables, nuts, legumes, mushrooms: you name it, I'll eat it, in abundance. And then there are the luscious colors and shapes and scents by means of which those flashy flowering plants call out to their pollinators. Was there ever anything more erotic than the delicate folds of a deep red rose or the arresting display of a canna lily? And then there is the sheer persistence of plants: how I admire their ability to make a way for themselves, taking root in the most unlikely of places! All it takes is the tiniest crack in the pavement and up they'll come and out they'll spread. The merest handful of soil can afford purchase for the especially plucky on a rocky escarpment. And how extraordinary are their capacities to communicate and congregate! When diverse plants and fungi get together, they go on to co-create stunning collectives in rambunctious company with other critters—microbes and mammals, birds and insects, reptiles and amphibians, the whole shebang—all sustained by the gracious ministry of water, sun, and soil.

I have had the good fortune to get to know one such collective quite well: a remnant of wet sclerophyll bushland nestling in the Dandenong Ranges east of Melbourne. Dominated by towering mountain ash, the tallest flowering plants on the planet, rivaling North American redwoods when fully grown, in partnership with their smaller companion, the blackwood, a gloriously winter-blooming acacia. Sherbrooke Forest is threaded through with ribbons of ancient temperate rainforest, flourishing beside the tiny creeks that flow from multiple subterranean springs.

Over the many years that we lived alongside it, I found myself falling ever more deeply in love with this patch of bushland. I was well aware that my acquaintance was superficial compared with that of old-timers and local naturalists, let alone its First Peoples, those of the coastal plains below and those of the Yarra Valley inland, who visited seasonally to source foodstuffs and other materials. Yet I came to consider the forest and its entrancing *creatures (from the more venomous of which, it must be said, it is best to keep your distance) a valued neighbor. Not long after we had moved up there from the eastern suburbs, an encounter with a recently road-killed red-necked wallaby with a newborn baby in her pouch nearly drove me to automotive vandalism. As it was, I contented myself with pulling her off the road (a piece of her exquisite jawbone fell out on the tarmac), whispering a tearful prayer, writing a bad poem, and cobbling together a cross to mark the spot. As my adoration deepened with growing familiarity of special nooks and crannies, I became fiercely protective of the many creatures whose entangled lives composed the forest. And as I began to realize how endangered they were likely to become as a consequence of climate change, I sickened with sorrow. Meanwhile, if anybody had approached once more with chainsaws, I felt ready to defend its still vibrant life with my own.[1]*

Thankfully, my fancied bravery has never been put to the test, and in the unlikely event that the Victorian government were to reverse the protected status granted to Sherbrooke Forest as part of Dandenong Ranges National Park in 1987, it is equally unlikely that any protesters would end up dying for their cause.

Elsewhere, however, on the frontline between resource extraction and forest protection, capitalist exploitation and Indigenous survival, that is precisely what is occurring right now. In the Amazonian rainforest, which takes pride of place in my meditations on this Third Day of creation, scores of forest defenders, most of them Indigenous leaders, have been murdered over the past five years alone. Under President Jair Bolsonaro in Brazil, illegal land clearing for commercial purposes expanded apace, contributing to the wildfires that have been intensifying in this region, ramped up by a warming climate.

---

[1] I have written about the Dandenongs elsewhere, including a short lyrical essay on my favorite rainforest gully in Sherbrooke Forest, "In a Eucalypt Forest," in SueEllen Campbell et al., *The Face of the Earth: Natural Landscapes, Science, and Culture* (Berkeley: University of California Press, 2011), 274–77.

In her account of a journey she made in a narrowboat on England's canals in the summer of 2018, wracked by a crippling sense of foreboding concerning the climate crisis, Rev. Frankie Ward reflects on the dire implications of the "burning of the rainforests, particularly—but not only—in the Amazon basin."[2] In addition to their terrible impact on the ecologies and peoples of the forests themselves, these fires threaten to further destabilize global climate, turning carbon sinks into carbon emitters, and disabling one of Earth's major life support systems. This realization brought Frankie to her lowest point on her inner journey, filling her with a desperation for which she found a voice in the Psalms:

> *I am utterly bowed down and brought very low;*
> *   I go about mourning all the day long.*
>
> *My loins are filled with searing pain;*
> *   there is no health in my flesh.*
>
> *I am feeble and utterly crushed;*
> *   I roar aloud because of the disquiet of my heart.*
>
> *O Lord, you know all my desires*
> *   and my sighing is not hidden from you.*
>
> *My heart is pounding, my strength has failed me;*
> *   The light of my eyes is gone from me.*

                                                    Psalm 38:6–10

Lying in a clearing in a remnant patch of Lancashire woodland as night fell, Frankie recalls how she heard, in the stillness, "the silent sobbing of the earth."[3]

To behold the bold burgeoning of vegetation in today's world cannot but bring to mind the forests falling and aflame, their peoples dispossessed and dying—but also resisting and fighting. To attend to plants and their fungal friends today is to apprehend Earth's cry: one that calls for solidarity with those who, at

---

[2] Frances Ward, *Like There's No Tomorrow: Climate Crisis, Eco-Anxiety and God* (Durham, UK: Sacristy Press, 2020), 174.

[3] Ward, *Like There's No Tomorrow*, 175.

this very moment, are defending the multispecies flourishing of
their forest home with their very lives. In seeking to respond to
this call, I find myself on my own journey in search of something
akin to the "fierce hope" that Frankie glimpsed on hers: one that
is capable of converting disabling despair into the fire in the belly
that fuels activism.

The Gathering of the Waters and the Greening of Dry Land

So far, this story has been all about the creation of spaces of possibility effected by *movement*. Starting with the shimmering, quivering, hovering movement of the divine breath/wind/spirit on the watery deep, followed by the pulsing alternation of darkness and light, the dynamic process of becoming unfolded further with the dramatic uplifting of a portion of those waters in order to open up the realm of air, the labile weather-world of Earth's protective atmosphere. Now, on the "Third Day," the pace picks up, the movement becomes multidirectional, and a whole new space of possibility heaves into view.

Notwithstanding its talk of the stately "gathering" of the waters, this passage actually invites us to imagine something rather more dynamic: the swirling, roiling, surging, and roaring as they gush into the place assigned for what Basil called the "Great Sea" (BaH, 294). In Milton's rendering, there was quite a commotion:

> *Immediately the mountains huge appear*
> *Emergent, and their broad bare backs upheave*
> *Into the clouds; their tops ascend the sky.*
> *So high as heaved the tumid hills, so low*

Down sunk a hollow bottom broad and deep,
Capacious be of waters. Thither they
Hasted with glad precipitance
... so the watery throng
Wave rolling after wave, where way they found—
... found their way

(VII, ll. 285–302)

This, too, was a separation that opened a space of possibility: this time it comes as a revelation, unveiling the land that had lain hidden beneath the primeval deeps. Yet neither did this separation establish a rigid divide. As many of the hexameral authors observe, the land retained its own life-giving waters: "Wherefore the earth," wrote Philo, echoing the ancient figure of Mother Earth, "had abounding veins like breasts" (OC, 31). Where they flow into rivers, these terrestrial waters are, as Basil put it, "received" by the sea, which, as we have already noted, in turn contributes moisture to the air through evaporation (BaH, 73). To this, Ambrose added that the sea also returns water to the land through underground streams, as was believed in the natural philosophy of his day (AmH, 83). In fact, as Abelard pointed out, the Hebrew word for "sea" in this passage encompasses fresh as well as salty waters, suggesting that the "gathering" actually entailed a distribution of interconnected waters across and beneath the land, as well as down into the depths of the ocean (ESW, 58). Moreover, as both Basil and Ambrose emphasized, Earth's mighty ocean itself connects as well as divides: "it girdles the isles, of which it forms at the same time the rampart and the beauty," writes Basil, "because it brings together the most distant parts of the earth and facilitates the inter-communication of mariners" (BaH, 73).

We will have much more to say about the sea in a couple of days' time. For now, though, the drama is all on land. And what a drama it is! Basil was patently beside himself with excitement at the thought of the land engendering vegetation. Repeating for the third time the phrase "let the earth bring forth," he added, "by itself without having need of any help from without" (BaH, 75). Many centuries later, Traherne framed Earth's participation in the divine act of creation as "co-operation": "As the Earth therefore co-oper-ates to the Production of her Fruits," he moralized, "so must we to the Production of all Virtues" (MoSDC, 34). Highlighting the land's generative powers, Basil intimated also the agency of plants in pursuing their own way in the world: "When the seed falls into the earth, which contains the right combination of heat and mois-ture, it swells and becomes porous, and *grasping* the surrounding earth, *attracts to itself* all that is suitable for it and has affinity to it" (BaH, 78, emphasis added).

Some commentators likened this remarkable springing forth of vegetal abundance to birthing: Earth "went into labor," remarked Chrysostom (CHoG, 72), while Ambrose elaborated on this idea: "The earth in labor brought forth new plants; girding herself with the garments of verdure, she luxuriated in fecundity," he added in a rather peculiar mixed metaphor whereby Earth's offspring became her attire, "and decked in diverse seedlings, she claimed them as her fitting adornments" (AmH, 92). While the visionary medi-eval abbess of Bingen, St. Hildegard (1098–1179), did not write a hexameron as such, her voice, too, must be recalled on this day, of all days. For it is to her that we owe the most marvelously vegetal image of the divine, a veritable phytotheology, in the guise of the "greening power," *viriditas*, that rises like—and as—sap from the life-giving land. As Hildegard declared in her *Book of the Rewards of Life* (*Liber Vitae Meritorum*):

The earth is at the same time
mother,
she is the mother of all that is natural,
mother of all that is human.
She is the mother of all,
for contained in her
are the seeds of all.[4]

In this way, the liberated land effects the birth of birth, or at least of reproduction: something that is common to all living things, however variously it is accomplished. And for at least some of the hexameral authors, in company with Hildegard, all living things were ensouled, albeit not all in quite the same way. Basil's brother, Gregory of Nyssa (c. 335–c. 385), for example, took care to differentiate between "vegetative," "animal," and "human souls" in his celebration of the "creation of man" (OMM, 177): a question to which we will return at the troubling end of the Sixth Day.

With this upsurge of luxuriant vegetation from the generative land, which comes into its own as the waters withdraw, such that, as Milton had it, "Earth now / Seemed like to Heaven" (VII, ll. 328–29), a new theme enters the hexameral literature: that of astounding abundance and mind-boggling diversity. Basil, once again, was especially effusive and sets the tone for later enthusiasts in this tradition. Marveling at the "ingenious contrivances of nature" (BaH, 83) manifest in the inexpressible variety of plants, each with their distinctive features, he exclaimed, "What shall I say? What shall I leave unsaid? In the rich treasures of creation it is difficult to select what is most precious; the loss of what is omitted is too severe"

---

[4] Hildegard of Bingen, quoted in Gabriele Uhlein, *Meditations with Hildegard of Bingen* (Santa Fe, NM: Bear & Company, 1983), 58. For an in-depth discussion of the meanings of "viriditas" in Hildegard's "ecological theology," see Michael Marder, *Green Mass: The Ecological Theology of St. Hildegard of Bingen* (Stanford, CA: Stanford University Press, 2021).

(BaH, 78). What was also clear to Basil was that these plants did not exist in isolation, but rather constitute what he termed an "elaborate system" (BaH, 87). By the time we come to Abelard, moreover, it is possible to discern a rudimentary recognition that that system is, as we would say, ecological, entailing regionally specific interrelationships among living organisms and their physical environs. As he observes, variety exists not only among individual types of plants but also among distinct plant communities in different climes: "many are born from the earth, of which some desire a hot land, others a cold, others a temperate" (ESW, 61).

Wondering how any "human mind" could "make an exact review, remark every distinctive property, unveil with certainty so many mysterious causes," Basil admitted to his listeners that "an insatiable curiosity is drawing out my discourse beyond its limits" (BaH, 85, 86). With the emergence of the biological sciences in the late eighteenth century, many human minds, motivated by that same curiosity (in conjunction, no doubt, with more instrumental agendas), were hard at work on just such an "exact review" of the Earth's extraordinary vegetal realm. Today, even as that realm is being decimated, this work continues to unveil new wonders. Now, though, it is being enriched by the independent insights—ethical as well as empirical—of Indigenous peoples, the colonization of whose lands had contributed to the expansion of Western botanical knowledge in earlier centuries.

Vegetal Histories, Mycorrhizal Networks, and the Rending of Earth's Raiment

The systematic study of plants within the prism of Western biological sciences took off with the work of the Swedish natural historian and physician Carl Linnaeus (1707–1778). His *Systema naturae* (*System of Nature*), first published in 1735, brought order into the overwhelming profusion that had left Basil so awestruck

by establishing a way of studying nature in accordance with a series
of taxonomic divisions. These are indicated in the full title of the
hugely influential tenth edition published in Latin in two volumes
in 1758 and 1759: "System of Nature through the Three Kingdoms
of Nature, according to Classes, Orders, Genera and Species, with
Characters, Differences, Synonyms, Places." Plants composed one
of those "kingdoms" (the others being animals and minerals), and
these he classified in accordance with their mode of reproduction.[5]

Linnaeus's "Systema Sexuale" excited a great deal of interest
in the love lives of plants. These were celebrated, for instance, by
the English natural historian, physiologist, and antislavery advocate Erasmus Darwin in one of the two long poems that make
up his immensely popular work of science communication, *The
Botanic Garden*.[6] He was by no means the first to do so. Basil, too,
waxed lyrical with respect to vegetal reproduction, observing of
palms, "sometimes we see those which they call female lower their
branches, as though with passionate desire, and invite the embraces
of the male" (BaH, 84). Among Darwin's enthusiastic readers was
William Wordsworth, who was led to speculate more generally on
the capacity of plants to take pleasure in their own existence. In his
"Lines Written in Early Spring," for example, he mused,

> *Through primrose tufts, in that green bower,*
> *The periwinkle trailed its wreaths;*
> *And 'tis my faith that every flower*
> *Enjoys the air it breathes.*[7]

---

[5] Carl Linnaeus, *Systema Naturae*, 10th ed. (Stockholm: Lars Salvius,
1758–1759).

[6] Erasmus Darwin, *The Botanic Garden* (1791; repr. London: Scolar Press,
1973).

[7] William Wordsworth, "Lines Written in Early Spring," in *The Works
of William Wordsworth: With an Introduction and Bibliography* (Ware, UK:
Wordsworth Poetry Library, 1994), 482.

Erasmus Darwin was the grandfather of the more famous Charles, and the former preempted the latter's theory of evolution. In his major scientific work, *Zoonomia* (1794–1796), Darwin the elder argued that sexual reproduction was the motor of those evolutionary processes, which, he surmised, began with micro-organisms in Earth's ancient oceans and had over time engendered the great abundance of diverse living kinds, including humans, in existence today. This evolutionary theory, within which extinction could be seen as a natural function of the struggle for existence, was popularized in verse in Darwin's *Temple of Nature*, published posthumously in 1803 (to which we will return on the Fifth Day).

Contemporary evolutionary theory, informed by the younger Darwin's theory of natural selection, together with much more empirical research, dates the emergence of plants and fungi to a staggering 350 million years ago. Their kinship relations are now being disclosed with the assistance of DNA sequencing, rather than in accordance with appearance or reproductive strategies. The older Darwin's hypothesis that plants were relative latecomers on this planet compared with sea creatures still holds, though. But then the idea that life started in the ocean, just as a babe comes into being in the waters of its mother's womb, is ancient and intuitive. Occurring in many creation myths, such as the "earth diver" stories of several Native American, Central Asian, and Finno-Urgic peoples,[8] it was also expounded by the pre-Socratic philosopher Thales (c. 624–c. 546 BCE), whom Johann Wolfgang von Goethe (1749–1832)—another avid plant-lover—turned into a spokesman for his own evolutionary theory in the second part of his great tragic drama *Faust* (1832).

In 1886 an ardent follower of Charles Darwin, German zoologist Ernst Haeckel (1834–1919), coined the term "ecology"

---

[8] See David Adams and Margaret Adams Leeming, *A Dictionary of Creation Myths* (Oxford: Oxford University Press, 1995), 79–80.

(*Oekologie*)—literally, the knowledge (*logos*) of the household (*oikos*)—to refer to the study of the relationship of animals with their organic and inorganic environment. As we have already seen, though, an appreciation of connectivities among living beings and their environs long predated that coinage and can already be glimpsed in the hexameral literature. Ambrose, for example, elaborating on a point made by Basil with respect to the existence of plants that are harmful for humans, insists that "not everything was created for our gourmandizing":

> Each and everything which is produced from the earth
> has its own reason for existence, which, as far as it can,
> fulfils the general plan of creation.... What you consider
> as useless has use for others.... What is harmful to you
> provides harmless fruit for birds or wild beasts. (AmH, 96)

Faith in divine providence as manifest in those connectivities that composed natural systems contributed to the distinctly custodial ethos that developed within some strands of Christianity. This can be seen in the frugal lifestyle and regenerative land care aspired to by many monastic orders of the Middle Ages, as laid down, for example, in the *Rule of St. Benedict* (516 CE). In Britain, this custodial ethos began to be articulated with greater urgency during the eighteenth century with growing recognition of the destructive potential of the intensification of agriculture and extractive industries, both at home and in the Americas, where native vegetation, formerly tended by Indigenous peoples, had been converted into monocultural plantations worked by African slaves. Alexander Pope (1688–1744), for example, in his "Essay on Man" (1743)—which, despite its anthropocentric title, is actually a celebration of the more-than-human world and its diverse living kinds—railed against human arrogance and tyranny, warning, "From Nature's chain whatever link you strike, / Ten or ten thousandth, breaks the chain alike" (Epistle 1, 1;. 245–46).[9] In the following century, this custodial ethic, in conjunction with a newfound aesthetic appreciation of places as yet undamaged by industrial regimes of farming or manufacturing, motivated the endeavors of Canon Hardwicke Drummond Rawnsley (1851–1920), cofounder of the National Trust, social reformer and animal welfare campaigner, to protect England's Lake District from slate mining and associated road and rail developments.[10]

With the emergence of the evolutionary thinking of the Romantic period, Pope's presupposition of a static and hierarchical "chain of being" was challenged by a new view of nature as a decentered mesh, weaving and reweaving itself in specific ways in different places over time. Alexander von Humboldt (1769–1859) set out to research this "interlinkage, not simply in a linear direction, but in an intricate netlike interweaving," on his travels in the Americas between 1799 and 1804.[11] When Charles Darwin ventured forth upon his own journey in the *Beagle* in 1831, he had Humboldt's travel writings in tow. This new understanding of nature as a process of evolutionary co-becoming rather than a static artifact of divine manufacture complicated Christian theologies of creation. There were, and are, certainly some Christians who cannot stomach Darwin's theory of natural selection. For others, though, the evolutionary paradigm could readily be reconciled with the long-standing premise of a creator who, in some mysterious

---

[9] Alexander Pope, "An Essay on Man," in *The Poems of Alexander Pope*, ed. John Butt (London: Methuen, 1965), 513.

[10] Michael Northcott, "The Romantics, the English Lake District, and the Sacredness of High Land: Mountains as Hierophanic Places in the Origins of Environmentalism and Nature Conservation," in *Eco-Theology: Essays in Honour of Sigurd Bergmann*, ed. Hans Günter Heimbrock and Jörg Persch (Paderborn: Brill-Ferdinand Schönigh, 2021), 74–90.

[11] Alexander von Humboldt, *Kosmische Naturbetrachtung*, ed. Rudolph Zaunick (Stuttgart: Alfred Körner, 1958), 342. My translation.

way, "lets be": one who was the "primary cause" of a physical reality that generated its own momentum, operating according to its own system of secondary and tertiary causes, which, unlike God, were amenable to scientific verification—a physical reality that might also be apprehended through the eyes of faith as radiant with divine presence and held in divine love.

Over the past two centuries, a bevy of botanists, evolutionary biologists, and ecologists have uncovered in ever more finely grained detail the complex connectivities among plants and other organisms and their shared environs. Reaching back in evolutionary time as well as out into ecological space, the lively interrelationships in which plants participate on land extend also beneath the waters and below the ground. Moreover, as I learned from my dear friend Wendy Wheeler, an expert in the fertile field of biosemiotics, these interrelationships are sustained by all manner of semiotic processes: forms of communication, that is, using signs—a phenomenon that can be traced throughout the living world, from the level of the individual cell to the online chatter of humans.[12]

Plants too, it seems, really do talk, if not in so many words! Rather they do so, for instance, through those scents and shapes and colors in which we too might delight, by means of which flowering plants call out to their favored pollinators, or, in the case of those scary carnivorous kinds, to their preferred prey. Rather more startlingly, they also do so through vibratory movements, such as those produced by plants that signal to one another by clicking their root tips. Touch also plays a role, both above and below ground, on what Anthony Trewavas has called the "plant dance floor." And so, it seems, does sound, according to researchers in the field of "phytoacoustics."[13] Most of the time, though, like all living

---

[12] Wendy Wheeler, *Expecting the Earth: Life/Culture/Biosemiotics* (London: Lawrence and Wishart, 2016).

[13] Anthony Trewavas, *Plant Behaviour and Intelligence* (Oxford: Oxford

beings (including ourselves), they are communicating chemically—and among their most crucial conversation partners are fungi.

I was first drawn into the wonders of the fungal realm by a special issue of the little journal of which I was then coeditor, *PAN* (*Philosophy Activism Nature*). In their editorial introduction, Alison Pouliot and John Ryan observed how fungi have "inspired the imaginations of scientists and aesthetes alike and are deeply enmeshed in the mythologies and traditions of many cultures." Just as microscopic phytoplankton are an essential ingredient of oceanic food webs, the neglected fungal "kingdom" beneath our feet, they noted, underpins "the earth's terrestrial ecosystems."[14] In truth, this "kingdom" is part of what might better be described as a multispecies "kindom."

To begin with, it was thanks to fungi, together with the algae they teamed up with, that plants made a place for themselves on dry land; until their own root systems evolved, their fungal friends served a similar purpose. The intimate entanglement of plants and fungi continues to this day: microscopic fungi in soil send out gossamerlike filaments that weave themselves into the tips of roots to form a mycorrhizal (fungal-root) network. Some 90 percent of all plants are thought to be reliant upon such mycorrhizal networks to supply them with nutrients and protect them from disease. In return, plants supply their fungal friends with sugars they have photosynthesized from sunlight. The connective tissue formed by fungi, known as mycelium, holds the soil together, helping it to retain water rather than being washed away by it, as well as storing significant quantities of carbon dioxide. Linking plants into wider networks, these fungal symbionts form what botanist Suzanne

---

University Press, 2014). On sound, see also Monica Gagliano, *Thus Spoke the Plant: A Remarkable Journey of Ground-Breaking Scientific Discoveries and Personal Encounters with Plants* (Berkeley, CA: North Atlantic Books, 2018).

[14] Alison Pouliot and John Charles Ryan, "Fungi: An Entangled Exploration." *PAN* 10 (2013): 1–5, 1.

Simard dubbed the "wood wide web," an intricately branching network along which water, nutrients, bacteria, and chemical signals—including news about water scarcity, insect attacks, and other hazards—are constantly passing to and fro.[15] Plants and fungi, it seems, have their own kinds of intelligence. And when they get together with other, more mobile creatures to form those larger collectives that we call woodlands and forests, something like a meta-organism emerges: one that those who have long lived in the midst of such fabulous plurisingularities, such as the Runa of Ecuador's Upper Amazon, know to have its own ways of thinking.[16]

Increasingly, modern Western science is disclosing the physical processes underlying phenomena that have long been recognized within the traditional knowledge systems and are integral to the resilient lifeways of many First Peoples: namely, that we have come to live and move and have our being in a world of multitudinous more-than-human intelligences that speak in a correspondingly diverse array of voices, to which, moreover, we would do well to attend. Tragically, this realization is dawning right at the time when so many of those voices are being silenced forever as a result of the ecologically destructive impacts of technologies and economies that were themselves enabled by earlier scientific advances.

A report published by Kew Gardens in 2020 bears the shocking tidings that 40 percent of Earth's "garments of verdure," as Ambrose put it—her plants and fungi, a great many of which are still unknown to science—are thought to be threatened with extinction. Indeed, a report from the previous year found that

---

[15] S. W. Simard in Peter Wohlleben, The *Hidden Life of Trees*, trans. Jane Billinghurst (London: William Collins, 2016), 11. For a wonderful introduction to the wonders of fungi, see Merlin Sheldrake, *Entangled Life: How Fungi Make Our Worlds, Change Our Minds, and Shape Our Futures* (London: Penguin, 2020).

[16] Eduoardo Kohn, *How Forests Think: Toward an Anthropology beyond the Human* (Berkeley: University of California Press, 2013).

571 plant species are known to have already been lost since 1750, but concluded that the actual number is probably far higher.[17] While the disappearance of particular species over time is a natural phenomenon, the rate of extinction has accelerated exponentially as the expansion of agriculture, mining, manufacturing, and urbanization has decimated native vegetation, with global heating now putting further pressure on plants and fungi and the multi-species worlds that depend upon them. According to this report, "The ongoing rate of plant extinctions is up to 500 times the pre-Anthropocene background extinction rate for plants."[18] Horrifically, a third of all free-living tree species are now believed to be at risk of disappearing forever.[19] Given that the interwoven lives of plants and fungi provide the fabric that supports the coexistence of all manner of other creatures within those larger collectives upon which humans are also dependent, this rapid diminishment of vegetal flourishing, rendering Earth's raiment ever more threadbare, is disabling the entire life-support system of what Pope Francis aptly calls "our common home."

Alexandre Antonelli, director of science at Kew Gardens, observes that most of the plants and fungi that scientists are yet to identify, quantify, and assess, both for their potential uses and their conservation status, are "already known and used by people in the region of origin—people who have been their primary custodians and often hold unparalleled local knowledge." Mindful, perhaps, of the colonial history of the collection housed in these Royal Botanic Gardens, assembled as it was from the ends of the empire,

---

[17] Damian Carrington, "40% of Earth's Plant Species at Risk of Extinction," *The Guardian*, September 30, 2020.

[18] A. Antonelli et al., *State of the World's Plants and Fungi 2020* (Kew: Royal Botanic Gardens, 2020). See https://www.kew.org.

[19] Botanic Gardens Conservation International, *State of the World's Trees, 2021*, www.bgci.org.

and concerned about the unsustainable exploitation (principally for the economic gain and insatiable appetites of outsiders) of plants that are precious to Indigenous peoples, Antonelli adds that it is "critical that any benefits derived from those species primarily contribute to the well-being of those people." He also acknowledges that "nature has a value of its own":

> Despite the fact that an exploitative view of nature has deep roots in our society, most people today would agree that we have no moral right to obliterate a species—even if it has no immediate benefit to us. Ultimately, the protection of biodiversity needs to embrace our ethical duty of care for this planet as well as our own needs.[20]

Yet the report is especially energetic in its consideration of the use value, and hence commercial potential, of the plants that are beginning to be studied in biodiversity hotspots, such as the Amazon. Indeed, in the *Guardian* article that carried news of this report, these are described as "an untapped 'treasure chest' of food, medicines and biofuels that could tackle many of humanity's greatest challenges."[21] To recall our dependence upon the fungal and plant kindom is clearly critical as it comes ever more under threat. Highlighting the benefits to be derived from particular species is doubtless a valuable way of garnering support for biodiversity conservation, especially in societies where that "exploitative view of nature has deep roots." But talk of "treasure chests," evoking images of pirate hoards on desert islands, simply reinforces that view.

This is a far cry from Indigenous understandings of plants as "persons." In the Americas, as elsewhere, a huge variety of plants has long been used for nutritional, medicinal, and ceremonial purposes by

---

20 Antonelli, *State of the World's Plants and Fungi 2020*.
21 Carrington, "40% of Earth's Plant Species at Risk of Extinction."

First Peoples. But these have typically not been considered mere "resources," there for the taking, a treasure chest waiting to be opened. Rather, as ethnobotanist Linda Black Elk of the Catawba Nation of South Carolina explained in a 2020 webinar hosted by the New York Botanical Gardens, among her people the "plant nations" are understood to be "relatives," with whom respectful relations need to be cultivated through communication—allowing space, building trust and a willingness to compromise and, when necessary, to apologize. In order to utilize a plant in such a way that you safeguard its nation's flourishing, you need to know its story. The plant's story informs you about its own requirements and relations with others, as well as your responsibilities toward it.[22] In referring to a plant as an "it," however, I've already got it all wrong. Speaking on "Indigenous Kinship and Multispecies Justice" in a series of webinars on "Species in Peril" hosted by the University of New Mexico, ethnobotanist Robin Wall Kimmerer, a member of the Citizen Potawatomi Nation and of European and Anishinaabe ancestry, explained that the Indigenous languages of the Americas "animate" the world. There is no word for "it," because all entities, including inorganic ones such as mountains and rivers, are persons. In this animate world, kinship relations arise from, and are cultivated by, practices of reciprocity keyed to mutual flourishing.[23]

---

[22] Linda Black Elk, "First Nations: Ethical Landscapes, Sacred Plants," New York Botanical Gardens, webinar, November 13, 2020, www.nybg.org.

[23] Robin Wall Kimmerer, "Indigenous Kinship and Multispecies Justice," University of New Mexico Biodiversity, webinar, November 19, 2020. See also Kimmerer's wonderful book *Braiding Sweetgrass: Indigenous Wisdom, Scientific Knowledge and the Teaching of Plants* (Minneapolis: Milkweed Editions, 2013), and Nancy J. Turner, ed., *Plants, People, and Places: The Roles of Ethnobotany and Ethnoecology in Indigenous Peoples' Land Rights in Canada and Beyond* (Toronto: McGill–Queens University Press, 2020).

"Amazonize Yourself!":
The Endangered Amazon and Its Ardent Defenders

The Amazon rainforest, one of those "treasure chests" that Antonelli is keen to have opened, is not only a biodiversity hotspot: it is also home to some 380 First Nations peoples, including a large number of "contactless" tribes, whose ancestral lands and lifeways, including soil-enriching and biodiversity-boosting forms of forest gardening and silviculture, are fast being eroded. This is happening with especial speed and brutality in Brazil, where the government of Jair Bolsonaro licensed large-scale industrial despoliation of the Amazon through the expansion of mining, logging, and agriculture, much of it occurring illegally on lands designated as Indigenous protected areas. Before turning to the voices of those who are so powerfully protesting this unfolding devastation and its associated, diabolically entwined genocide, ethnocide, and ecocide, it is worth recalling how the fate of Amazonia concerns us all.

It is impossible to talk about this region without gushing superlatives. Watered by the most voluminous river on Earth—the mighty Amazon, with its more than one thousand tributaries—this is the largest area of tropical rainforest in the world, covering some five and one-half million square kilometers. Most of the Amazon rainforest is situated within the borders of Brazil, with a further 13 percent in Peru, 10 percent in Colombia, and smaller areas extending into Bolivia, Ecuador, French Guiana, Guyana, Suriname, and Venezuela. Brazil alone is home to around 30 percent of the world's remaining tropical forests, covering 58 percent of its territory.[24] An estimated 12 percent of the world's freshwater reserves

---

[24] Marcilio de Freitas, "The Future of Amazonia: Inheritance or Ruin?" Seeing the Woods: A Rachel Carson Center, blog, September 2, 2020, https://seeingthewoods.org. See also Marcílio de Freitas and Marilene Corrêa da Silva Freitas, *The Future of Amazonia in Brazil: A Worldwide Tragedy* (Frankfurt a.

are also located in Brazil, together with around 10 to 20 percent of Earth's dwindling biodiversity.[25] Every year, hundreds of the plants that are new to science are being identified in Brazil, which topped the world for new plant identifications in 2019.[26] All of this incredibly lush vegetation might be metaphorically breathtaking, but it literally gives us the air we breathe, pumping out around 20 percent of Earth's oxygen supply while absorbing huge quantities of carbon dioxide. Some 10 percent of the world's carbon store is currently safely tucked away in the Amazon rainforest.

The extent of forest cover in the Brazilian Amazon has been dwindling for some time. Following the intensification of deforestation that began in the 1970s, this had extended to 792,979 square kilometers by 2014, equaling a loss of about 19 percent of its estimated total at the time of the European colonizers' arrival in 1500.[27] Under the previous presidency of Luiz Inácio Lula da Silva (2003–2010) and his minister of environment, Marina Silva (2003–2008), the rate of deforestation was significantly slowed. During this period, 73 percent of the total protected areas worldwide were located in Brazil, and by the end of 2010, 43.9 percent of the Amazon forest was protected by various kinds of reserves.[28] In recent years, however, deforestation, largely for cattle ranching

M: Peter Lang, 2020). Marcilio has also self-published a three-volume collection of his own poetry in praise of, and lamentation for, the *Amazon: Amazônia nosso tesouro* (n.p.: Amazon Kindle Direct Publishing, 2022).

[25] José-Augusto Pádua, "The Dilemma of the 'Splendid Cradle': Nature and Territory in the Construction of Brazil," in *A Living Past: Environmental Histories of Modern Latin America*, ed. John Soluri, Claudia Leal, and J.-A. Pádua (New York: Berghahn, 2018), 92.

[26] Antonelli, *State of the World's Plants and Fungi 2020*, 9.

[27] José-Augusto Pádua, "Civil Society and Environmentalism in Brazil: The Twentieth Century's Great Acceleration," in *The Great Convergence: Environmental Histories of BRICS*, ed. S. Ravi Rajan and Lise Sedrez (Oxford: Oxford University Press, 2018), 118.

[28] Pádua, "Civil Society and Environmentalism in Brazil," 133.

and soya production, but also mining and logging, has expanded exponentially. In conjunction with changes to weather patterns associated with climate change, deforestation is the main contributor to the massive fires that have begun to ravage Amazonia. In 2020, they were worse than ever, affecting Argentina, Bolivia, and Paraguay as well as Brazil, reaching even into wetland regions that have hitherto been strangers to fire. Currently, it is thought that as much as 40 percent of the Brazilian rainforest is at a tipping point of turning into savannah.[29] Were this to occur, global heating would be ramped up to a level that could prove intolerable for much of life on Earth. For this reason, the devastation that is currently unfolding in Amazonia, and especially in Brazil, concerns us all.[30] Yet it concerns some of us rather more closely in another way as well: those of us, that is, who end up consuming the produce of deforestation, such as chicken or beef fattened on soya grown on once-forested lands now transformed into monocultural plantations.

Those most immediately impacted by this unfolding ecocide, however, are the First Peoples of Amazonia. In Brazil—the diverse demography of which includes the descendants of African slaves as well as European colonizers, more recent immigrants, and a great many of mixed heritage or *mestiza*—the Indigenous population had already been decimated by the diseases, weaponry, and environmental changes brought by Portuguese invaders, plummeting from an estimated 2 million to 3 million prior to 1500 to 817,000 in the 2010 census.[31] Among this population, which is home to more uncontacted tribes than anywhere else in the world, hundreds

---

[29] C. A. Boulton et al., "Pronounced Loss of Amazon Rainforest Resilience since the Early 2000s," *Nature Climate Change* 12 (2022): 271–78.

[30] Timothy J. Killeen, *A Perfect Storm in the Amazon Wilderness: Success and Failure in the Fight to Save an Ecosystem of Critical Importance to the Planet* (Winwick, UK: White Horse Press, 2021).

[31] Instituto Brasileiro de Geografia e Estatística, "Population Census 2010—Main Results," accessed March 30, 2023, www.ibge.gov.br.

of different languages are spoken.[32] Rendered voiceless in their own country, they are now speaking out to the world, using the media and lingua franca that predominate in those global systems of production, consumption, and trade that are ravaging their lands. Here, in part, is what they have to say:

> A few years ago, the tributaries of the Amazon dried up for the first time in living memory. If we don't act now, in ten years, the Amazon ecosystem will collapse. The heart of this planet will stop beating.... We will disappear if we don't act.... There is no turning back. But we can't let it destroy us anymore. Now is the time for you to be silent. The time has come to listen. You need us, the prisoners of your world, to understand yourselves. Because the thing is so simple: there is no gain in this world, there is only life.[33]

This is a translation into today's globally dominant language from the settler-colonial language of Brazil—Portuguese—of words spoken by the Indigenous performer and activist Sara Kay. She is speaking in a video recording from the forested banks of the Oiapoque River in northern Brazil, which screened internationally

---

[32] FUNAI, the National Indian Council of Brazil, estimates that there are at least one hundred isolated communities in the Brazilian Amazon. Survival International, "The Uncontacted Indians of Brazil," accessed March 30, 2023, www.survivalinternational.org. Aryon D. Rodrigues, "The Present State of the Study of Brazilian Indian Languages," in *South American Indian Languages: Retrospect and Prospect*, ed. Harriet E. Manelis Klein and Luisa R. Stark (Austin: University of Texas Press, 1985), 405–42.

[33] Sara Kay, "This Madness Has to Stop!," Wiener Festwochen "School of Resistance—Episode One," May 16, 2020, www.youtube.com. See also Teresa Millesi, "'This Madness Has to Stop!': Indigenous Voices on the Destruction of the Amazon," Rachel Carson Center, "Seeing the Woods" blog, October 14, 2020, https://seeingthewoods.org.

on the opening night of the Vienna Theatre Festival, May 16, 2020. Sara was meant to have been there in person, performing the lead role in an activist production of Sophocles's *Antigone* (c. 441 BCE), set on an occupied road in the Amazon, with a chorus comprising Indigenous survivors of a massacre caused by the Brazilian government. But then the pandemic intervened. Allowed to spread unchecked by the Bolsonaro regime, this novel disease (the origins of which are probably linked with the commercial exploitation of rainforests elsewhere) has had an appalling impact on Indigenous people, as well as on diverse inhabitants of the Amazonian capital, Manaus. There, Sara tells us, at the time of the recording, the dead "lie in mass graves filled up by tractors. Others lie in the street, unburied like Antigone's brother." Meanwhile, amid the chaos, the agents of destruction seize the opportunity to "penetrate even deeper into the forest."

Sara explains that her name means "she who cares for others," and that, on her father's side, she comes from the Tariano Clan, the "Clan of Thunder," making her a Daughter of the Thunder God. Both—the care and the thunder—are palpable in her speech, and among her targets are Christian missionaries. "First came the soldiers," she recalls, "then came the clergy.... They murdered in the name of God and the one civilization. In the name of progress and profit." For most of the last five hundred years of colonial oppression, the clergy were predominantly Catholic. Today the missionaries are largely Evangelicals in the US mold. Extremely well-subsidized, they are penetrating far deeper into Indigenous territory—and to even more culturally and ecologically destructive effect—than the Catholics ever did. They are peddling a version of Christianity that takes a particularly aggressive view of the human calling to "subdue the earth." This interpretation is highly congenial to those extractive industries favored by Bolsonaro. The former president has also been able to curry favor among conservative Catholics, but his base is solidly Evangelical, and he sought to shore up his power by means of a form of "Christofascist" propaganda.[34] From his perspective, Indigenous sovereignty and lifeways are simply an impediment to an allegedly God-given right to complete the colonial conquest of the Amazon in the name of progress and profit.

Yet the peoples and ecologies of Amazonia are also able to count some Christians among their staunchest allies. One such is the eminent botanist Sir Ghillean Prance, a former director of Kew Gardens, who spent many years researching in the Brazilian Amazon. The significance of his work on plant diversity there, conducted in association with Woarani People, earned him the 1993 International Cosmos Prize, and in 2004 he became the first recipient of the Graziela Maciel Barroso Prize from the Brazilian Botanic Garden Network. Ghillean is a deacon in the Lyme Regis Baptist Church and a patron of Green Christian, a UK-based organization originally established by Christians within the British Green Party. In his concluding keynote lecture for Green Christian's Annual Festival held online in October 2020, he shared his frustration that concerted action to arrest extinctions and global heating had not been taken long before now. Ghillean is among those scientists who have been sounding the alarm for decades, notably in publications such as *Extinction Is Forever: The Status of Threatened and Endangered Plants of the Americas* from 1977 and *Tropical Rainforests and the World Atmosphere* from 1986.[35] In his gentle and

---

[34] Fàbio Py Murta de Almeida, "Bolsonaro's Brazilian Christofascism during the Easter Period Plagued by COVID-19," *International Journal of Latin American Religions* 4 (2020): 318–34. "Christofascism" is a term first coined by feminist theologian Dorothee Sölle, to refer to the use of Christian idiom and imagery in Nazi propaganda, together with the collusion of some Christian church leaders, Protestant and Catholic, within the Hitler regime.

[35] Ghillean T. Prance and Thomas S. Elias, eds., *Extinction Is Forever: The Status of Threatened and Endangered Plants of the Americas* (New York: New

restrained way, Ghillean also shared his deep dismay at the accelerating rate of rainforest destruction, especially in the Amazon, and
his grief at the deaths of so many Indigenous people in Brazil, both
through murder and disease, including some forest defenders known
to him personally. But he also had words of encouragement. He
spoke of Indigenous initiatives, such the Ceibo Alliance cofounded
by the remarkable Woarani activist Nemonte Nenquimo, and the
recovery of organic farming methods consistent with maintaining
high levels of biodiversity. Ghillean told us of the rainforest conservation and restoration work to which he had himself contributed
with REGUA (Reverva Ecológica da Guapiaçú), an eight-thousand-
hectare reserve along Brazil's Atlantic coast, which also provides
environmental education, including a Young Ranger program
for local children. Beginning with lamentation and stressing the
urgency of acting against escalating extinctions and global heating,
in alliance with Indigenous peoples, Ghillean sought to coax us
gently but surely along the path to hope in faith.[36]

There are also grounds for hope in the work of REPAM,
the Pan-Amazon Ecclesial Network of the Catholic Church.
Established in 2014 REPAM embodies the "integral ecology"
outlined by the Argentinian Pope Francis in *Laudato si'* (2015),
and expounded further, with respect to Amazonia, in *Amazonia:
New Paths for the Church and for an Integral Ecology* (2019), the
outcome of a special synod meeting within which Indigenous
people were key participants. The theology underlying these
documents is informed by the liberation theology advanced by
Leonardo Boff, himself a Brazilian, which brought a strong emphasis
on social justice to the spectrum of Brazilian environmentalisms in

---

York Botanical Gardens, 1977); Ghillean T. Prance, ed., *Tropical Rainforests
and the World Atmosphere* (1986; repr. London: Routledge, 2018).

[36] For a video of Ghillean Prance's address, "Re-imagining the Promised
Land," see the Green Christian 2020 Festival site, https://greenchristian.org.uk.

the 1970s.[37] Having been censured under previous popes, liberation theology's staunch critique of prevailing socioeconomic systems that entrench injustice and damage creation has now become something akin to official church policy. REPAM's work includes "enabling Indigenous leaders to be heard on the world stage"; creating a "School for the Promotion of Rights" to train community and pastoral leaders in their human and environmental rights; supporting human rights defense cases, in particular those recognized under the UN Declaration of the Rights of Indigenous Peoples to "free, prior and informed consent" concerning any commercial developments on their ancestral lands; and advocating "protection for the 137 'contactless tribes' of the Amazon and affirmation of their right to live undisturbed." In these and other ways, REPAM seeks to reinforce the promise that Pope Francis made in the Amazon town of Maldonado in Peru in January 2018, to affirm "a whole-hearted option for the defense of life, the defense of the earth and the defense of cultures."[38]

One of the early members of REPAM was the social researcher and community worker Márcia Maria de Oliviera, who wrote to me about her involvement with this and other Catholic organizations in January 2021, following her recovery from a bout of COVID-19.[39] Her own religious formation and social engagement

---

[37] Pádua, "Civil Society and Environmentalism in Brazil," 122.

[38] Caritas, "REPAM: The Church in the Heart of the Amazon," accessed March 30, 2023, www.caritas.org; Synod of Bishops for the Pan-Amazon Region, "Amazonia: New Paths for the Church and for an Integral Ecology," June 8, 2018, https://press.vatican.va.

[39] As Márcia Maria speaks Portuguese and an Indigenous language, but not English, I am indebted to Talitta Reitz at the Rachel Carson Center for translating my questions into Portuguese, and to Clarice Corfield in Keynsham and Rita Sousa-Silva at the Freiburg Institute for Advanced Studies for translating her responses into English. I am also immensely grateful to Fábio Py Murta de Almeida for putting me in contact with Márcia Maria, and to Márcia

have been strongly informed by liberation theology. Her family was "very committed to the Rural Workers' Union and the Pastoral Land Commission (Comissão Pastoral da Terra)," created in 1975 by the then bishop of the Diocese of Goiás, Dom Tomás Balduíno, a leading proponent of liberation theology and "a role model in the fight for justice." During her seventeen years of religious life with the Scalabrinian Missionaries of Saint Charles, she worked extensively with migrants, and between 2004 and 2011 in public education with the Jesuit organization, Social Service for Action, Reflection and Social Education (Serviço de Ação, Reflexão e Educação). In the course of her studies in sociology, from a bachelor's degree through to the postdoctoral level, she was able to "delve deeper into the migration issue in the Amazon" and share her knowledge with institutions dealing directly with the migrants in this region, such as Cáritas, CPT, and the Migrants' Pastoral Service (Serviço Pastoral dos Migrantes—SPM). These organizations contributed to the establishment of REPAM, which was cofounded by the Latin American Catholic Episcopal Council (Conselho Episcopal Latino-Americano [CELAM]), the National Conference of Bishops of Brazil (Confêrencia Nacional dos Bispos do Brasil [CNBB]), the Latin America and Caribbean Secretariat of Caritas (Secretariado da América Latina e Caribe de Caritas [SELACC]), and the Confederation of Latin American and Caribbean Religious (Confederação Latino-Americana e Caribenha de Religiosos e Religiosas [CLAR]).

Márcia Maria's role in REPAM has been both advisory and as a contributor to the training of team leaders and the coordination of regional committees, in particular in Brazil's northernmost and most geographically isolated state, Roraima. The learning, though, has clearly been two-way. She began to question the "instrumental

Maria herself for her profound responses to my questions, which are quoted here with her kind permission.

anthropocentric" view of the natural world as a mere resource as she meditated upon *Laudato si'*. Studying this extraordinary encyclical with seminaries and dioceses in Amazonia in 2015, she came to recognize nature instead as "a subject of law" and humans as "creatures of Earth," participants in what Pope Francis has called the "universal communion." However, it was in dialogue with the First Peoples of Amazonia that her emancipatory faith acquired a deeper ecospiritual dimension, arising from experiences of interconnectivity and informed by practices of care, grounded not in fear but in love. Though she admits that the confluence of Christian and Indigenous spirituality is strongly resisted in some quarters, Márcia Maria recalls the words of a song by Imbaúba, a group that takes its name from a tree also known as "mother-of-the earth": "We are part of the earth and the earth is part of us.... With great wisdom our grandparents used to say: if we take care of the earth, the earth takes care of us." For her, this insight is inseparable from social justice: "Caring for our common home implies first of all caring for each other in an attitude of respect for the life and dignity of each and every one." Countering the "depredatory processes of colonization" and rejecting interpretations of "dominion" as "domination," spiritualities that foster sharing, solidarity, and care for the Earth can be a source of resilience, she believes, as well as inspiring resistance and facilitating transformation toward a "just, equitable and sustainable civilization." This she sees as consistent with Christian teaching on the "kingdom of God," not in a "strictly temporal meaning," but as something to be practiced here and now.

It was nonetheless not in the Amazon rainforest, but in the Catacomb of Santa Domitila near Rome, that Márcia Maria recalls experiencing the most profound moment hitherto in her journey of faith. It was there, where early followers of Jesus once sheltered from persecution at the hands of an earlier empire, that she joined with other participants in the Synodal Assembly on the Pan-Amazon region in a Mass to celebrate the signing of the "Catacomb Pact for the Common Home" on October 20, 2019: a fitting place to commit to "place ourselves on the side of those who are persecuted for their prophetic service of denouncing and repairing/repaying injustices." Among the other highlights of this document, in her view, are the commitments "in the face of extreme global warming and the depletion of natural resources, to defend the Amazon jungle"; "to recognize that we are not the owners of Mother Earth, but rather the sons and daughters, formed from the *dust of the ground*"; "to welcome and renew every day the covenant of God with everything created"; "to renew in our churches the preferential option for the poor, especially for Native peoples"; "to abandon, consequently, in our parishes, dioceses, and groups all types of colonist mentality and posture"; "to denounce all forms of violence and aggression"; and "to announce the liberating novelty of the gospel of Jesus in welcoming the other and the one who is different."

While the Ecclesial Conference of the Amazon, arising from the synod, has now largely subsumed the work that REPAM initiated, the latter remains important in helping to coordinate its activities. In response to the pandemic, REPAM also became involved in the distribution of food, medicines, respirators, and personal protective equipment to the remotest communities, and joined the campaign to "Amazonize yourself" (*Amazoniza-te*). Recalling that the "first documented call to 'amazonize' dates back to 1986, in a pastoral letter by Dom Moacyr Grechi of the Diocese of Rio Branco, Acre, in which he called on the people to take up the cause of the Amazon and the defense of its peoples," Márcia Maria told me that this call resounded anew in the synodal process. It has also been taken up by the Global Assembly for the Amazon, convened in the lead-up to COP 26 by Indigenous leaders, members, and ecclesial organs of the Church in the Amazon, artists, scientists, and opinion makers to protest the ongoing ethnocide, ecocide, and extractivism in the Amazon aggravated by the COVID-19 pandemic. In her words,

> The call to "Amazonize" implies the recognition of the struggles and resistance of the Peoples of the Amazon, who are facing more than five hundred years of colonization and development projects based on the unrestrained exploitation and destruction of the forest and natural resources at the risk of driving thousands of species, which have not even been properly studied, into extinction. The call to "Amazonize" is the awakening of all people in defense of the Amazon, its biome and its peoples threatened in their territories, wronged, expelled from their lands, tortured and murdered in agrarian and socio-environmental conflicts, humiliated by the powerful agribusiness and large economic developmental projects that do not respect the limits of nature or its preservation.

In Márcia Maria's assessment, these ills will not be overcome by a "greener" version of "postcolonial" capitalism-as-usual. This has been brought home to her by the COVID-19 pandemic, which to her mind "endorses Friedrich Engels's prophetic warning from the first century of capitalist industrialization: 'Let us not flatter ourselves overmuch on account of our human victories over nature; for each such victory, nature takes its revenge on us.' The pandemic represents a symptom of something that is not right in this current stage of the capitalist system and alerts us to review our selfish, individualistic, predatory lifestyle . . . before it is too late."

The Amazon was dubbed such by the European invaders who were startled to see Native women fighting alongside men, like the fabled female warriors of Greek myth. They might not be bearing arms, but Indigenous Amazonians like Sara clearly inherit their foremothers' fighting spirit: one that is also shared by their allies, such as Márcia Maria. In her address, Sara says that she is glad that instead of acting the part of a Greek tragic heroine on the stage in Vienna, she had the chance to speak in her own voice about a tragedy that is unfolding "here and now, in the world, before our very eyes." Yet something is to be learned from the play that was not performed when read through Indigenous eyes looking keenly at today's power-wielders, including all of us who are complicit with those systems of production and consumption that are destroying her world—and, ultimately, our own. Creon, Sara discerns,

> Knows what he is doing is wrong ... that it will bring his fall, the fall of his family, the Apocalypse. And yet he does it, he criticizes himself, but he still does what he hates. This madness has to stop. Stop being like Creon. Let's be like Antigone. Because when lawlessness becomes law, resistance becomes duty. Let's resist together; let's be human—each in his own way and place, united by our differences and our love for the life that unites us all.

Sara, like Márcia Maria, is among those defenders of the Amazon and its peoples who had cause to celebrate when Luiz Inácio Lula da Silva succeeded Bolsonaro as Brazilian president in October 2022, only to hold their breath as Bolsonaro's supporters launched an unsuccessful insurrection a few months later. The return of Lula, and his environment minister, Marina Silva, promises to give the Amazon, and us all, a fighting chance of survival. The longevity of their leadership is not guaranteed, though, and the extractivist interests that oppose them remain powerful, while the damage already runs deep. Yet for people like Frankie Ward and me to give way to despair would be to leave people like Sara and Márcia Maria in the lurch.

Pondering this day of creation—the day of the burgeoning of vegetal life, its primordial goodness in Elohim's eyes, and how it is being undone in our own day—has made me realize that when the outlook for what Pope Francis calls "our common home" seems most bleak, it is not, in the end, hope, nor even faith, but love that gets me out of bed in the morning.

Love, that is, in all its colors: creaturely love of my own existence, no matter how difficult and painful it becomes at times; biophilial love, rejoicing in the existence of manifold others, creatures of land and sky, air and water, mountains and seas, plants and fungi and the amazing collectives they co-create with others; companionable love of special friends; familial love, with all its highs and lows; erotic love, with its risky yet ecstatic intensities; attentive love for those in our care, including, in my case, my poor, neglected pot plants; empathetic love that reaches out a hand to a neighbor in need, be they stranger or even enemy; resolute love that allies us with all those standing up to their oppressors and seeking to over- turn ecocidal systems of domination.

Some of these many-splendored loves can conflict with one another. Love can be possessive and oppressive, overbearing and undermining. Much harm can be done in its name. Yet it is love—above all, in its self-giving, other-regarding, and life- affirming dimensions—that reigns at the heart of the promised "kingdom of heaven," which is even now, and ever was, coming into being in and through the earthly creation. The "kingdom of heaven," Jesus is reported to have said once, "is like a mustard seed that someone took and sowed in his field; it is the smallest of all the seeds, but when it has grown it is the greatest of shrubs and becomes a tree, so that the birds of the air come and make nests in its branches." But then again, he added, it is "like yeast that a woman took and mixed in with three measures of flour until all of it was leavened" (Matt. 13:31–33). Mustard seed and yeast: plant and fungus. Well, then, here's another simile:

The kin(g)dom of heaven is like the mycorrhizal wood wide web.

It is what branches in darkness, supporting all that glories in the light.

It is how we unite across our differences, enabling us to resist and restore and give rise to new possibilities of shared flourishing.

It is the stirring in the depths that brings forth the burgeoning on the surface: the vegetal splendor that paints the sky blue and moderates Earth's climate; the vegetal creatures with whom all we animals exchange breath; the plant nations to whom all peoples are beholden.

FOURTH DAY

*And God said, "Let there be lights in the vault of the heavens
to divide the day from the night, and they shall be signs for
the fixed times and for days and years, and they shall be lights
in the vault of the heavens to light up the earth." And so it
was. And God made the two great lights, the great light for
dominion of day and the small light for dominion of night,
and the stars. And God placed them in the vault of the
heavens to light up the earth and to have dominion over day
and night and to divide the light from the darkness. And God
saw that it was good. And it was evening and it was morning,
fourth day.*

                                                    Genesis 1:14–19

⌒

*When I relocated to England from Australia, I quickly real-
ized that one of the things I was going to miss most was the
night sky. It was not only that northern skies are so much more
sparsely populated than southern ones, although that, too, I
found dispiriting. If you are fortunate in your location and
conditions are right, you can certainly take pleasure in the array
of circumpolar stars that are sometimes visible in English night
skies. But Australia is positioned in such a way as to reveal a
great many more celestial marvels, especially where the atmosphere is clear and electric lights are few (which goes for most of*

the continent).[1] *Among these marvels, in the nomenclature of Western astronomy, are the "Jewel Box," a glittering open cluster of a hundred or so stars; Omega Centauri, a dazzling congeries of several million stars; the multihued "Tarantula Nebula" and "Eta Carina Region," situated within those portions of the Milky Way only visible from the southern hemisphere; and, of course, the Southern Cross, which graces the settler-colonial flag. I am only now beginning to appreciate how very bright and busy were the skies I left behind! Yet what I really missed to begin with was not so much the abundance of celestial lights as the deep darkness of the night.*

Here in England's rural southwest, we live in a tiny village tucked into a hidden valley. It is accessible by road only by driving cautiously along narrow winding laneways lined with hedgerows and frequented by horses and riders, dogs and their companions, farmers on tractors, an occasional bevy of sheep or cows, and, if you're very lucky, and manage to avoid hitting them, sundry forms of dwindling wildlife of the furry or, more commonly, feathered variety. There are no streetlights in the village, but it is never, ever truly dark. This valley is only five miles from Bath and twelve from Bristol, and our night sky is perpetually illumined by the ghastly glow of electric lighting.

I discovered my urgent desire for the dark when we were residing in one of Melbourne's southeastern suburbs close to my then workplace, Monash University. There, too, the nights were never properly dark, and only rarely were they truly quiet. We lived on a leafy street that terminated in a dead end, with a tree-lined golf course on the other side of our back fence. But two busy roads, one of them multilaned, crossed nearby, and there always seemed to be a background hum, as if the city were resisting rest. The longer we remained there, the more desperate I became for

---

[1] The Australian Astronomical Observatory explains in more detail why the night sky is better in Australia. See "We Get Asked That a Lot," https://aat.anu.edu.au.

peaceful nights of deliciously inky darkness. For me, this was a driving factor in our move to the Dandenongs. There is the odd streetlight in The Patch, although none are near our home on the outer edge of the village. There, on nights unillumined by the moon, it can get pitch-black. Many is the guest who has become bushwhacked trying to walk down our drive without a flashlight! And then there was the time when a couple of young lads drove their stolen car into the steep gully opposite our house, having stealthily, if stupidly, failed to turn on their headlights. (They ran off unharmed before the police arrived, but I daresay the resident wildlife was unimpressed.)

Only after moving to the hills did I discover something else about where we had previously been living, about the place where our son was born, spent his early years, and started school. Many a morning, as my bus wound down to the city on the plains in the direction of Monash, I could see a shroud of smog blanketing Melbourne. This smog sets in when prevailing atmospheric conditions trap the constantly accumulating automotive and industrial emissions close to the ground. These conditions, known as a "weather inversion," are likely to become more frequent and intense across Melbourne as the planet heats up.

At the same time that we have bedimmed the stars with our electric lights, we have smudged the sunlight with our smog. And both, as it transpires, pose serious risks to the health and well-being of vulnerable communities and individuals, human and otherwise. In many parts of the world, the air quality is considerably worse than it tends to be in Melbourne (except for those increasingly frequent occasions when the surrounding bushland has, once more, gone up in smoke). And while my family and I were able to distance ourselves from the glare and smog for a time, the direction of travel for many people globally is rather the reverse: from the country to the city, into sprawling conurbations that are growing ever larger. There, the urban poor, disproportionately people of color, are among those most likely to suffer the adverse consequences of poor air quality.

To contemplate the celestial lights of the biblical Fourth Day of creation in our world today, then, is to be confronted with anthropogenic pollutants that have robbed them of their shine. And to behold this bedimming of sun, moon, and stars is to uncover an unheavenly host of injustices arising from the despoliation of the living Earth.

The Celestial Luminaries:
Brother Sun, Sister Moon, and All Stars

Having told of how the liberated Earth adorned herself in vegetal verdure, the biblical narrative now returns our gaze to the heavens above to ponder the populating of the firmament. Sky evidently proving less fecund than soil, Elohim steps in to accomplish this "himself." Once again, abundance is the name of the game: in addition to the majestic sun and more modest moon, Elohim makes a multitude of lesser lights, the "thousand, thousand stars, that then appeared / Spangling the hemisphere," as Milton put it (VII, ll. 383–84). Movement, too, comes into play: that primordial pulsing of light and dark now gets translated into the alternating passage across the sky of the sun by day and moon by night, while entire congregations of stars move through their paces in longer cycles. New connectivities are forged: the lifeways of plants become keyed to seasonal variations in sunlight and temperature, while the waters below get caught up in the dance on high, as the ebb and flow of ocean tides fall into step with the waxing and waning of the labile moon, who, as Basil marveled, must be "of enormous size and power to make all nature thus participate in her changes" (BaH, 105–6). As Grosseteste observed, human bodies also experienced her pull in the influence exerted over the menstrual cycles of women (SDC, 184).

That question of power, though, requires delicate handling. Within the culture of the Babylonian imperialists from whose creation narrative this one so decisively departed, the sun and moon were revered as deities. Ancient commentators on the hexameron were well aware of the dependence of vegetation, and hence all life, on sunlight, and most do not assume that the sequence of "days" in the narrative corresponded in reality to a historical succession. Instead, they generally follow Philo in surmising that the point of postponing the description of the creation of the celestial luminaries was to demonstrate the superordinate power of the creator, thereby guarding against the temptation to deify these admittedly awesome creatures.

Similarly, all are at pains to distinguish the sort of "signs" that might be discerned in the heavens from those projected onto them by astrologers. Abelard put the case particularly clearly, reasoning that it was crucial to differentiate between "natural causes" and what he called "future contingents, which so equally have the potential to be and not be" (ESW, 67). The "signs" to which Abelard referred pertain to the former, functioning as indicators of natural events, such as meteorological phenomena, as well as providing orientation in space and a means of computing time. For Abelard, the study of such natural causes was the proper pursuit of astronomy, and quite a different matter from the "diabolical conjecture" concerning "future contingents" practiced by astrologers. This was not only a question concerning what is knowable and how. It was also a moral matter. Demoting sun, moon, and stars from their exalted position within astrology of governing human fortunes was essential to safeguard a space for ethical discernment and self-determination. Astrological fatalism, Ambrose observed, tends to "deprive man of his humanity, if no room is left for character, no outlet for education or for freedom of action" (AmH, 136).

The celestial luminaries, widely assumed to be far larger than they appear due to their vast distance away, are nonetheless honored in the hexameral literature as extraordinary creatures in their own right, exerting a major influence on earthly existence. The cosmos of early and medieval Christianity was still a vibrantly animate one. Saint Francis (c. 1182–1226) famously hailed the celestial lights as "Brother Sun" and "Sister Moon and the stars" in his "Canticle of the Creatures." Many centuries later, a trace of that ancient Christian animism resurfaced in Gerard Manley Hopkins's poem "The Starlight Night," the opening lines of which exhort the reader to "Look at the stars! look, look up at the skies / O look at all the fire-folk sitting in the air."[2] Back in the ninth century, John the Scot had argued, "Even the lowliest body—a stone, for example, is not wholly devoid of life, although we cannot discern it.... Every creature, then, is either living in itself or participating in life in some fashion" (DN, 204). Eriugena's philosophically reasoned pan-vitalism, as noted in the first chapter, was later regarded as heretical, and his work was condemned to the flames by the Council of Paris in 1210. Thankfully, though, some copies survived, and his thought appears to have left its trace in both scholastic metaphysics and mystical theology.[3] Abelard nonetheless expressed himself with greater caution, but even he was loath to rule out the possibility that the luminaries were "celestial animals" with a degree of independent agency, as Paul appears to suggest in Ephesians 6:12 (ESW, 66).

Whatever their view on this question, all of the hexameral writers concurred that the delegated "dominion" of the sun and moon in the heavens had a powerful effect upon the terrestrial realm as well. While Basil got carried away in consideration of

---

[2] Gerard Manley Hopkins, "The Starlight Night," in *Poems and Prose of Gerard Manley Hopkins*, ed. William Henry Gardner (Harmondsworth, UK: Penguin Classics, 1963), 27.

[3] Jean A. Potter, "Introduction," in John the Scot, *Perephyseon: On the Division of Nature*, trans. Myra I. Uhlferler, with summaries by Jean A. Potter (Indianapolis: Bobbs-Merrill, 1979), xxiv.

lunar influences, Traherne was spellbound by the "marvellous Efficacy" of the sun, whose beams "do quicken and make the Plants, and other living things, to grow, helping all things both in their Life and Conversation" (BaH, 40). With the strengthening of the sun's rays and the lengthening of days in the springtime, Traherne observed, "Calves leap and dance in the Meadows, the Birds sing Notes and Ditties, build their Nests, bring forth their Young; and all the Earth is covered with Variety of curious little Creatures." Yet he laments that "ungrateful Man ... notes it not, altho' this Sun fills his Veins with Spirits too, his Flesh with Warmth, his Limbs with Agility, that he might walk comfortably and wisely, thankfully and cheerfully, among the glorious Works of God" (MoSDC, 43).

What is happening in the heavens, then, might not determine human fortunes, at least not in the ways foretold by astrologers—but it could certainly affect how we feel about the world in the present. This is how Hugh of St. Victor theorized this connection: "all the stars, the planets in particular, have specific effects through the air on bodies subsisting below them. And when the body is changed, its affinity with the soul inside causes the soul to change as well, receiving joy or sadness or other such affections from outside" (NoG, 66). We might put it somewhat differently today, but I think many would concur that Hugh and Traherne were onto something concerning the mood-altering propensities of our physical environs under the influence of the changeable skies above our heads. Even for those who are unable to walk about, as Traherne recommended we should do, a spell of sunshine or the sight of its gentle reflection on the moon on a star-spangled night can make all the difference.

For Philo, though, the greatest boon afforded to humanity by the celestial luminaries was not so much physical or emotional as intellectual, in that they pique our hunger for knowledge. Gazing up at the night sky, he wrote,

Man ... saw the well-ordered circuits of fixed stars and planets.... He marked the rhythmic dances of all these, how they were marshalled by the laws of a perfect music, and the sight produced in his soul an ineffable delight and pleasure. Banqueting on sights displayed to it one after another, his sight was insatiate in beholding. And then, as usually happens, it went on to busy itself with questionings.... It was out of the investigation of the problems that philosophy grew, than which no more perfect good has come into the life of mankind. (OC, 41–43)

Awesome Astronomy, Appalling Pollution: Reintegrating Facts and Values

Within that branch of philosophy that morphed into modern Western science right around the time that the hexameral tradition petered out, plenty of questions about the cosmos remained unanswered. Since Traherne's day, astronomers have learned a fair bit about the sun and moon, and a good many stars and planets, including, of course, our own. Eric Idle helpfully pulled some of this together in the song he wrote with John De Prez and Trevor Jones for Monty Python's *The Meaning of Life*:

> *Whenever life gets you down, Mrs. Brown,*
> *And things seem hard or tough,*
> *And people are stupid, obnoxious or daft,*
> *And you feel that you've had quite eno-o-o-o-ough!*
>
> *Just remember that you're standing on a planet that's*
> *   evolving*
> *And revolving at nine hundred miles an hour*
> *It's orbiting at nineteen miles a second, so it's reckoned*
> *The sun that is the source of all our power*

Now the sun, and you and me, and all the stars that we
    can see,
Are moving at a million miles a day,
In the outer spiral arm, at fourteen thousand miles an hour
Of a galaxy we call the Milky Way

Our galaxy itself contains a hundred billion stars
It's a hundred thousand light-years side to side.
It bulges in the middle sixteen thousand light-years thick,
But out by us it's just three thousand light-years wide
We're thirty thousand light-years from Galactic Central Point,
We go 'round every two hundred million years
And our galaxy is only one of millions of billions
In this amazing and expanding universe

The universe itself keeps on expanding and expanding,
In all of the directions it can whiz.
As fast as it can go, that's the speed of light, you know,
Twelve million miles a minute and that's the fastest speed
    there is
So remember, when you're feeling very small and insecure,
How amazingly unlikely is your birth
And pray that there's intelligent life somewhere out in space
'Cause there's bugger all down here on Earth![4]

According to Paul Kohlmiller's fact-check of the song in the San Jose Astronomical Association's newsletter *Ephemeris* for December 2003, this accorded pretty well with the scientific consensus at that time, the only correctives being that the "sun (and therefore the earth and at least all the stars that you can see with the naked eye) are moving through the galaxy at … more

---

[4] "Galaxy Song," written by Eric Idle and John Du Prez, copyright © Python (Monty) Pictures Limited, reprinted with permission from Kay-Gee-Bee Music Ltd.

than six million miles per day," and that the arm of our galaxy is moving correspondingly faster: more like 250,000 miles per hour.[5] It is in the nature of scientific discovery, though, that ongoing updating would be required to keep up with new findings in the awesome field of astronomy. Indeed, physicist Brian Cox, who had already worked with Idle on a revamped version in 2012, commented in a tweet to Idle from 2023 that he thought they "should invest in a Foundation to re-evaluate The Galaxy Song every decade, for as long as there is a civilization on this planet, or beyond, and tweak the lyrics when necessary."[6]

Meanwhile, here are a few more astounding findings to add to Idle's that I have managed to track down. In addition to eight planets, it seems our solar system contains 5 "dwarf" planets; over 170 moons; more than 5,500 comets; and, scarily, almost 700,000 known asteroids (it is believed that one of these triggered the mass extinction event that wiped out most of the dinosaurs, among other species, sixty-six million years ago). In company with the other planets, Earth took shape out of the dust that was whooshed away from our big Brother Sun, now roughly middle-aged, as he began to form over four and a half billion years ago. Sister Moon is believed to have come into being out of debris blasted away from the proto-Earth when something Mars-sized plowed into her. Earth ended up orbiting the sun at what proved to be a sweet spot for the emergence, evolution, and intercommunication of an abundance of diverse living beings. We earthlings all contain carbon and oxygen molecules manufactured in ancient stars and dwell on a medium-size planet neither too close nor too far away from our fiery benefactor. As Brother Sun ages, though, he is going to get bigger and hotter and, in his death throes, is anticipated to engulf

---

[5] Paul Kohlmiller, "A Study of the Galaxy Song by Eric Idle," Ephemeris, July 19, 2007, https://ephemeris.sjaa.net.

[6] Brian Cox, twitter.com, @ProfBrianCox, February 16, 2023.

Mercury, Venus, and possibly Earth as well.[7] You can get too much of a good thing.

There is, of course, a knowing irony in Idle's song. To discover all those things about Earth's place in space—about which, scientists stress, much remains uncertain—requires a fairly prodigious amount of intelligence. And yet, the singer insists, there's "bugger all down here on Earth." While an atheist might read this as poking fun at the persistence of "religious superstition" in a scientifically enlightened age, it could also be interpreted as spotlighting the discrepancy between the cleverness entailed in scientific discoveries and the wisdom required to know what best to do with them. Part of the problem, I think, is the severance of "facts" from "values" that became institutionalized in the separation of the "natural sciences" from the "humanities"—including philosophy, religion, and poetics—during the nineteenth century. This was, of course, right at the time when the growth of industrialization was accelerating those Earth system changes that had begun with the European colonization of the New World and the intensification of agriculture in parts of the Old. The "natural philosophy" that Philo praised integrated facts and values, and so did that strand of the hexameral tradition that was in conversation with it. And it is precisely in the interests of a contemporary reintegration that I think it is worthwhile endeavoring to revivify the hexameral tradition at this time of profound planetary imperilment.

Though human intelligence per se may not have failed, the creation of collective living spaces hostile to human health and well-being, and that of many other creatures besides, clearly manifests a failure of human intelligence within modern industrial civilization. Take London, for example, which has the distinction of being the world's first city to have reached a population of over 5 million.

---

[7] British Natural History Museum, "Space," is a great source for further information on all of this. See www.nhm.ac.uk.

Britain's imperial capital became the largest city in the world from around 1825, growing from an estimated 1 million or so in 1801, to 5.567 million by 1891. It was overtaken by New York only in 1925.[8] Complaints about air pollution in London go back at least to Shakespeare's day, but fossil-fueled industrialization, conjoined with the expansion of housing heated by dirty "soft coal," made matters infinitely worse. William Blake was already railing against those "Satanic mills" in the early 1800s, referring to the city's proliferating smokestacks in his famous poem "Jerusalem." His prophetic vision, however, failed to alter his industrial capitalist society's direction of travel. By midcentury, the phenomenon of "pea-soupers," smog so bad that it turns day to night, was casting a pall over the London that is so atmospherically invoked in Charles Dickens's novels. A century later, an extreme smog event of this kind caused an estimated four thousand deaths over a space of five days in December 1952. This Great Smog disaster prompted legislation to mandate the use of "clean fuels" within specified "smokeless zones."

The United Kingdom's Clean Air Act of 1956 was effective in significantly decreasing domestic coal usage, and the days of pea-soupers in London, and in other cities of the Global North, are no more. Elsewhere, however, in the growing cities of the more recently industrialized and industrializing world, they have become a hazardous reality. Although compounded of elements less visible to the naked eye, air pollution continues to reach lethal levels in the older industrial nations as well. In Britain, for example, while emissions released from the exhaust pipes of motorized transport have reduced significantly since the 1990s,

---

[8] Great Britain Historical GIS Project, University of Portsmouth, "Population Statistics | Total Population," A Vision of Britain through Time, Visionofbritain.org; Matt Rosenberg, "Largest Cities throughout History: Determining Population prior to Census-Taking Was No Easy Task," ThoughtCo, November 4, 2019, www.thoughtco.com.

concern is growing about the impact of tiny particles that separate from the tires of moving vehicles. Once airborne, they are inhaled by pedestrians, ferrying toxins deep into their lungs.[9] Along with other tiny particles, such as those occurring from wear and tear on road surfaces and their paint markings, these minuscule meanies are adding to the burden of fine particulate pollution (PM_{25}) pumped out by the combustion of fossil fuels from factories, motor vehicles, and domestic stoves and fireplaces. Worldwide, a study from 2018 found that PM_{25} was implicated in the premature deaths of an estimated 8.7 million people. These deaths represent one in ten of all deaths in Europe and the United States, and nearly one in three across eastern Asia, including India, Southeast Asia, and China, where the smog in Beijing had become so extreme that the terms "airpocalypse" and "airmageddon" started circulating on social media in 2013.[10]

For every premature death, moreover, there are countless lives blighted by smog-borne ill-health. In addition to respiratory and cardiovascular disease, fine particulate pollution can impair children's cognitive function and hasten their elders' cognitive decline, as well as contributing to anxiety and depression.[11] A study of 186

---

[9] Zhengchu Tan et al., "Tyre Wear Particles Are Toxic for Us and the Environment," Imperial College London, 2023, https://spiral.imperial.ac.uk.

[10] Karn Vohra et al., "Global Mortality from Outdoor Fine Particle Pollution Generated by Fossil Fuel Combustion: Results from GEOS-Chem," *Environmental Research* 195 (April 2021): 110754, www.sciencedirect.com. Pollution mitigation measures in China from 2012 to 2018 were successful in reducing smog-related mortality, which dropped from an estimated 3.9 million to 2.4 million premature deaths between these years. On smog in social media in China, see Greta Gaard, "(Un)storied Air, Breath and Embodiment," *ISLE* 29, no. 2 (2022): 295–322.

[11] Kirsten Weir, "Smog in Our Brains: Researchers Are Identifying Startling Connections between Air Pollution and Decreased Cognition and Wellbeing," *American Psychological Association* 43, no. 7 (July/August 2012), www.apa.org.

young residents of Mexico City, ranging from eleven months to twenty-seven years old, found markers for Alzheimer's, Parkinson's, and motor neurone disease (MND) linked to the metal-rich nanoparticles from vehicular pollution that had lodged in their brainstems.[12] Recent research in London found that, within a test group of thirteen thousand residents, even a small rise in exposure to the nitrogen dioxide in London's air increased their risk of requiring community care for mental illness by around a third, and of hospitalization by nearly a fifth.[13] Air pollution, it seems, may well be damaging every organ in our bodies.[14] Nor are humans the only creatures suffering from the sullying of the air that we all share. Smog impairs the capacity of plants to absorb carbon dioxide, reduces immune response in amphibians, and causes cardiovascular disease in birds and mammals, including, of course, our domestic companions.

Among our own kind, the burden of smog, together with other types of less visible air pollution, is not equally shared. In a landmark legal ruling in the United Kingdom in 2020, the inner South London coroner Philip Barlow found that exposure to nitrogen dioxide and fine particulate pollution in excess of World Health Organization guidelines, primarily from traffic emissions, together with the lack of public education about the risks

---

[12] Technology Networks, "Alzheimer's Biomarkers Found in Brains of Children Exposed to Air Pollution," Neuroscience News and Research, October 7, 2020, www.technologynetworks.com.

[13] J. Newbury et al., "Association between Air Pollution Exposure and Mental Health Service Use Among Individuals with First Presentations of Psychotic and Mood Disorders: Retrospective Cohort Study," *British Journal of Psychiatry* 219, no. 6 (2021): 678–85.

[14] Dean E. Schraufnagel et al., "Air Pollution and Non-communicable Diseases. A Review by the International Forum of Respiratory Diseases' Environmental Committee. Part I: The Damaging Effects of Air Pollution," *CHEST Journal* 155, no. 2 (2019): 409–16.

of living on busy roads, contributed significantly to the asthma attack that took the life of a nine-year-old girl, Ella Kissi-Debrah, in February 2013. It is no coincidence that Ella was Black. Writing in *The Guardian* in the wake of Ella's mother Rosamund's successful efforts to have the cause of her daughter's death reexamined, Anjali Raman-Middleton, a former schoolmate of Ella's and cofounder of Choked Up, a campaign for clean air founded by Black and Brown sixth-formers (twelfth-graders), pointed to research from Imperial College London showing that the poor and people of color are most at risk from traffic pollution across the United Kingdom.[15]

Pollution, Racism, and Eco-Justice:
Initiatives from the United States

In the United States, the association between pollution and racial disadvantage has long been recognized, thanks not least to the efforts of the United Church of Christ (UCC) to expose and redress what became known as "environmental racism." This term was coined by Rev. Benjamin Chavis Jr. in response to a different type of pollution caused by the dumping or incineration of toxic waste, typically in poor and Black neighborhoods. Chavis co-organized a campaign to prevent the creation of such a dump site in Warren County, North Carolina, in the late 1970s. He later became the leader of the UCC's Commission for Racial Justice. The commission's landmark report, "Toxic Wastes and Race in the United States" (1987), confirmed that race was the top variable associated with the location of a toxic waste facility. This study also found that three out of five Black and Hispanic Americans resided in a neighborhood that housed what the Environmental Protection Agency called an

---

[15] Anjali Raman-Middleton, "I Breathe the Same Same Polluted Air That Ella Kissi-Debrah Did. Change Must Be Her Legacy," *The Guardian*, December 17, 2020.

"uncontrolled toxic waste site," that is, a closed or abandoned site that posed a threat to human health and the environment.[16]

The first National People of Color Environmental Leadership Summit followed in October 1991 in Washington, DC. The summit was attended by over one thousand participants, who collectively agreed to adopt seventeen "Principles of Environmental Justice." This remarkable document conjoins concern for social justice and equity, respect for cultural diversity, and recognition of the sovereignty and self-determination of the United States' First Peoples, with an affirmation of the "sacredness of Mother Earth, ecological unity and the interdependence of all species, and the right to be free from ecological destruction."[17] From the searing experience of environmental racism, linked in the first instance to toxic waste but lodged within a longer history of slavery and colonialism, an inclusive vision of justice had emerged, embracing the wider communion of earthly creatures pursuing their diverse lives under the same sun and stars and the one moon.

When I interviewed then minister of environmental justice in the UCC, Brooks Berndt, in January 2021, it was just under a year since the church had released its third report on toxic pollution.[18] Titled *"Breath to the People": Sacred Air and Toxic Pollution*, this report recalls Isaiah 42, where we read that "the Creator of the heavens, who stretches them out, / who spreads out the earth with all that springs from it … gives breath to its people, / and life to those who walk on it" (42:5).[19] As Berndt writes in the moral and

---

[16] United Church of Christ, Commission for Racial Justice, "Toxic Wastes and Race in the United States," 1987, www.ucc.org.

[17] United Church of Christ, Environmental Justice Ministries, "Principles of Environmental Justice," accessed March 30, 2023, www.ucc.org.

[18] My interview with Brooks Berndt took place on January 20, 2021, and is quoted here with his kind permission.

[19] United Church of Christ, "'Breath to the People': Sacred Air and Toxic Pollution," accessed March 30, 2023, www.ucc.org.

theological postscript to the report, "Our faith tradition teaches us that the air is sacred. It is the very breath of God given to us. We could not live for a moment without it." Yet that divine breath has become tainted by industry, with grievous consequences for those most exposed to its hazardous by-products.

Whereas the UCC's second report, *Toxic Wastes and Race at Twenty: 1987–2007*, followed the first in focusing on toxic waste facilities, the third looked at a range of industrial emissions and examined the population profile of those living in close proximity to the one hundred top emitters of toxic chemicals and heavy metals as identified by the US Environmental Protection Agency in 2018.[20] While the second report came to the same conclusion as the first, with race still figuring as the foremost risk factor for living in proximity to a toxic waste facility, the third report broadened its remit to consider age, alongside income and race, in recognition that the very old and the very young are more vulnerable to the adverse health impacts of the toxins under examination. The findings were sobering and, in some respects, surprising. Across the United States, an estimated 169,654 people, including 11,500 children under the age of five, live within a mile of a facility on the Toxic 100 list, and 1.6 million people, including 112,500 children under the age of five, live within three miles of one. Given that these facilities are spewing forth a mix of toxins that are known to cause cancer, birth defects, and brain damage, this was seen to constitute "a moral crisis" for the nation.[21]

Compounding this moral crisis is the connection between polluted air and racial and economic disadvantage that this study also has reconfirmed: "At the national level, the percentage of people of color or Hispanics or Latinos, low-income residents, and

---

[20]   United Church of Christ, "Toxic Wastes and Race at Twenty: 1987–2007," accessed March 30, 2023, www.ucc.org.

[21]   United Church of Christ, "Breath to the People," 3.

children under five living within one mile of the Toxic 100 were all higher than national averages."[22] Those who live downwind from such facilities are particularly at risk, and these people are often subject to other types of pollution as well, such as those residing in Louisiana's infamous "cancer alley," a stretch of industrial toxic territory extending from Baton Rouge to New Orleans.

In addition, this report showed that, among the Toxic 100, some "hide in plain sight," emitting hazardous materials under a cloak of invisibility.[23] One such location is sited not far from the UCC's offices in Ohio. As Berndt notes in his Postscript to *Breath to the People*,

> There are no giant smokestacks belching clouds into the air, no tall columns sending burning flares into the air for all to see.... But this facility spews chromium, copper, formaldehyde, nickel, nitric acid, trichloroethylene, and lead into the air. This is in a community that has also suffered from one of the worst lead crises in the country. Disturbingly, 565 children under age five live within one mile of the plant, while 4,408 live within three miles.[24]

Clear skies, it seems, can be deceptive: even where the sun shines unimpeded, industrial hazards might lurk unseen. Among these, of course, are also those ozone-depleting chemicals, which, far from blocking sunlight, allow more of its potentially harmful rays to beam down upon the Earth.

It was no coincidence that *Breath to the People* was released on Ash Wednesday, for it issued a call to "repentance" in the original sense of "turning around and changing course to go in a new and better direction." The recommendations of the report chart a way forward, with a range of technical, legal, and political measures to

---

22 United Church of Christ, "Breath to the People," 9.
23 United Church of Christ, "Breath to the People," 4.
24 United Church of Christ, "Breath to the People," 31.

mitigate toxic pollution and its inequitable burden, underpinned by the religious and moral imperatives of creating a more just society and caring better for creation.

My conversation with Berndt took place on a momentous day in American politics: the day on which Joe Biden and Kamala Harris were inaugurated at the new president and vice president of the United States. This brought to an end the presidency of Donald Trump, whose administration had overseen a systematic assault on environmental protections and the weakening of the enforcement of those that remained. As well as inspiring hope for renewed action to tackle toxins, the new administration boded well for a reversal of course on climate change. Berndt, who in 2019 published a "church handbook for the climate crisis," *Cathedral on Fire*, has long been concerned about this issue.[25] As a young pastor in his first post in Vancouver, Washington, he led his church in campaigns to shut down an old coal-fired power plant and to oppose the construction of a large oil terminal. With the inauguration of a new administration, Berndt was planning to take up the fight against fossil fuels once more in earnest, lifting climate crisis to the top of the UCC's environmental agenda.

In addition to its worldwide climatic and associated ecological impacts, together with the lethal pollution unleashed by the combustion of fossil fuels on the ground, global heating is already increasing the incidence and severity of wildfires, which themselves become a further source of toxic smog. While the cardiovascular effects are well known, only recently has it been discovered that the inflammation caused by smoke from wildfires also increases the risk to pregnant women of going into premature labor. A Stanford University study estimates that this may have caused seven thousand additional preterm births in California between

---

[25] B. Brooks, *Cathedral on Fire: A Church Handbook for the Climate Crisis* (Cleveland: United Church of Christ, 2020).

2007 and 2012.[26] Afflicting all who share breath, smoke pollution possibly even contributed to the mass die-off of migratory birds witnessed in the wake of the huge wildfires across California, Oregon, and Washington State in 2020.[27]

Given the inevitability of more frequent and intense weather-borne extremes, Berndt also sees an important role for the church in enhancing resilience, both psychological and practical, to the impacts of climate change. Creation Justice Ministries, an ecumenical organization that grew out of the National Council of Churches' Eco-Justice working group, is actively pursuing a project to turn churches into hubs of "climate resilience."[28] In a similar way to the Principles of Environmental Justice ratified by the 1991 People of Color Environmental Leadership Summit, Creation Justice Ministries links social equity with care for the Earth.

Smog and presumably other less visible forms of air pollution as well harm nonhuman as well as human creatures. So, too, does light pollution. A 2020 review of the current scientific research on

---

[26] Sam Heft-Neal et al., "Associations between Wildfire Smoke Exposure during Pregnancy and Risk of Preterm Birth in California," *Environmental Research* (January 2022): doi: 10.1016/j.envres.2021.111872. Epub August 14, 2021.

[27] Kari Paul, "Dying Birds and the Fires: Scientists Work to Unravel a Great Mystery," *The Guardian*, October 18, 2020.

[28] Creation Justice Ministries, "Faithful Resilience," https://www. creationjustice.org/resilience.html. See also Brianna Baker, "They're Turning Churches into Climate Resilience Centers," *Grist*, January 13, 2021, https:// grist.org. As Laurel Kearns explains, this was inspired by the Eco-Justice Project founded at Cornell University in 1974. Laurel D. Kearns, "Ecology and the Environment," in Michael D. Palmer and Stanley M. Burgess, eds., *The Wiley-Blackwell Companion to Religion and Social Justice* (Chichester, UK: Wiley-Blackwell, 2012), 591–606. On Christian antipollution activism in the United States, see also Laurel D. Kearns, "Con-spiring Together: Breathing for Justice," in Laura Hobgood and Whitney Bauman, eds., *The Bloomsbury Handbook of Religion and Ecology: The Elements* (London: Bloomsbury Academic, 2018), 117–31.

this problem, which has grown to the point of "systemic disruption" of terrestrial ecosystems, found that light pollution was endangering a vast array of organisms, from the microbial level through to plants, insects, birds, and mammals, especially bats, by interfering with migration patterns, nighttime pollination, and predator-prey relations; injuring or killing birds outright should they fly into illuminated windows; and encouraging surface algae on still water bodies.[29] Given the pivotal role of insects within the entire mesh of life, the deleterious impact of light pollution, in conjunction with other causes of insect decline, is especially worrisome. LED lighting, though introduced to reduce energy consumption, has made matters even worse. A study of moth caterpillar numbers in hedgerows along illuminated rural roads in England found numbers of them 52 percent lower than in unlit areas, compared with 41 percent lower under sodium lights.[30] Statistics like this are a valuable reminder of the need for holistic thinking if our technological fixes for one environmental hazard are not to engender or exacerbate others.

Human health is also placed at risk by the artificial illumination of the night. Humans have poor night vision, and require light to get about when the sun no longer shines and the moon is inadequate to guide their steps. Yet too much artificial illumination during the night has been associated with sleep disruption; increased incidence of headache, fatigue, stress, anxiety, and obesity; decreased sexual function; and breast and prostate cancer. As is the case for other diurnal creatures, darkness triggers the release of melatonin. Melatonin prepares us for the refreshment of sleep and the blessing of dreams, and acts as an antioxidant,

---

[29] Dirk Sanders et al., "A Meta-analysis of Biological Impacts of Artificial Light at Night," *Nature Ecology and Evolution* 5 (2021): 74–81.

[30] Douglas H. Boyes et al., "Street Lighting Has Detrimental Impacts on Local Insect Populations," *ScienceAdvances* 7, no. 35 (August 25, 2021): 1–8.

helping to hold back the aging process and protecting every cell of our bodies from potentially carcinogenic damage.[31] Less measurable, but possibly also grievous, is the aesthetic and spiritual deprivation of living in a world in which ever fewer stars are visible in ever more places.[32] Meanwhile, the dominion of the heavens that Elohim granted to Brother Sun and Sister Moon is being usurped by human technologies. The sky is becoming littered with space junk, the darkness pierced by the gleaming shafts of Elon Musk's StarLink satellites, launched in batches of sixty at a time, as the deep reaches of space are opened up as a new terrain for colonial conquest.

Given the limited public appreciation of the dangers of light pollution, it is perhaps unsurprising that there are as yet few, if any, Christian initiatives to redress this problem. I can't help wondering, though, whether the widespread failure to protest the despoliation of the night sky might not also relate to the cultural legacy of light veneration in the Christian West. The "Word," which, as we read in the poetic opening of John's Gospel, was with God in the beginning, brought the "life" that became "the light of all people. The light shines in the darkness, and the darkness did not overcome it" (John 1:4–5). This privileging of light is manifest, for example, in the name of the multifaith environmental organization in association with which Berndt hosts a monthly webinar: Interfaith Power and Light.

Yet the Bible also affords a different view. As we have seen on that First Day with which the hexameron opens, the creation of light did not quench the darkness, but came graciously to alternate with it. And as any number of Christian mystics who pursue

---

[31] International Dark Sky Initiative, "Human Health," www.darksky.org.

[32] Christopher C. M. Kyber et al., "Citizen Scientists Report Global Rapid Reductions in the Visibility of Stars from 2011 to 2022," *Science* 379, no. 6629 (2023): 265–68.

the path of the via negativa have shown, night also holds its blessings, for the divine might be most truly encountered only in the darkness of unknowing. The abolition of the night as a source of spiritual deprivation appears to be gaining wider recognition today, including among Christians. Some months after our interview, Berndt alerted me to a short article on light pollution that had been posted on the United Church of Christ website in the interim. In this article, Anne Hayek, a member of the Congregational Church of Needham, UCC, and of the Massachusetts Chapter of the International Dark Sky Association, observed,

> In the quiet of the night, we are given a break from daytime stimulation, allowing us to focus inward and listen to our Creator's voice. If we are fortunate enough to view it, the starry night sky against a dark backdrop offers a sense of abundance, often diminished elsewhere on our planet by human activity. If Abraham lived in a modern, light-polluted city, what would he think of God's promise of descendants as numerous as the stars in the sky?[33]

In a similar vein, Michael Bledsoe, minister of Riverside Baptist Church in Washington, DC, writes of the blessed nights he spent in the Catskills, "remote and unlinked from the bustling matrix of the city." There, he discovered that, in the absence of light pollution, it was "the depth of the night which provided the opportunity to see," in the starry heavens, an intimation of the "Light of God" that is ever present "even when you walk in a dark valley or a night of sorrow."[34]

---

[33] Anne Hayek, "For the Beauty of the Sky: International Dark Sky Week: A Christian Perspective," United Church of Christ, The Pollinator: UCC Environmental Justice Blog, www.ucc.org.

[34] Michael Bledsoe, "Silence, Dark Sky: Spirituality," Riverside Baptist Church, Washington, DC, February 10, 2014. The Episcopal Church of the

Getting to such places, however, requires time, transport, and money, all of which are in desperately short supply for many people. In this respect, light pollution is also an environmental justice issue, as well as a contributor to biodiversity loss, since it tends to be worse in areas where disadvantaged communities suffer disproportionately from a range of environmental harms as well. Moreover, as Anne Hayek observes, such communities are "often less able to afford to travel to the few remaining dark sky places and experience awe at our shared natural heritage."[35] While the creation of Dark Sky Parks is to be welcomed and defended, far more needs to be done to balance the needs of human safety with the restoration of the night in those urban spaces, where, as Erazim Kohak laments in *The Embers and the Stars*, "the glare of electric light extends the day far into a night restless with the eerie glow of neon."[36]

Beholding the fire-folk who only appear in the night sky when electric lighting down here below is dimmed, no less than breathing fresh air in sunlight unimpeded by smog should surely not be the privilege of the few.

Tilt back your head, or lie down on the ground, and lift your eyes to the sky: behold the fire-folk, Brother Sun and Sister Moon and stars, beaming down from on high.

There are signs in the heavens, if you know how to look. Some might give guidance, as they have done of old, but others bear witness to new ways here below.

Redeemer, Cincinnati, OH, summarizes research on the adverse impacts of light pollution as a springboard for reflection on spiritual "artificial light." See "Rise and Shine," January 7, 2021, RedeemerCincy.org.

[35] Hayek, "For the Beauty of the Sky."

[36] E. Kohak, *The Embers and the Stars: A Philosophical Inquiry into the Moral Sense of Nature* (Chicago: University of Chicago Press, 1984), 10.

Look up, look around, recall all you can't see: behold, in breath-taking smog and star-quenching glare, a call to repentance. Turn away, turn around, chart a new course.

Arise and let shine. Return the skies to the fire-folk through better care of the Earth, that all might breathe freely, that all might sleep deeply. Give thanks for the light, but let there be night.

Fifth Day

*And God said, "Let the waters swarm with the swarm of living
creatures and let fowl fly over the earth across the vault of the
heavens." And God created the great sea monsters and every
living creature that crawls, which the water had swarmed forth
of each kind, and the winged fowl of each kind, and God saw
that it was good. And God blessed them, saying, "Be fruitful
and multiply and fill the water in the seas and let the fowl
multiply in the earth." And it was evening and it was morning,
fifth day.*

Genesis 1:20–23

What is it about rock pools?

*There they are, just down the beach, always beckoning, calling
you away from the surf and sand, promising glimpses of all
manner of peculiar beings, if you've got something to protect your
feet, and go slow, and keep your eyes peeled.*

*Out beyond the rocks, there's the awesome vastness of the open
sea. You know it's full of marvels, but they're hidden from your
gaze. Then again, your attention might be caught by the calls
of seabirds, prompting you to lift your eyes to the sky; but unless
there are cliffs nearby where they have found a perch, they're
generally on the wing and don't stick around for you to really
take them in. Here among the crevices and pools in the rutted*

sea-worn rocks, though, you can sometimes find a window onto a marine world in miniature, with strange critters of many colors that scuttle and whiz and open and close and waft about in the watery breeze. This is a labile world that alters with every tide as the shutters go down and things get unmoored and mixed around. When you come back tomorrow, each and every window will open onto a somewhat different scene.

The most surprising thing I've ever encountered in a rock pool was a baby shark. I guess it was about a foot or so in length, and it did not look happy about finding itself marooned on the shoreline. I was with my big brother, who told me to stand back while he picked it up gingerly by the tail. Dashing to the perilous edge at the highest point of the rocks, he swung his arm out wide and landed that little shark safely back in the deep, dark waters swirling below.

Evening was coming on as we hurried home to have our tea and tell our tale. On the way, Richard wondered whether he had done the right thing: after all, that hapless little shark—we imagined it might have been a Great White—could well grow up to bite off somebody's leg one day, maybe even his own! But we both knew that it simply had to be done. Without saying as much, what my brother showed me that day was that the neighbor-love I'd learned about in Sunday school was not just for the person next door, but also for strangers, and not only those of our own kind. Neighbor-love did not depend upon any capacity or willingness of the other to reciprocate, and it extended even to those who might, in other circumstances, do us harm.

The lesson of that rock pool is one I have never forgotten. It is also one that I will never quite fathom.

The Peopling of Water and Air:
"Bourne beyond Bounds" by Creatures of Breath

Having lit up the heavens, Elohim's attention returns to the Earth, homing in on those waters that had been separated on the Second Day. As had the land on the Third Day in the bringing forth of vegetation, so now the waters "co-operate," as Traherne had it, in the creation of great swarms of diverse living beings: those that teem in the lower waters, as well as others that swarm through the aerial realm opened up by the raising of the firmament (MoSDC, 58). Some of these creatures were of monstrous proportions— but whether great or small, all are said to have been gifted with a kind of animation that distinguishes them from plants: *Nephesh chayyah* in Hebrew—literally, a living breath. And all were pleasing in Elohim's sight. Addressing them directly, their creator exhorts them to get together and make more of their own kind so that the seas and the skies should be jam-packed with abundant and ebullient animal life. Now, this was something new under the sun, moon, and stars on this good Earth that was getting ever better, ever busier: filling up with all manner of highly mobile creatures that scuttle and swim and float and fly and open and close.

One of the puzzling features of this passage is the "big question," as Augustine put it, as to why Elohim is said to have "allotted flying things . . . to the waters and not to the air" (LCG, 143). Some commentators attribute this to the similarity in their mode of locomotion, which is highlighted through their designation as mobile creatures that are variously said to "swarm," "fly," and "crawl." As Philo observed, aquatic and aerial animals are "both things that float" (OC, 149). For landlubbers like ourselves, I would add that there is a certain lightness of being in the lives of both. They appear to us less weighed down by the force of gravity. By no means do all aquatic critters have fins, but those that do seem to fly through the water as birds do through the air with their wings, as both Basil (BaH, 124) and Ambrose (AmH, 197) observed. And then there are those large fish and marine mammals (as we classify them today)—whales, dolphins, and porpoises—who like to leap out of the water and arc through the air, while some seabirds, such as puffins and terns, dive down and fly underwater for minutes at a time.

Augustine nonetheless hazarded another line of reasoning, in his cautious and qualified way. He wondered whether "this air that is contiguous to the land" is called "by the name of water, since it proves itself by dew-fall to be damp even on the finest of nights, and because it also condenses into clouds" (LCG, 143). This interpretation was taken up by some of the medieval commentators as well. Robert Grosseteste, noting the "connaturality of air and water," understood swimming things to have been "brought forth from moist thicker water, and the flying things from moist water in suspension" (SDC, 188, 187). In that sense, then, aerial creatures might also be said to have been waterborne at the beginning.

Another uncertainty is whether those aerial creatures also included flying insects. Basil evidently thought they did, as he made special mention of bees, for whom he expressed particular admiration on account of their cooperative industry; artistic constructions, by comparison with which "the discoveries of geometry are mere by-works to the wise bee" (BaH, 128); democratic governance; and of course the "precious nourishment" they produce, in which humans, whether "kings or men of low degree," might also partake and thereby be "brought to health" (BaH, 127). Whether or not you believe the legend that Basil's eloquence was gifted to him by the bees who fed him their honey as he slept, he was clearly big on bees. Ambrose, who became known as *doctor mellifluous* (honey-flowing doctor) on account of his sweet rhetoric,[1] followed Basil,

---

[1] Claire Preston, *Bee* (London: Reaktion, 2006), 13.

together with Vergil's *Georgics* (29 BCE), in his praise for honey-bees. He also mentions the "sweet chant" that issues from the "tiny throat of the cicada" (BaH, 217), the silken chrysalis woven by the "Indian worm" (BaH, 218), and the alleged self-restraint of locusts, unless enjoined from on high to administer divine vengeance for human wrongdoing by devouring the crop. Most commentators, however, take their cue from the word translated by Alter as "fowl" and assume that the winged creatures of day five refer only, or primarily, to the feathered variety.

All commentators affirm the inherent goodness of these strange fellow creatures, however defined, who teem in the seas and swarm through the skies in such abundance and variety as to "beggar counting," as Chrysostom observed (CHoG, 96). Aware that not all of them might be to human liking or serve human purposes, he stressed that "it was not simply for our use that everything was created" (CHoG, 98) and insisted that "although you stand in ignorance of the reason for the created things, don't presume to find fault with their creation" (CHoG, 97). Basil, who found himself "borne beyond bounds" (BaH, 135) in view of the manifold wonders of the seas and skies, went further in noting the limits not only of human knowledge but also of power with respect to some of these creatures. Of fish, for instance, he observed that theirs is "special nature … a life apart"; as such, "they cannot be tamed and cannot bear the touch of a man's hand" (BaH, 111).

While this view was not widely held within ancient natural philosophy, the topos of alterity and untamability recalls the lauding of the Leviathan in the book of Job, precisely in terms of its resistance to human dominion: "Will it make a covenant with you to be taken as your servant forever?" asks the Lord. "Will you play with it as with a bird, / or will you put it on leash for your girls?" (Job 31:4–5). Ambrose also saw the seas as a domain that exceeds human dominion. Whereas some humans greedily "claim the sea for themselves by right of ownership and boast that they have subjected fishes like slaves to a condition of servitude" (AmH, 181–82), Ambrose asserted that the life of the ocean was "given for common use," including, and initially only, that of its nonhuman inhabitants, such that "you were not to claim anything as your own personal property" (AmH, 160). Traherne, by contrast, preempting the momentous (some might say calamitous) blessing bestowed upon the first humans on the Sixth Day, insisted, "Man, by thy divine Providence, hath the Possession of all this Sea, and Dominion over it, as he hath over the Earth." Yet he also affirmed the wisdom and goodness of all waterborne creatures, recalling the "great and wide sea" of Psalm 104, "wherein are things creeping innumerable, both small and great; there go the Ships and there is that Leviathan which thou hast made to take his Pastime therein" (MoSDC, 58).

With the emergence of this new kind of creature came novel capacities and proclivities, including the evident delight in their own existence manifested by the Leviathan of Psalm 104, who, in newer translations, "sports" in the sea. "Fish leaped from the rivers," Ambrose exclaimed, "Dolphins frolicked in the waves. Shell-fish clung to the rocks. Oysters adhered to the depths and the sea-urchins waxed strong" (AmH, 160). Reveling in their own existence, these creatures were also "provided with a sense of self-preservation and with the instinct of shrinking from death" (AmH, 160). Moreover, as Grosseteste averred, they were equipped with a desire to reproduce: something that he framed as a virtue, since "goodness is the desire of giving not only one's things but oneself, for the ease and benefit of another. In generation, the generator gives its substance for the establishment of the substance of that which is generated" (SDC, 193).

Manifesting as amorous desire, this mode of self-giving might be considered inherent to the creaturely being of animals.

Additionally, Basil and those who followed his lead observed avian virtue expressed in the care for their young and, in the case of the stork, their elderly. Birds also have the capacity to bring incidental benefits to others, including those not of their kind, through their power of song. While not all birdcalls are equally melodious (as I am reminded at this moment by the croak of the raven who, thrillingly, has taken to hanging out in the churchyard next door), "From branch to branch," as Milton's Raphael recounted so exquisitely,

> the smaller birds with song
> Solaced the woods, and spread their painted wings,
> Till even; nor even then the solemn nightingale
> Ceased warbling, but all night tuned her soft lays.

(VII, ll. 433–36)

Yet not all was sweetness and light in this rambunctious new realm of animal life. Predation is now part of the picture, with smaller creatures providing sustenance for larger ones all the way up the food chain. And with predation came clever strategies both to hide and to hunt. Such, for example, is the "cunning and trickery of the squid, which takes the color of the rock to which it attaches itself. Most fish," Basil observed, "swim idly up to the squid as they would to a rock, and become the prey of the crafty creature" (BaH, 113). While he admonished his human listeners not to follow such examples of predatory guile, nor to be deceived by those who seem innocuous but have malign designs upon the innocent, Basil was confident that "a wise and marvelous order reigns among these animals." This is manifest in particular in the "law of nature, which according to the needs of each kind, has allotted to them their dwelling places with equality and justice" (BaH, 114).

The observation that aerial as well as aquatic creatures have their own dwelling places—and, it was fondly thought, respected those of others—was taken up by other commentators as well. Ambrose parsed this concept in terms that preempt the modern concept of the "ecological niche," with different kinds of fish inhabiting those places best suited for their nourishment, such that "each one is by nature constrained to keep itself within the bounds of its native habitat" (AmH, 181). Recalling the "great sea monsters" singled out in the biblical text, Ambrose observed how the whales of the Atlantic "cherish their habitat as their native land and consider it a delight to dwell therein" (AmH, 183).

In the case of migratory creatures, their habitat is geographically dispersed, and Ambrose, like Basil, marveled at the indwelling intelligence that enables them to traverse such huge expanses with such surety. Different creatures, as Ambrose put it, "follow diverse customs" (AmH, 163), which are perfectly fitted to ensure their collective flourishing. In this respect, such creatures put humans to shame: some men, in their "monstrous greed" (AmH, 182), are forever encroaching on the dwelling places of others, laying claim to their possessions, and transforming the land and sea "in compliance with individual whims" (AmH, 181). Basil, notwithstanding his questionable assumption that aquatic animals have "no memory, no imagination, no idea of social intercourse" (BaH, 122), exclaimed that humans are "less reasonable about our own affairs than the fish" (BaH, 117). Indeed, according to Ambrose, it is precisely our much-lauded superior "reason" that is wont to lead us astray, opening us up to rhetorical persuasion to act against our own best interests, not to mention those of others (AmH, 185).

As in the case of the land's role in the generation of vegetation, so, too, the agency of the waters as participants in Elohim's world-making project is sometimes likened to childbirth. "The command was given," proclaimed Basil, "and immediately the rivers and lakes becoming fruitful, brought forth their natural broods; the sea travailed with all kinds of swimming creatures; not even in mud and marshes did the water remain idle; it took its part in creation" (BaH, 109). Many centuries later, Traherne would be more explicit: the "Sea, like a Mother, both brings them forth and sustains them" (MoSDC, 58).

Within the creation stories of some other cultures, all life is said to have emerged from the sea, albeit through the intermediary of the formation of land. Such, for example, are the "earth diver" narratives of several Native American, Central Asian, and Finno-Urgic peoples, in which a divine being generally sends an animal of some kind into the primeval waters to find mud or sand with which to form dry land, thereby rendering Earth habitable for the emergence of terrestrial life forms.[2] Within contemporary scientific narratives, Earth's ancient waters are thought to have played an even more pivotal role in their own right in both bringing forth and sustaining the entire meshwork of life on this planet. While many mythic traditions have revered "mother earth" deities, with Christian writers of the Middle Ages still deploying the metaphor of *Terra Mater*, it seems that we living beings actually owe our existence to the watery deep, our ancient *Aqua Mater*.

Oceanic Origins, Degraded Wetlands, and the Depopulation of Earth's Aquatic and Aerial Realms

Although the mysteries of biogenesis have not yet been fully revealed (with seeding from the aerial depths of outer space remaining in contention), the scenario that evolutionary biologists currently favor points to the thermal vents through which elements from the hot, steamy, and seething *tohu va bohu* beneath Earth's crust come into contact with salty waters, creating a warm,

---

[2] David Adams and Margaret Adams Leeming, *A Dictionary of Creation Myths* (Oxford: Oxford University Press, 1995), 79–80.

mineral-rich soup that is conducive to the mysterious chemical reaction that produced the building blocks of life some four and one-half billion years ago. Contemporary science suggests that the sea not only birthed those first "forms minute, unseen by spheric glass," as Erasmus Darwin conjectured in *Temple of Nature* (1803), those briny deeps also created and continue to maintain conditions conducive to the burgeoning of terrestrial life.[3]

The molecular structure of the waters covering some 71 percent of Earth's surface makes our precious planet warmer and more hospitable to life as we know it than it would otherwise be, given its distance from the sun. Meanwhile, the great ocean conveyor belt, in distributing heat north and south from the equator, plays a crucial role in transporting toward the poles some of the immense warmth that the seas absorb. Without our mighty Aqua Mater, then, Earth would be as inhospitable as Venus or Mars, and any organisms who came into being in the ocean would have been unlikely to have taken the momentous step that brought some of them, beginning with adventurous plants in partnership with their fungal friends, onto land. Without our great Aqua Mater, life might have started, as it almost certainly has elsewhere, but it could not have burgeoned in the gloriously biodiverse way that it has on our predominantly blue planet.[4]

The life forms that continued to make their home in the seas, together with those that adapted to the fresh waters, whether flowing or still, are indeed, as the hexameral commentators

---

[3] Erasmus Darwin, *The Temple of Nature; or, The Origin of Society*, Canto 1, "The Production of Life" (London: T. Bentley, 1803), ll. 295–302, produced for Project Gutenberg by Stephen Gibbs and Christine P. Travers, October 9, 2008. See "Third Day," 62.

[4] Kate Rigby, "Oceanic Extinctions and the Dread of the Deep," in Jeremy Kidwell and Stefan Skrimshire, eds., *Extinction and Religion* (Bloomington: Indiana University Press, forthcoming 2024).

enthused, mind-bogglingly many and various. The blue whale grows up to one hundred feet and weighs in at two hundred tons—a "great sea monster" reputed to be not only the largest animal species still in existence, but the largest to have ever inhabited this planet. With the help of powerful variants of that "spheric glass," the microscope, we also now know that these life forms include a multiplicity of tiny critters, collectively called zooplankton, who feed on the phytoplankton, which also helps to oxygenate the air breathed by those of us with lungs. Zooplankton might not be as charismatic as the mighty blue whale, but whales of all kinds, together with the other sea mammals, fish, mollusks, and crustaceans, persist only by the grace of these, their tiniest compatriots, who form the swarming base of the oceanic food web.

Birds, biologists tell us, only came much later, evolving piece-meal over millions of years from theropods, a type of dinosaur, during the Jurassic Period (around 165 million to 150 million years BCE), and then reemerging, phoenixlike, from the scorched Earth following the gargantuan meteor strike that appears to have precipitated the most recent mass extinction event on this volatile planet some 67 million years ago. Only in the wake of this global cataclysm, which killed off their larger dinosaur kin and brought an end to the Cretaceous Period, did birds really come into their own, diversifying into the ten thousand species that are now known to be distributed worldwide.[5] As an Australian I am rather chuffed to learn that the songbirds that solace all Earth's woods, fields, towns, and their peoples are now thought to have originated on the ancient supercontinent of Gondwana, evolving as a subspecies

---

[5] Stephen L. Brusatte, Jingmai K. O'Connor, and Eric D. Jarvis, "The Evolution and Diversification of Birds," *Current Biology Review* 25, no. 19 (2015): R888–R898.

of "passerines" (perching birds) in the region that became Australia around 50 million years ago.[6]

Winged insects had evidently made their appearance far earlier, coevolving with the first land plants around 400 million years ago in that marvelous dance of life that Lynn Margulis, following the work of Russian botanist Boris Kozo-Polyansky (1890–1957), termed "symbiogenesis."[7] Around 130 million years ago, some plants developed an ingenious mechanism for attracting pollinators by means of the alluring aromas and hues of their flowers. In tandem with those flowering plants, Basil's beloved bees came into being—although it took around another 50 million years for those first solitary bees and wasps to be joined by others who acquired the complex social existence so admired by humans, whose societies are frequently far less well ordered.[8]

Here, though, I am going to keep with the designation of "fowl" and follow those commentators who consider the winged ones to be exclusively of the feathered variety, those saurian survivors of the last mass extinction, whose drastically dwindling numbers and diversity have led them to be dubbed "canaries in the coal mine," signaling the strife that human activities are visiting upon Earth's web of life. In the words of Patricia Zurita, CEO of Birdlife International, we "need to listen and act upon what birds are telling us, as they disappear ever faster."[9] Heeding Zurita's call on this Fifth Day, I am concerned in particular with those birds who favor a watery habitat, bringing my attention to those aquatic as well as avian creatures whose intertwined flourishing is contingent on the health of wetlands and oceans.

---

[6] Tim Low, *Where Song Began: Australia's Birds and How They Changed the World* (Melbourne: Penguin Random House, 2014).

[7] Lynn Margulis, *Symbiotic Planet: A New Look at Evolution* (New York: Basic Books, 1998).

[8] Dave Goulson, *A Sting in the Tale* (London: Vintage, 2013), 42–50.

[9] Quoted in Damian Carrington, "'Canaries in the Coalmine': Loss of Birds Signals Changing Planet," *The Guardian*, May 5, 2022.

Long before the manufactories of Europe's industrial era started pouring their waste into rivers and streams, wetlands were targeted for "development." Within the Western cultural imaginary, swamps, marshes, fens, and bogs have commonly been reviled as malign places, associated with melancholia, madness, disease, and death.[10] In Milton's *Paradise Lost*, the swamp features as the lair of Satan. Compounding these negative cultural associations was the practical consideration of acquiring more land for livestock and crops. Unsurprisingly, it was the low-lying Netherlands that pioneered the expansion of agriculture from the twelfth century onward through the construction of polders and canals, along with dikes to hold back the sea. In Britain, those who sought to follow the Dutch example by transforming noisome swamps and mires into productive farmland set to work in earnest during Shakespeare's day, when an ambitious scheme to drain the Lincolnshire fens was launched with the legal support of the General Drainage Act of 1600.

Yet these ambitions were not unopposed. For the smallholders who had dwelt in the fens for generations, this miry water country was hearth and home. "Its stores of thatch and sedge provided a modest livelihood; its peat offered a ready supply of fuel; its grasslands, when dry, were ideal for seasonal grazing; and its lakes and streams teemed with fish, eel, and waterfowl."[11] While these subsistence farmers were excluded from the political process, voices of opposition were raised by some in Parliament, whether on the grounds of impracticability or concern about the loss of existing natural resources, or out of respect for what was seen as a praiseworthy part of God's earthly creation. The aquatic and avian life of

---

[10] Rod Giblett, *Postmodern Wetlands: Culture, History, Ecology* (Edinburgh: Edinburgh University Press, 1996).

[11] Todd Andrew Borlik, "Caliban and the Fen Demons of Lincolnshire: The Englishness of Shakespeare's *Tempest*," *Shakespeare* 9, no. 1 (2013): 21–51, 24.

the fens also had supernatural champions, spirits of place, who were said to cause trouble for any who sought to drain the swamp. The story of St. Guthlac, a seventh-century Anglo-Saxon hermit, was revived in association with the debates over the fens. Indeed, a lost play from the late 1500s called *Cutlack* may well have been one of the sources Shakespeare drew on for *The Tempest*, which contains in the figure of Caliban a reminiscence of the fen bogey said to have been known as Tiddy Mun.[12]

In the long run, though, the program of disciplining and draining these unruly waterscapes prevailed over all opposition and was ramped up another notch toward the end of the eighteenth century in association with a new wave of enclosures of erstwhile common land. Among the many songs and ballads written to protest the first wave is one that takes the perspective of a fish that was endangered by the drainage of the Lincolnshire fens. First published in 1611, "The Powtes Complaint" invited the "Brethren of water" to "treat upon this matter, which makes us quake and tremble," for "where we feed in Fen and Reed, they'll feed both Beef and Bacon."[13] Their fears were warranted: "powte" is thought to be a local name for the burbot: a once-common freshwater fish that is now considered extinct in the United Kingdom.[14]

Wetlands are protean places that are flooded either permanently or seasonally with waters that might be fresh, salt, or brackish,

---

[12] Borlik, "Fen Demons," 24–41.

[13] "The Powtes Complaint" (anon.), in R. Palmer, *A Ballad History of England from 1588 to the Present Day* (London: B. T. Batsford, 1979). I am indebted to my environmental humanities master's student Jess Nock for introducing me to this ballad, for which she has recorded her own setting, along with settings of other antienclosure ballads and poems, including one of her own. You can find them on Soundcloud at jess-55.

[14] Todd Borlik and C. Egan, "Angling for the 'Powte': A Jacobean Environmental Protest Poem," *English Literary Renaissance* 48, no. 2 (2018): 256–89.

depending on where they are located. Different kinds of wetland are characterized by different vegetation types, which are all uniquely adapted to their unoxygenated, or anoxic, soils. According to the more inclusive definition of wetlands used in the Ramsar Convention—which includes also rivers and floodplains, estuaries and deltas, mudflats, mangroves and coral reefs, as well as paddy fields and fish ponds—40 percent of Earth's plants and animals depend upon these places of abundance where land and water meet and mingle. As well as supporting a huge diversity of endemic aquatic and avian species, they also provide crucial waystations for the millions of migratory birds who breed, rest, and refuel there.

Wetlands are vital in other respects as well. They are among the most effective carbon sinks on the planet, with peatlands (which include bogs and fens) storing as much as all the world's forests combined; they provide flood mitigation, with mangroves and salt marshes helping to protect over half the world's human population from coastal flooding, as well as reducing air temperature and helping to mitigate droughts; and they are the Earth's kidneys, purifying water by filtering pollutants, removing up to 60 percent of metals and 90 percent of nitrogen. It is estimated that one billion people depend upon wetlands directly for their livelihood, and that the diet of around half the world's population incorporates wetland-grown staples, such as rice. Additionally, and incalculably, for those suffering from stress, anxiety, and depression, spending time around wetlands might also afford a deep sense of peace and release.[15]

Thanks to the efforts of national organizations such as the Wetland Wildlife Trust (WWT), founded in 1946 by Peter Scott (son of the Antarctic explorer), several wetlands in the United Kingdom, including parts of the Lincolnshire fens as well as the

---

[15] Wetland Wildlife Trust, "Why Wetlands: Why Wetlands Are Amazing," accessed March 30, 2023, www.wwt.org.uk.

Somerset Levels, have been restored. Others are being created, often in former industrial sites, such as the Royal Society for the Protection of Birds' Saltholme nature reserve on the site of a former saltworks at Cleveland in Tees Valley. The crucial importance of wetland protection was recognized internationally with the adoption of the Convention on Wetlands in Ramsar (Iran) in 1971. Coming into force in 1975, this was the first global intergovernmental environmental agreement. Yet while the improved fortunes of wetlands in the United Kingdom and elsewhere in the Global North has been facilitated by the outsourcing of much of its mining and manufacturing, the "Brethren of water" are seriously embattled in those more recently industrialized and industrializing nations.

Take India, for example. India is awash with wetlands. Forty-six Indian wetlands have been designated under the Ramsar Convention as "Wetlands of International Significance," affording a range of crucial benefits to local populations as well as vital habitat for a dizzying number and variety of aquatic and bird species. Several of these wetlands are also sacred sites—and most of them are in trouble, to a greater or lesser degree. Reading through Ramsar's "Annotated List of Wetlands of International Significance" for India has filled me with wonder and worry in roughly equal measure.

The vast congregations of migratory birds who visit some of these sites must be a marvel to behold: two hundred thousand ducks, geese, swans, and other waterfowl have been known to overwinter on Harike Lake in the Punjab, for instance. Among the species of birds and fish who inhabit or frequent India's Ramsar wetlands, many have been identified as at risk of extinction. These include the critically endangered Deolali minnow, red-headed vulture, white-rumped vulture, Indian vulture, Baer's pochard, and sociable lapwing (whose society is dwindling); the endangered catfish, Egyptian vulture, steppe eagle, Pallas's fish eagle, saker falcon, woolly necked stork, black-bellied tern, spotbilled pelican, black-necked crane, lesser and greater adjutant stork, and white-eyed pochard; and the vulnerable Asian woollyneck, lesser white-fronted goose, spoon-bill sandpiper, grey pelican, Dalmatian pelican, marbled teal, sarus crane, greater spotted eagle, grey-headed fish eagle, ferruginous duck, and common pochard (which is fast becoming a rarity). One marshland reserve in the Punjab also affords refuge to an endangered reptile, the spotted pond turtle, while other wetlands are also home to endangered mammals, such as the Indus River dolphin, snow leopard, hog deer, Indian wild ass, Indian pangolin, tiger, and smooth-coated otter.

These precious places of aquatic and avian abundance, some of which are human-made and most of which have been used sustainably for countless generations, are themselves at risk. Of the forty-six, Ramsar lists thirty-six as being encroached on by human settlements, thirty-one by other modifications to natural systems, thirty-three by unsustainable agriculture and aquaculture, twenty-two by other forms of biological resource extraction, and twenty-three by interference with water flow. Roads and service corridors are eating into sixteen, while thirty-five are threatened by pollution and six by energy production and mining. Invasive plants and animals are affecting twenty-seven. Three are vulnerable to naturally occurring geological events, but thirteen are already beginning to experience the adverse impacts of anthropogenic climate change, which are set to worsen and spread.

Defending the "Brethren of Water": Initiatives from India and Kenya

When I spoke with Dr. Mathew Koshy Punnackad in March 2021 about his work with the Church of South India (CSI), he was quick to highlight the plight of India's wetlands.[16] With a

---

[16] Interview with Dr. Mathew Koshy Punnackad took place on March 19, 2021, and is quoted here with Mathew's kind permission.

master's in chemistry, a doctorate in environmental science, and independent studies in theology and biblical hermeneutics, Mathew is exceptionally well qualified for his role as Honorary Director of CSI's Synod Department of Ecological Concerns, a position he has held since 2014. Water matters have been high on his agenda for a long time. As the principal of Bishop Moore College, Mavelikara, he organized conferences on Water Crisis and Climate Change (2008) and The Impact of Climate Change on Food Security (2011), as well as initiating an award-winning rain harvesting project at his college.[17] This was part of a larger "green campus" initiative, including plantings to recharge groundwater and prevent soil erosion and the installation of solar-powered lighting.

Drawing on over three decades of teaching experience, Mathew's work with CSI has a strongly educational focus, entailing the provision of ecotheological training to clergy and working with some two thousand teachers to enhance ecological literacy and environmental engagement among schoolchildren. I was delighted to discover that, in the workshops he has run for over three hundred clergy members (around 30 percent of the entire clergy of CSI), he has been using the eco-justice approach to biblical hermeneutics pioneered by Hebrew Bible scholar Norman Habel, my friend and fellow Australian, Lutheran minister, and founding coeditor of the Earth Bible series (we encounter Norm again on the Sixth Day). Among the outcomes of these workshops are two edited collections, *Green Parables* (2016) and *Green Miracles* (2020).[18] In addition to

---

[17] The college was recognized with the Palathully Award of Malayala Manorama in 2008 and the Dr. P. S. Job Memorial Award from the All India Association for Christian Higher Education in 2010.

[18] Among Mathew's many other publications are edited collections of *Earth Bible Sermons* (3 vols., 2015–2016), *God Is Green* (2004), *A Christian Response to Ecological Crisis* (2009), *Green Gospel* (2011), *Green Church* (2014), *Climate Emergency: People's Stories of Adaptation and Mitigation* (2019), and

teaching and publishing, Mathew has also initiated several eco-programs, including the Green Parish Award, Green Home Award, and Green School Award. At the time we spoke, he was working toward the creation of twenty-three "climate resilient" schools and communities in South India in the lead-up to COP 26.

Mathew's journey toward becoming an environmental educator, writer, and campaigner began when he attended a conference in Japan in 1989. Visiting Minamata, he was dismayed to meet people whose hands and legs had been lamed by organic mercury poisoning as a consequence of the toxic waste that a local factory had dumped into the waters from which they fished. Subsequently, his concerns about the unjust human suffering wrought by environmental degradation expanded to include passionate advocacy for the protection of wildlife, entailing a theologically informed ethos of respect for the discrete domains within which different species are best able to flourish. Commenting on the increased incidence of human-elephant and human–big cat conflict in India today, he observed that this was a consequence of human incursion into their habitat, against which they were, as he put it, quite rightly "protesting."

Mathew is particularly concerned about the loss and degradation of Indian wetlands. In this connection, he told me of the case of one small wetland in Kerala State, adjacent to the UNESCO-listed village of Aranmula, home to the famous Sree Parthasarathy Temple. Here, the "Brethren of water" include humans and their rice paddies together with the aquatic and avian life of the

---

Sustainable Living (2020). He has also coauthored two books for children, *Silent Rhythm: Eco-tales for Children* (2017) and *Green Stories for Sunday School Children* (2019), as well as guides for Sunday school teachers and for the "green church." His monograph, *The Green God of the Bible: An Ecological Reading of the Bible Illustrated*, was published in 2020. All these books are published by CSI, with some copublished with the Indian Society for Promoting Christian Knowledge.

adjoining naturally occurring wetlands along the Pampa/Pamba River. This river flows into the Ramsar-listed Vembanad Kol Wetland, a complex ecosystem covering 2,114 kilometers, which encompasses the largest lake in Kerala, a chain of lagoons, and mangrove swamps. Like other Ramsar wetlands in South India, this major site is itself "in crisis."[19]

In 2004 part of the wetlands that had allegedly been bought for fish cultivation was instead filled in for an airstrip. This grew into plans for the creation of an international airport under the aegis of the Chennai-based transnational KGS Group, leading to over two hundred hectares of land, including the Aranmula wetlands, being declared an industrial development site in 2011. With a much larger area likely to be affected, this would have been ecologically devastating and would have led to the loss of livelihood and eviction for thousands of villagers, none of whom had been consulted in the planning process. Local people, in collaboration with their extended support network, including Mathew, campaigned tirelessly: planting trees, protesting, petitioning, and engaging in civil resistance modeled on Gandhi's *satyagraha*. Their efforts were successful: in July 2013 the Kerala government, which had a 10 percent share in the planned airport complex, canceled its in-principle sanction of the project. The following year, India's National Green Tribunal revoked the environmental clearance that had previously been awarded on the grounds that this approval was based on insufficient information.[20] Though this was not the end of the story, Aranmula's more-than-human Brethren of water, it seems, are not to be banished by tarmac and planes.

---

[19] South Asia Network on Dams, Rivers and People, "Ramsar Wetlands in Crisis 2020: South India," March 3, 2020, https://sandrp.in.

[20] I have supplemented Mathew's interview, and a press report that he sent me separately, with an online report from Global Justice Now, "Victory for Campaign against Airport in Aranmula," June 20, 2014.

This one instance underscores the importance of the work that CSI is undertaking in fostering environmental understanding and advocacy among Christians at this perilous time of transition in India. CSI's endeavors have received international accolades, including the 2009 International Environment Conservation Award instituted by the Alliance of Religions and Conservation in association with the United Nations Development Programme (UNDP). More recently, Mathew was invited to address the 2019 UN Environment Assembly in Nairobi to share "stories of commitment and hope from India," and later that year he hosted the Faith for Earth conference of the United Nations Environment Programme (UNEP) at CSI's Synod Centre in Chennai.[21]

The religious demographics of India are an important factor in Mathew's work. Christianity is a minority religion in India, representing only 2.4 percent of the population nationally, of whom nearly half are concentrated in the South. By comparison, the 2011 census recorded 81 percent Hindus and 12.9 percent Muslims, nearly 2 percent Sikhs, and less than 1 percent each of Buddhists, Jains, and "other religions."[22] For this reason, Mathew is very committed to interreligious dialogue and collaboration and takes personal inspiration from what he sees as the more "holistic" religions and philosophies of the East, including Daoism, Shintoism, Zen, Hinduism, and Buddhism.[23] Although originally associated with European imperialist and capitalist expansion, Christianity in India, which some believe can be traced back to the first century CE, has acquired its own multiform character, absorbing cultural influences from other traditions (including in the North, those of

---

[21] "Dr. Mathew Koshy Represents CSI in the Fourth Environmental Assembly of the UNEP," Church of South India News, March 15, 2019.

[22] Pew Research Center, "Religion in India: Tolerance and Segregation," June 29, 2021, www.pewresearch.org.

[23] Mathew Koshy Punnakadu, "How I Became a Christian with Environmental Concern," accessed March 30, 2023, https://drmathewkoshy.com.

Indigenous tribal peoples), which enjoin respect and reverence for the natural world.[24]

While working in India for about ten years around the turn of the millennium, another of my conversation partners for this Fifth Day, marine biologist Robert Sluka, began to question the "dualistic anthropocentric individualistic" style of the American Evangelical Presbyterianism in which he had been raised.[25] Bob did not take his faith lightly. On the contrary, he was a devout believer and had even been involved in church planting work. His other great passion was the ocean. This childhood love, ignited by beach holidays in Florida and nurtured by the documentaries of Jacques Cousteau, eventually propelled him into a career in marine biology. Yet he kept these two sides of his life completely separate.

The connections that Bob began to glimpse between them during his time in India were consolidated and deepened when he moved to England around 2006. Talking with Christians in science there and reading more widely in theology brought about "a real paradigm shift" in which he realized that his marine conservation work was itself the way in which he expressed his devotion to God. During this time, he also came to draw spiritual sustenance from the Anglican liturgy and was licensed to preach in his local parish. Crucially, this was also when he began volunteering for the international interdenominational Christian conservation organization A Rocha, initially in the United Kingdom, but subsequently as the lead scientist with A Rocha Kenya's Marine and Coastal Conservation Programme. Bob now works for A Rocha International, heading up their Marine Conservation Programme, and living in Florida, where he also leads a local project.

---

[24] Pew Research Center, "8 Key Findings about Christians in India," July 12, 2021, www.pewresearch.org.

[25] Robert Sluka, interviewed by the author, December 1, 2020, and quoted with Bob's kind permission.

As Bob puts it in his short video profile for A Rocha, the aim of this program is nothing less than to "see the ocean and the people who use it transformed from a place of scarcity and problems to a place of abundance and teeming," as it is pictured in Genesis 1.[26] A Rocha's first marine conservation initiative, with which Bob was closely involved from the start, centers on Kenya's Watamu Marine National Park and Reserve. When A Rocha sent him to Kenya to undertake the first survey of this marine park, Bob and his team discovered that it was home to a number of critically endangered or threatened species. As he explained to me, Watamu is part of the National Park system in Kenya. Deriving from Euro-American notions of "wilderness" and originally imposed in many parts of Africa by colonial legislatures, this system was initially based on a model of conservation—"fortress conservation"—that presupposes that people should be excluded, except as visitors. Such a model has had adverse consequences for traditional landholders, including those who live along this stretch of Kenya's coast and for whom the sea has always been an important food source. In addition to their work of monitoring and habitat protection for both avian and aquatic sea life, initiatives to redress poverty, secure sustainable livelihoods, and mediate conflicting interests and perspectives are therefore also integral to the marine conservation project of A Rocha Kenya. Bob has found inspiration for this work in the "integral ecology" espoused in Pope Francis's encyclical *Laudato si'*, interlinking care for creation, justice for the poor, and inner peace.

A crucial participant in A Rocha Kenya's community engagement work is Queen Elizabeth Hare, whom I also interviewed in August 2021. As a member of the Giriama community, in whose traditional territory Watamu is located, Queen told me she was thrilled to be back working among her own people, having

---

[26] A Rocha International, "Dr. Robert Sluka Archives," People, accessed March 30, 2023, https://arocha.us.

left home to study for her bachelor's in environmental resource conservation at Machakos University.[27] Before taking up her position with A Rocha Kenya in 2020, she had worked as an attaché with the National Environment Management Authority, volunteered with Kenya Forest Service, and contributed to a social economic survey for the Friends of Arabuko Sokoke Forest NGO. Although she is twenty-four, Queen tells me with a chuckle that because she is "tiny" and still looks so young, the schoolchildren she works with frequently mistake her for one of their own. You don't have to talk with her for long, though, to discover that Queen is a real dynamo, bursting with energy and bubbling with ideas (she has to keep a notepad beside her bed because so many of these ideas come to her in the night, when, she says, God most often seems to speak to her). She had never considered educational employment before joining A Rocha, but she has become passionately committed to it.

Most of the children whom Queen works with have no idea what lies beneath the sea's silken surface, despite living along the coast. As funding for her initial role with A Rocha came from the Shark Conservation Fund (a project of the Rockefeller Philanthropy Advisory), she has been teaching children in particular about Watamu's endangered sharks, rays, and guitarfish, and how they can be better protected. As well as seeking to awaken their interest, curiosity, and concern about sea life more generally, she involves the children in beach cleanups to remove the plastic waste washing up along Kenya's shoreline from the staggering eight million tons that are currently ending up in Earth's interconnected oceans every year.[28] Along the way, Queen endeavors in the schools

---

[27] Interview with Queen Elizabeth Hare, August 8, 2021, quoted with her kind permission.

[28] UNEP News and Stories, "Our Planet Is Drowning in Plastic Pollution —It's Time for Change!", May 25, 2018, https://www.unep.org/news-and-stories/story/our-planet-drowning-plastic-pollution. Bob has himself written a

program to be a role model for young girls, too many of whom miss out on the advantages that might be enjoyed by their brothers and are at risk of being pressured into sexual activities that leave them pregnant in their teens, derailing their education and limiting their future prospects.

Queen's role also entails working with local fishermen, many of whom have been driven to poaching in the marine protected area in order to feed their families, especially during the pandemic lockdown that further diminished their earning capacity. For this reason, she instigated an Artisanal Fishing Competition in December 2021, in order to engage the local community in a celebration of the traditional skills of sustainable fishing.[29] These people, her people, are doing it tough, and Queen feels immensely grateful for the opportunity she has to stand by them and hear their concerns while helping them to better appreciate the importance of marine conservation. She has come to understand marine conservation as intrinsic to the Christian calling to both "rule" and "care" for God's creation (an understanding that she would like to foster within her own Catholic Church community, which, at the time of our conversation, had not yet taken on board Pope Francis's prophetic teaching on "care for our common home").

To be sure, the present is a painful time for marine conservationists and all who love the ocean and are entranced by the multifarious multitudes of life, both avian and aquatic, that it

---

booklet about marine plastics for use in Christian communities and is a strong advocate of beach cleanups, not only for their practical value in waste reduction but also as an embodied practice of care for creation, and as such, an act of worship, with physical, psychological, and spiritual benefits for participants. Robert D. Sluka, *Marine Plastics* (Cambridge: Grove Books, 2021).

[29] Queen told me about this inspired initiative and much more in a follow-up interview on May 29, 2022, also quoted here with her kind permission. See A Rocha Kenya, "Community Fishing Competition," accessed March 30, 2023, www.arocha.or.ke.

enabled and sustains. Earth's seas are in strife. In the passage from Job that I cited earlier, the voice that speaks from the whirling winds proceeds to humble humans further by asking rhetorically about the Leviathan, "Will traders bargain over it? / Will they divide it up among the merchants? Can you fill its skin with harpoons, or its heads with fishing spears?" (Job 41:6–7). The ancient author of this text could not have foreseen the industrial-scale commercial whaling that brought several species to the brink of extinction. While international agreements have now curtailed whaling significantly, other threats abound. Six out of the thirteen great whale species are currently classified as endangered.[30]

The conservation status of many other marine mammal species is uncertain, and where there are clear signs of trouble, the causes are not fully understood. Underwater sound pollution is likely to be interfering with their communication, and ship-strikes and gear entanglement are becoming more common as sea traffic has increased. PCBs (polychlorinated biphenyls)—organic compounds formerly used in capacitators, oil paints, and cool-ants—although banned in many countries, are still leaching into the sea and can persist for a long time in marine environments. They have been found to cause infertility in porpoises and orcas, harming their immune systems and even altering their behavior.[31] Changes in sea temperature and ocean circulation related to anthropogenic global heating are a further hazard for some species. Between January and May 2019, for example, thirty-one emaciated Pacific grey whales were found dead along the West Coast of North America between Baja California and Puget Sound. Dozens more seen making their way south to their summer breeding grounds

---

[30] World Wildlife Fund, "Whale," accessed March 30, 2023, www.worldwildlife.org.

[31] J.-P. Desforges et al., "Predicting Global Killer Whale Population Collapse from PCB Pollution," *Science* 361, no. 6409 (2018): 1373–76.

were also clearly malnourished. While the cause of their plight remains uncertain, the receding Arctic ice cap is forcing the whales further north to breed and feed, thereby lengthening their journey to the Baja.[32]

At the other end of the spectrum of sea life, the tiniest of marine creatures are also at risk as a consequence of climate change. Phytoplankton appear to be declining due to the warming temperature of the ocean, while the zooplankton who feed on them are threatened by increasing acidity levels arising from anthropogenic carbon dioxide emissions, which interfere with the formation of their calcareous shells.[33]

For a myriad of creatures in between, both avian and aquatic, their marine habitat is also becoming an ever less congenial dwelling place for a variety of reasons:

- Trawlers continue to deplete fish populations and scrape the sea floor, ravaging the plants that are so vital to marine ecosystems.
- Heat pulses are bleaching coral reefs, including those in the Watamu Marine National Park, and sending many species scurrying into cooler climes.

---

[32] A report in *Oceanography* from June 2019 indicates that endangered Atlantic right whales are also being adversely affected by warming oceans in the Gulf of Maine, where ecosystem changes are driving the whales to alter their foraging behavior and bringing them into waters where they are at greater risk from ship strikes and gear entanglement. Nicholas R. Record et al., "Rapid Climate-Driven Circulation Changes Threaten Conservation of Threatened Atlantic Right Whales," *Oceanography*, June 2019, 163–69. In July 2020 the IUCN accordingly moved this species into the "critically endangered" category.

[33] J. A. Gittings et al., "Impacts of Warming on Phytoplankton Abundance and Phenology in a Typical Marine Ecosystem," *Nature: Scientific Reports* 8 (2018): article 2240, https://doi.org/10.1038/s41598-018-20560-5; N. Bednarsek et al., "Extensive Dissolution of Live Pteropods in the Southern Ocean," *Nature Geoscience* 5 (2012): 881–85.

- Ghost nets are causing abrasion to corals and sponges and continue to entangle sea creatures long after they have ceased to be used to catch them.

- Nanoplastics that can transport viruses and toxic chemicals, as well as other noxious substances—including radioactive waste and per- and polyfluoroalkyl substances (PFAS), a family of about ten thousand chemicals valued for their nonstick and detergent properties—continue to find their way into the ocean, accumulating up the marine food chain.

- Invasive species are hitchhiking into other creatures' habitats by means of international shipping.

- Wild weather and reduced food sources are undoing the efforts of seabirds to raise their young, who are also liable to be fed bits of plastic that their parents have mistaken for tasty morsels, while many aquatic birds are dying in droves as new strains of avian influenza find their way into free-living populations from intensive chicken farms.

- Dwindling sea ice is undoing the lifeways of Arctic sea mammals, driving walruses, for example, to seek to breed onshore—a perilous business, since it places their young at risk from predation by hungry polar bears, whose capacity to breed and feed is also becoming increasingly difficult as their Arctic environs melt away.

According to UN secretary general António Guterres, having for too long taken Earth's seas for granted, we are now facing an "ocean emergency. We must turn the tide."[34]

Yet for all that, Queen and Bob radiate good cheer. Their faith, I think, is part of it, for it is a source of encouragement, strength, and hope. For Bob, trust in God's love for the entire living world

---

[34] Quoted in Karen McVeigh, "UN Head Declares 'Ocean Emergency' as Global Leaders Gather in Lisbon," *The Guardian*, June 27, 2022.

is foundational. Those people who are striving to safeguard and restore the earthly creation are not going it alone. His recognition of the cruciform quality of the natural order is also crucial. From this perspective, suffering, death, and loss, whether at the level of individual lives or evolutionary processes, are understood to be inextricably interwoven with abundance, renewal, and transformation. Moreover, referring to the concept of "ultimate" rather than "proximate" hope, such as that conveyed in Revelation with its promise of redemption not only for the human "saved" but for other living beings as well, Bob trusts that God will carry the earthly creation beyond this time of escalating extinction and entrenched injustice. The Christian churches, he thinks, could be "a huge force for good" in these perilous times if they truly embraced both the scientific knowledge and theological understanding that are in the service of renewed collective flourishing.[35]

The marine conservation work that he and Queen are doing with A Rocha Kenya exemplifies this shift. The opportunities they have been afforded to apply their own gifts in making a positive difference is surely a further source of their good cheer, and so too is the evidence they are seeing of growing understanding and engagement in the local community, and of the sea life that is returning to the national park and spilling out to repopulate its surroundings. Yet the creation of marine reserves such as Watamu, vital though they are, will not stop the seas from growing warmer and more acidic; nor will it hold back the tide of toxins and plastics. Just as our experience of sun, moon, and stars is affected by our treatment of the Earth, so the life of the oceans is afflicted by what

---

[35] Bob notes that most ecotheology and biblical studies hitherto have tended to be land-oriented, but the collaboration between oceanographer Meric Skrokosz and biblical scholar Rebecca S. Watson has resulted in a wonderful resource for reimagining human relations with the sea through a biblical lens: *Blue Planet, Blue God: The Bible and the Sea* (London: SCM Press, 2017).

we get up to on land. While new rules, regulations, policies, and technologies will be necessary to redress these problems, a deeper shift in human minds and hearts is vital.

For Bob, as a Christian, this conversion has entailed the revelation that God delights in the existence of all living creatures, who share in praise for their creator and in the promise of redemption, and that the "neighbors" whom we are called to love as ourselves are by no means only human. This ethos underpinned his statement to the 2017 UN For the Ocean Conference on behalf of A Rocha International: "We will continue to expand our marine program and are committed to utilizing the sustainable development goals to help us reflect on how well in particular we are loving our neighbors, both our fellow humans and all life on our planet."[36] In keeping with this ethos, the marine conservation project at Watamu has given special prominence to a little nondescript coral, the Crisp Pillow Coral (*Anomastraea irregularis*), which can be found in the rock pools along the shore. As Bob stresses, this little critter "isn't pretty, you would never notice it, it doesn't do anything for us." Yet it has "intrinsic value" as a fellow creature, beloved by God, and it has an ethical call upon us as a neighbor in need.

⁓

Not unlike Basil, I have been "bourne beyond bounds" by the wonders of this day: those "marvels of creation, coming one after another in constant succession, like the waves" (BaH, 330). Yet, unlike him, I have had to confront also the appalling damage that industrial societies have wrought upon the lives and homes

---

[36] Text available from A Rocha, "Robert Sluka." See also R. Sluka, "Faith and Science Directing A Rocha's Marine Conservation Work in Kenya," in R. Borde, A. A. Ormsby, S. M. Awoyemi and A. G. Gosler, eds., *Religion and Nature Conservation: Global Case Studies* (London: Routledge, 2023), 284–86.

of so many creatures who dwell in or alongside watery places. There is a further twist to this tale. In "The Powtes Complaint," the fish entreats the "ancient water nurses" of the Fens to "send us good old Captain Flood to lead us out to battle." Today, at the same time that water life is ailing, the oceans are rising. Among those human communities most at risk of coastal flooding are those that have done least to cause this problem. They, too, must be counted among the endangered Brethren of water.

So come, dive deep beneath the waves and spread your wings on high.

Cherish your swamps, guard your bogs, and defend your rivers and streams.

Join in common cause with the Brethren of water, from the tiny to the mighty, and do not abandon the neighbor you might find among the rocks.

Sixth Day

And God said, "Let the earth bring forth living creatures of
each kind, cattle and crawling things and wild beasts of each
kind." And so it was. And God made wild beasts of each kind
and cattle of every kind and crawling things on the ground of
each kind, and God saw that it was good.

And God said, "Let us make a human in our image, by
our likeness, to hold sway over the fish of the sea and the fowl
of the heavens and the cattle and the wild beasts and all the
crawling things that crawl upon the earth."

> And God created the human in his image,
> in the image of God He created him,
> male and female He created them.

And God blessed them, and God said to them, "Be fruitful
and multiply and fill the earth and conquer it, and hold sway
over the fish of the sea and the fowl of the heavens and every
beast that crawls upon the earth." And God said, "Look, I have
given you every seed-bearing plant on the face of all the earth
and every tree that has fruit bearing seed, yours they will be
for food. And to all the beasts of the earth and all of the fowl
of the heavens and to all that crawls on the earth, which has
the breath of life within it, the green plants for food." And so it
was. And God saw all that He had done, and, look, it was very
good. And it was evening and it was morning, the sixth day.

Genesis 1:24–31

⌒

My foster mother was a cocker spaniel.

I had a human mother, too, and a loving one at that. But she was often ill in my early years, and she was utterly devoted to her work with intellectually disabled children and their families, so she could not always be there for me.

When I was still in nappies, Lucy had puppies. I was utterly entranced by them. Somewhere in the family slide collection, there's a photo of me in the kennel, beaming, with puppies crawling all over me. If memory serves, one of them is hanging from the ribbon in my hair.

The puppies were all sent away to other homes in due course. But I remained, and Lucy took care of me as if I were her own. One day when I was only a toddler, I wandered off away from home. Crossing Jansz Crescent, I made my way down to the playing fields along Flinders Way. Fortunately, I avoided the creek (not that there was much water in it most of the time, but it doesn't take much to drown a child who ends up in it face down). When my anxious family found me at last, I was sound asleep under the sheltering canopy of a weeping willow tree, with Lucy sitting beside me, keeping guard.

In the following years, whenever I got into trouble, I would seek out Lucy. I remember the deeply comforting sensation of wrapping myself tearfully around her soft, warm body as she lay curled, forbearingly, in her basket. I knew she would never judge me but simply love me as I was, as only dogs know how.

When I was seven, and we were living far away in England, Lucy died peacefully of old age in the care of family friends. The news came in the depths of a gloomy London winter, which had already sent me spiraling into a depression so bad that it was thought I required medication (although I had taken to secreting my tablets in the snow). On our return to Australia, before we had even left Sydney's international airport terminal, my father had purchased a copy of the Canberra Times *and circled the "For Sale" item for a litter of cocker spaniel pups. And so, sweet Trish, dear friend, followed hard on Lucy's heels. Several more utterly wonderful canine companions have brought joy and, inevitably, sorrow into my life over the intervening years. Yet Lucy was the one who first opened me up to loving communion with otherkind, and her death left a hole in my heart that has never entirely healed.*

☞

Of Land Animals and Sovereign Man:
Discordant Notes in the Choir of Creation

And so we come at last to the work of the Sixth Day: the day on which the land, having already brought forth a luxuriant array of vegetation, now collaborates with the creator once more. Together, land and creator generate all manner of animals, from the tiniest of insects to the mightiest of mammals. This was the day on which our own kind is said to have been made directly by Elohim and not only blessed, like all the rest, but charged also with holding sway over our fellow earthlings. With respect to these last-made late-comers to what Basil celebrated as the "universal choir of creation," I approach the Sixth Day with a degree of dread, and with a deepened sense of the profound historical distance between myself and earlier commentators on the hexameron. As I have discovered, however, I am not entirely alone in my trepidation.

Aware of his listeners' longing to hear of the making of their own kind, Basil conceded with evident reluctance, "Let me speak of it, since it is necessary, and let me put an end to my hesitation. In truth the most difficult of sciences is to know one's self" (BaH, 150). Accordingly, his ninth homily concludes with the assurance, "If God permits, we will later say in what way man was created in the image of God, and how he shares this resemblance" (152).

Perhaps, when it came to it, Basil felt that this permission had not been granted, or perhaps he was simply perplexed as to what to say on this difficult matter. Only toward the end of his life did he appear to have been able to bring himself to comment on the momentous culmination of the Sixth Day of creation (although the authorship of these two homilies is disputed).[1] As it is, his meditations leave us with a view of creation chock full of gloriously diverse living beings, among whom are humans, both male and female, made equally in the image and likeness of their creator. We are creatures, then, who are special in some way, but who have not yet been elevated to the perilous position of sovereign species.

Other commentators, by contrast, did not hold back on holding forth on the matter of humankind's elevated status in the scheme of things. Their celebration of human exceptionalism makes for painful reading when we realize the breadth of human culpability in silencing ever more of the other-than-human voices that graced the polyvocal choir of creation. For, at least in the West for the past few hundred years, the ruthless exploitation of Earth and its diverse denizens as a mere storehouse of "natural resources" to be extracted, traded, transformed, and set to work for exclusively human benefit has been granted religious legitimacy precisely with reference to our biblical calling to "Be fruitful and multiply and fill the earth and conquer it, and hold sway over the fish of the sea and the fowl of the heavens and every beast that crawls upon the earth" (Gen. 1:28). For that very reason, I cannot join Basil in avoiding this painful passage. In company with many other ecologically inclined biblical scholars, theologians, ethicists, and activists today, I nonetheless hear and respond to it rather differently from earlier authors in the hexameral tradition. I approach it through a lens that at once seeks to honor what might be considered distinctive—

---

[1] Virginia Burrus, *Ancient Christian Ecopoetics: Cosmology, Saints, Things* (Philadelphia: University of Pennsylvania Press, 2019), 258.

if not necessarily in humankind per se, then at least in the position in which we now find ourselves—while at the same time affirming our continuities, and indeed kinship, with other creatures, with whom we are connected not only biologically and ecologically but also morally and spiritually.

It might seem surprising, and perhaps even perverse, to preface my meditations on the day that confronts us with the question of the complicity of Christian texts and traditions with the unfolding extinction crisis with a personal narrative about a childhood animal companion. To be sure, like anything else I might have penned on this occasion, that story is entirely inadequate to the enormity of this terrible wrong. Yet I find it telling that, despite the ancient history of human-dog coevolution, few of the hexameral authors whom I have studied pay much heed to the affectionate relations that humans might enjoy with our canine companions, let alone other creatures.[2] Domestic "pet ownership" might be a relatively modern phenomenon, and a questionable one at that, since it implies both possession and infantilization of the animal other. Yet canine companionship, not to mention close working collaborations with herding and hunting dogs, was certainly well known in previous centuries. Basil, for instance, wrote of the "gratitude of the dog," alleging that "many are said to have fallen dead by their murdered masters in lonely places" (BaH, 147). But what of the gratitude and affection of humans for their animal companions?

There are many delightful stories of saints featuring loving, ethical, and sometimes surprisingly intimate relationships with free-living creatures. Several of these can be found on the website of Catholic Concern for Animals (CCA), a sister organization of Pan-Orthodox Concern for Animals, which features in my meditations on this momentous day. The best known among them (especially

---

[2] Raymond Pierotti and Brandy R. Fogg, *The First Domestication: How Wolves and Humans Coevolved* (New Haven, CT: Yale University Press, 2017).

since the current pope, remarkably enough, took his name) is St. Francis, who is reputed to have persuaded a wolf to stop attacking the townspeople of Gubbio if they promised to feed said predator for the rest of his life.[3] According to his biographer, Bonaventure, St. Francis took this view: "Not to hurt our humble brethren is our first duty to them, but to stop there is not enough. We have a higher mission—to be of service to them wherever they require it."[4]

One of my favorite animal-loving saints, who does not currently appear on the CCA list, is St. Giles, a sixth-century hermit who dwelt in the woodlands of the Lower Rhone region. Like many saints, he is said to have been a vegetarian. According to some stories, his plant-based diet was supplemented by his animal companion, a red deer hind, who voluntarily fed him on her milk. When she came to him one day seeking refuge from the king's hunters, he shielded her, taking the arrow intended to kill her in his own hand, and sustaining a wound that never entirely healed. In consequence, Giles is remembered as the patron saint of the physically disabled. But he might also be revered as a patron saint of animal welfare, as is the seventh-century Welsh saint Melangell, who is said to have protected a terrified hare who ran to her to escape the prince's hunting party. The prince was so struck by the hare's trust in Melangell that he made his lands available to her as a place of asylum (she was fleeing a forced marriage in Ireland) and of sanctuary for others, including hares, which still enjoy protected status there to this day.

Such saints' stories offer welcome possibilities for affirming human kinship with fellow creatures within a Christian horizon of

---

[3] Catholic Concern for Animals, "Saints Who Loved Animals: The Saints and Their Feast Days," accessed March 23, 2023, https://catholic-animals. com. See also Edward C. Sellner, *Celtic Saints and Animal Stories: A Spiritual Kinship* (Mahwah, NJ: Paulist Press, 2020).

[4] Quoted in J. R. Hyland, *God's Covenant with Animals* (New York: Lantern Books, 2000), xii.

understanding. Historically, though, these tales have been largely sidelined by the dominant narrative of Man's separation from and mastery over those beings cast as beasts. For my own part, I am convinced that my familial relationship with Lucy has been foundational for my concern about the unjust suffering of other animals at human hands. To move away from the intense instrumentalization of nonhumans as, for instance, mere providers of "ecosystem services," I believe that it is important to cultivate relationships with particular fellow creatures that are founded on friendship and love. These relationships, as Metropolitan Kallistos of Diokleia, cofounder of Pan-Orthodox Concern for Animals (POCA), observes, "contain within themselves an element of eternity."[5] Their cultivation could well be key to the fundamental cultural reorientation that is required to arrest the pace of species extinctions and declining wildlife numbers.

Despite the strain of human supremacism—one that is stronger in some commentators than others, but rarely entirely absent—the hexameral tradition does also open pathways for revaluing other animals and reimagining our relationship with them and with Earth. As in the case of those vegetal, watery, and airy creatures formerly brought forth by the land and sea, the animals that Earth now births are celebrated in their marvelous variety and staggering abundance. The biblical narrative assumes three broad categories of other-than-human land animals: "cattle," referring to domesticated (or domesticable) herd animals; "crawling things," generally understood as encompassing insects, but in some cases also reptiles and amphibians; and "wild beasts," free-living animals, principally those that would later be classed as mammals.

[5] Metropolitan Kallistos of Diokleia (Ware), "An Integrated Theology: Compassion for Animals," in *Climate Crisis and Creation Care: Historical Perspectives, Ecological Integrity and Justice*, ed. Christina Nellist (Cambridge: Cambridge Scholars Publishing, 2021), 2–19, 5.

Several commentators nonetheless also attend to finer differences among kinds, all of whom are, according to Basil, "equally to be honoured," regardless of their usefulness or otherwise to humans, "even venomous ones" (BaH, 150).

Augustine was particularly emphatic on this point, freely confessing, in his treatise *On Genesis: A Refutation of the Manichees* (c. 388–89), "that I have not the slightest idea why mice and frogs were created, and flies and worms." Yet, he continued,

> I can still see that they are all beautiful in their own specific kind, although because of our sins so many of them seem to be against our interests. There is not a single living creature, after all, in whose body I will not find, when I reflect upon it, that its measures and numbers and order are geared to a harmonious unity.[6]

For Augustine, as indeed for other commentators on the hexameron, such marvels testify to the ineffable wisdom of the creator. Yet precisely because of their belief that all things originated in and were sustained by the creative agency of a loving God, they were spurred on to defend the primordial goodness of a vibrantly more-than-human world against those, such as the matter-hating Manicheans, for whom the material realm was simply so much muck.

In commenting on the wondrous variety of land animals, several of the hexameral writers follow classical natural historians, principally Pliny the Elder (23/24–79 CE), in observing the fitness of their form to their way of life, such as the fangs that enable carnivores to devour their prey; the multiple stomachs that help ruminants to digest grasses; or that magnificent trunk that the elephant, hailed by Basil as "the greatest of terrestrial creatures, created for the terror of those who meet it," is able to use not only as a nose to take breath, but also like a hand to pick up food and

---

[6] Augustine, *On Genesis*, 40.

draw up drink (BaH, 148). Some, preempting the concept of the ecological niche, also point to the evident fit between particular kinds and their habitats. Traherne, for example, described all of these "divers Species" with their "wonderful Forms, Properties and Instinctiveness" as being "placed," in an appropriate "Climate, or Soil" (MoSDC, 65). Certain moral values are found among those properties, including parental care and types of intelligence that are superior to those of humans. According to Ambrose, land animals may have capacities, such as the apparent ability to preempt changes in the weather and avoid harmful substances, that have been dulled in humans by luxury or muddled by presupposition. Of dogs' extraordinary tracking skills, for example, Ambrose opined that "sense perception has taken up the trapping of reason" (AmH, 242).

Since, as Ambrose affirmed, the "divine wisdom penetrates and fills all things ... of more value is the testimony given by nature than is the proof presented by doctrine" (AmH, 239). To that testimony belonged the recognition that all creatures, notwith-standing their varied levels of awareness, seek to take pleasure and persevere in their own existence, each after their own kind. This is how Gregory of Nyssa imagined the life of the land prior to the creation of humans: "all the beasts that had come into life at God's command were rejoicing, we may suppose, and skipping about, running to and fro in the thickets in herds according to their kind, while every sheltered and shady spot was ringing with the chants of the songbirds" (OMM, 167).

But then, God said, "Let us make a human in our image, by our likeness, to hold sway over the fish of the sea and the fowl of the heavens and the cattle and the wild beasts and all the crawling things that crawl upon the earth."

Despite the fact that Elohim, as discussed at the outset with respect to that big "one day," is grammatically plural in Hebrew, all of the hexameral writers puzzle over the sudden appearance in this passage of the pronoun "us." Philo speculated that God must have enlisted the assistance of some of the angels to accomplish this tricky business, while the early church fathers take their cue from the Gospel of John, according to which the Word was there from the beginning of the world, made flesh in the person of Jesus of Nazareth only later. During the medieval period, two turns into three, as it becomes more common to give a Trinitarian spin to that mysterious "us," in keeping with their rendering of the "breath" that hovers over the primordial deep as the Holy Spirit.

Most commentators make much of the fact that this mode of divine making distinguishes humans from all the other living beings that were brought forth either by the land or sea. The gender-neutral Hebrew word for "human," 'adam—from *Adamah*, earth, which becomes the proper name of the first man in Genesis 2—attests, however, that we are also bodily beings made from the good soil of the land and destined to return there. As is sometimes noted, humans were not the only creatures fashioned directly by God: so, too, were Sun, Moon, and Stars. That association could be seen as reinforcing, as well as delimiting, our sovereignty: as they hold sway in the sky, so we are to lord it over other creatures of land and sea. This is how Origen read it, exclaiming, "How great is man's greatness, who is made equal to such great and distinguished elements" (OHoG, 62–63). Yet, as Origen, in company with all the other commentators, went on to stress, we alone were made in the "image" and "likeness" of God as we shine brighter even than the majestic celestial lights.

Our being made in Elohim's likeness and image is also a matter of puzzlement given the general agreement on the ineffability of the divine. Among the hexameral writers, John the Scot made my favorite comment on this. "I confess," he wrote, "that I am wholly unaware of why God wished to make man in particular, rather than any other visible or invisible creature, in His own image" (DN,

234). Others, though, were in little doubt. While the Scriptures are silent on the question of in what respect men and women were made in the divine image and likeness, Philo set the pattern for Christian commentators by following Plato and the Stoics in locating human uniqueness in our allegedly unique powers of rational understanding.

According to this reading, it was by virtue of our intellectual capacities that we were to lord over other living beings and even, according to Robert Alter's translation, to "conquer" the Earth. "So the Creator made man after all things," observed Philo, "as a sort of driver or pilot, to drive and steer the things on Earth, and charged him with the care of animals and plants, like a governor subordinate to the chief and great King" (OC, 16). While Philo construed human sovereignty in custodial terms more reminiscent of Genesis 2 than Genesis 1, in keeping with ancient Hebraic notions of kingship as entailing brotherly care for subject peoples (Deut. 17:14–20), he also opened the door to a predominantly instrumental view of nonhuman others by suggesting that it was for human benefit that they had been created first.[7] "Apparently," Philo surmised, God "desired that on coming into the world man might at once find both a banquet and a most sacred display" (63): nourishment, that is, for both body and mind. Creation has an anthropic telos, then, for it tends toward the making of humankind. This thought leads him to fantasize how the sudden appearance of "man" must have caused the other animals "to be amazed and do homage to him as to a born ruler and master" (69).

While the Greco-Roman conceptual world within which the hexameral tradition took shape did not presuppose so stark a divide between spirit and matter as Rene Descartes later articulated,

---

[7] Richard Bauckham, *Living with Other Creatures: Green Exegesis and Theology* (Milton Keynes, UK: Paternoster, 2012), 5.

it commonly privileged certain kinds of stuff over others.[8] These value hierarchies in turn informed Christian designations of the privileges accruing to humans as made in the image and likeness of God (*imago dei*, as this became known in Latin). Augustine, affirming that all living things have souls, followed Philo in identifying reason as our distinguishing feature. Other commentators speak instead of the particular nature of the human soul (vis-à-vis "animal" and "vegetal" souls), as uniquely "rational" and/or "immortal," while the Anglo-Saxon Aelfric (contrary to the implication of the Hebrew text) denied any kind of soul at all to the "beasts, which have no understanding concerning their Creator" (LCG, 19). Abelard made a further distinction along gendered lines, suggesting that whereas both men and women are like God in their possession of an immortal soul, the former more fully embody the *imago dei* in their superior faculty of reason (ESW, 78). One wonders what Eloise and her sisters, who had requested Abelard's exposition of this most mysterious of texts, might have made of that!

The distinctions in play here do not necessarily imply a rigid binary opposition. Basil, Gregory of Nyssa, Chrysostom, John the Scot, and Traherne in particular all valued the inherence of the heavenly within the earthly and of the mind or soul within the body. Elsewhere, however, a sharper divide is evident. Origen, for example, read the creation of land animals as an allegory for "the impulses of our outer man, that is, of our carnal and earthly man" (OHoG, 60–61), recalling, with Paul, that "nothing good comes of the flesh," as distinct from the "incorporeal, incorruptible inner man" (63). Similarly, Ambrose, despite following Basil in his celebration of other creatures, and Gregory in extolling the "grace and beauty" of the human body, betrayed a positively

---

[8] Patricia Cox Miller, *In the Eye of the Animal: Zoological Imagination in Ancient Christianity* (Philadelphia: University of Pennsylvania Press, 2018), 167.

Pauline distaste for messy fleshiness in declaring that "God preferably seeks after the soul when it is alone, thus dissociating Himself from the slime of the body and from the cupidity of the flesh" (AmH, 259).

However variously defined, the unique possession of a particular kind of soul or mind is commonly identified as entitling humans to the dominion vouchsafed in Genesis 1:26. This in turn poses some interpretive challenges, considering the extent to which some creatures do not in fact appear to serve human interests or obey our rules. Basil took a decidedly nonanthropocentric view on this, maintaining that "all has not been created in view of the wants of our bellies," and that things that are harmful to humans afford nourishment for other creatures (BaH, 79). Others, like Augustine, were at pains to explain away the evident fact that much in nature resists our sway, not least those beasts for whom we ourselves are prey, as a consequence of the fall. Anastasios took a different tack, reasoning that the evident counterfactuality of human dominion points to the nonliteral meaning of this passage, and indeed of the whole creation narrative: *Adamah* here refers not to ordinary human beings but exclusively to Jesus Christ, to whom alone all creatures are subject (AnH, 197). Yet none of the writers entirely escaped the pull of the anthropic principle, according to which humans, and the salvation story in which they are to play the leading role as followers of Christ, constitute the primary purpose of creation. Even Traherne, whose hexameron is rich in references to the Psalms and to Job 38–39, with their decentering of humans amid the vastly more-than-human choir of creation, succumbed to human exceptionalism in exclaiming that, before Man,

> The rest of the Creatures were without a Head.... They were worthless before, because they serv'd nothing, and were to no Purpose, even as a Clock is nothing til the Weight be put on, tho' the Wheels be in order, but the

Weight being once on, it is suddenly put into Motion. Even so the World became useful in a Moment, which before was unprofitable, dead, and useless. (MoSDC, 82)

In light of the damage that was licensed by this view of our own kind as the "Sum" and "End of all Creatures," as Traherne put it (82), "the master-work, the end / Of all yet done," as we read in Milton's *Paradise Lost* (VII, ll. 5005–6), it is hard to avoid the conclusion that this creation narrative was, and remains, an extremely dangerous religious inheritance.

An "Inconvenient Text"?
Interpretive Challenges for the Age of Extinction

How are we to handle this "inconvenient text," as Australian biblical scholar and Lutheran pastor Norman Habel has termed it?[9] In his book of that name, Habel identified this as one of several passages in the Bible that seem resistant to an ecological hermeneutic. How do we read in a way that is, as fellow Australian eco-biblical scholar Anne Elvey put it, "*with* Earth as habitat, agent, judge," that is attentive to "the cry of Earth in this moment" and oriented toward decolonizing human relations both with one another and with otherkind?[10] In Habel's collaboration with Aboriginal scholar Anne Pattel-Gray, informed by his long-standing conversations with other elders among Australia's First Peoples, he has reached the conclusion that nothing less than a

---

[9] Norman Habel, *An Inconvenient Text: Is a Green Reading of the Bible Possible?* (Adelaide: ATF, 2009). Habel had previously initiated an Earth Bible project, which generated a series of books bringing an ecological perspective to bear on selected biblical texts, beginning with Norman C. Habel and Shirley Wurst, eds., *The Earth Story in Genesis* (Sheffield: Sheffield University Press, 2000).

[10] Anne Elvey, *Reading with Earth: Contributions of the New Materialism to an Ecological Feminist Hermeneutic* (London: T&T Clark, 2022), 5.

full-blown rewording will do. This, then, is their proposal for a decolonial rendering of Genesis 1:26–28:

> Then the Wind, the Creator Spirit, said to the Land, "You have brought forth many Land beings. Let us now together make human beings in our image, male and female, and let their nature reflect both Land and Spirit; and let them be at peace with their kindred Land beings and let them be custodians of the Land." And it happened. Then the Wind blessed the human Land beings and said, "It is very good."[11]

I rejoice in this endeavor and in the deep listening from which it has arisen and the transformative promise that it bears. But for those for whom the words of sacred Scripture cannot so easily be altered, there are other options.

In a first step, in a long tradition of biblical hermeneutics inaugurated by Friedrich Schleiermacher in the nineteenth century, we might resituate the text historically. This creation narrative, as noted previously, is thought to have been composed, or at least redacted, in the aftermath of the Babylonian conquest of the kingdom of Judah by Jewish priests who were, or had been, living in exile. In this context, their insistence that *all* humans, regardless of gender or any other markers of difference, were made in the image and likeness of God bears a decidedly democratic and anti-imperialistic thrust. According to their imperial overlords and in keeping with the cultures of many other agrarian civilizations, only the king could claim likeness to the divine. Elevating all humans equally over other living beings and subduing the Earth itself was quite likely also bound up with their effort to distinguish their own monotheistic vision, the vision of what was then an

---

[11] Norman Habel, Anne Pattel-Gray, and Australian First Nations, *De-colonising the Biblical Narrative: The First Nations De-colonising of Genesis 1–11* (Adelaide: ATF Press, 2022), 17–18.

oppressed people, aspiring to restore their nation on land that was not altogether well suited to agriculture. Here, it is important to recall also that the word commonly translated as "earth" (*seret*) is ambiguous, referring variously to the whole Earth, an area of land, or the ground. In this context, it is perhaps better rendered, as do Habel and Pattel-Gray, not as earth or Earth (i.e., the whole planet) but the land to which the people were being restored—land they would need to work to afford their sustenance.

Reading on with this in mind, humans were to be neither entirely separate from otherkind nor unbounded in their rule. In company with all the other terrestrial animals, we were to be exclusively herbivorous:

> And God said, "Look, I have given you every seed-bearing plant on the face of all the earth and every tree that has fruit bearing seed, yours they will be for food. And to all the beasts of the earth and all of the fowl of the heavens and to all that crawls on the earth, which has the breath of life within it, the green plants for food." (Gen. 1:29–30)

Elohim hails the creation in its wholeness, as completed on the Sixth Day, as "very good." Furthermore, all living beings are equally proclaimed "good," and humans join the creatures of air and water as called upon to "be fruitful and multiply." The scriptural narrative, then, entails that the sovereignty vouchsafed to our kind with respect to our terrestrial living spaces was not intended to harm other creatures, let alone eliminate them from the "very good" and wildly polyphonic choir of creation.

In a second step, we might revisit the hexameral tradition itself to discern countervailing tendencies. Although their approach to this text is very different, earlier hexameral commentators sometimes qualify the human supremacism that it might be seen to imply. As we have already noted, for Philo, sovereignty was parsed not as conquest, but rather as enjoining "care of animals and plants" (OC, 73). For Traherne, echoing a call to self-restraint found also among the early church fathers, our earthly rule was to be exercised with, "Thankfulness, wise Consideration, and Moderation," lest we forfeit God's "eternal Mercies, either by sinful Ingratitude, stupid Heedlessness, or inordinate Love or Excess in the Use of any of them" (MoSDC, 69), for "they are all given unto us conditionally" (69), and we are called to render "to all Creatures, in thee and for thee, their due Esteem" (86).

Moreover, none of the hexameral writers doubt the inherent worth of other creatures in themselves, and several stress that our differentiation from them is partial rather than absolute. Augustine, for example, observed "both a certain connection with and a distinction from the animals. On the one hand it says man was made on the same day as the beasts; they are all of them land animals after all. And yet, on the other hand, because of the pre-eminence of reason ... it speaks separately about him" (LCG, 149–50). For Bede, the dispensation to hold sway over other creatures, to the extent that we are able to exercise this through our superior use of reason, was granted in compensation for our inadequacies in other respects, so that "man could care for his fragility, gaining from them both nourishment and clothing and assistance in labour and travel" (BeH, 94).

For some commentators, our continuities with other creatures are traced along a scale of increasing complexity. Philo, for instance, noted that the account of the creation of animals begins with the "least elaborately worked out" (fish) and proceeds to those "worked out in the greatest detail" (humans), with this growing complexity corresponding to greater levels of awareness and what he termed the "life principle" (OC, 51). Along similar lines, Grosseteste linked such degrees of liveliness to the capacity for conscious self-willed movement (SDC, 212–13), observing that the "sequence of nature, then, goes up by a sort of series of steps, I mean by the properties of life, from lower things to more perfect things" (240). Similarly, Grosseteste maintained that human likeness to the creator was merely a matter of degree: "God is all things in all things: the life of living things, the form of things with form, the species of things with species: and human beings are in all things God's closest likeness and resemblance" (222). This account, of course, still privileges humans, who appear as a culmination of creation. For John the Scot, too, the last day is "a climax," with humans manifesting "understanding like an angel, reasoning like a man, sensing like an animal, and living like a plant" (DN, 204). Yet he added that "even the lowliest body—a stone, for example—is not wholly devoid of life, although we cannot discern it. . . . Every creature, then, is either living in itself or participating in life in some fashion" (204). Moreover, while all creatures are understood to be inherently "good" in themselves, each bearing witness to divine wisdom, creative agency, and loving-kindness, some commentators also stress that they are interconnected in such a way as to compose something that is more than the sum of its parts. As Grosseteste put it, "All things are woven together, in a highly ordered way, by natural connections" (SDC, 214), such that "Any creature, then, so long as it preserves the good in which it was created, is good in itself, without qualification. In its relation to the ordering of the whole, it is better. The whole is very good" (257).

Ecological Connectivities, Evolutionary Continuities, and Human Kinship with Otherkind

Over the past century or so, the biological sciences have provided abundant empirical evidence for such continuities and connectivities in ever more fine-grained detail. On one measure, for instance, human kinship with other animals might be traced in our DNA, differing from that of our closest living relatives among the other Great Apes (chimpanzees and bonobos) by between only 1.2 percent and 5 percent, depending on how differences in the genome are counted. According to the Smithsonian Museum's website on human origins, evolutionary biologists have deduced that we share a common ancestor with monkeys as well as apes who lived around twenty-five million years ago, and our lineage is likely to have parted company from the ancestor we share with our closest cousins only around six to eight million years ago.[12] Yet a small degree of genetic divergence can result in significant differences among species, since each gene codes for many different traits, and the way that they manifest is affected by external factors. After all, humans also share around 75 percent of our genes with laboratory mice.[13]

Another measure, and one that I find infinitely more interesting, is afforded by research into animal behavior, or ethology. Increasingly, the painstaking work undertaken by contemporary ethologists such as Marc Bekoff and Norbert Sachser is confirming the hunch, which Charles Darwin voiced in *The Expression of the Emotions in Man and Animals* (1872), that the differences between humans and animals, whether cognitive, emotional, or in some cases, at least, moral and perhaps even spiritual, are more a matter of degree than of kind.[14] It seems that barely a day goes past without some intriguing new facet of animal conduct coming to light that puts pressure on the premise of human exceptionalism. The

---

[12] Smithsonian Institution, "Human Origins: Genetics," August 15, 2022.

[13] National Human Genome Research Institute, "Human Genome Project Completes Genetic Map of Mouse DNA," May 16, 2010, www.genome.gov.

[14] See, e.g., Marc Bekoff, *Minding Animals: Awareness, Emotions, and Heart* (Oxford: Oxford University Press, 2002); Norbert Sachser, *Much Like Us: What Science Reveals about the Thoughts, Feelings, and Behaviour of Animals* (Oxford: Oxford University Press, 2022).

one that caught my eye most recently is particularly enchanting: rats, it seems, share the human proclivity to move in time with rhythmic music, instinctively swaying their furry little bodies and bobbing their bewhiskered heads in a way that had been thought to be uniquely human. Moreover, they evidently share a preference for precisely the same tempo: 120 to 140 beats per minute. The music to which the rodent and human participants in this study were spontaneously moving, Mozart's Sonata for Two Pianos in D Major, was originally composed at 132 beats per minute, "suggesting we share a 'sweet spot' for hitting the beat."[15]

One by one, the alleged hallmarks of human hyperseparation from other animals have been falling away. Take tool use, for example. By getting out of the laboratory and spending time getting to know a troupe of chimpanzees on their home turf in Gombe Stream National Park, Jane Goodall made the momentous discovery in October 1960 that they had learned to fashion twigs into implements to fish termites out of their nests.[16] Furthermore, this is a cultural accomplishment that younger chimps have to learn from their elders. Tool use has since been found in many other species as well. At least three Australian raptors, for instance, have figured out how to use burning branches to intentionally start fires to flush out prey—an avian pyrophytic prowess long recognized among those Indigenous Australian peoples whose country they share.[17]

What about language, though? Articulate human speech is doubtless extraordinary both in its complexity and in what it

---

[15] Hannah Devlin, "Slaves to the Rhythm: Rats Can't Resist a Good Beat, Researchers Say," *The Guardian*, November 11, 2022.

[16] Jane Goodall, *Through a Window: My Thirty Years with the Chimpanzees of Gombe* (Boston: Houghton Mifflin, 1999).

[17] Mark Bonta, Robert Gosford, Dick Eussen, Nathan Ferguson, Erana Loveless, and Maxwell Witwer, "Intentional Fire-Spreading by 'Firehawk' Raptors in Northern Australia," *Journal of Ethnobiology* 37, no. 4 (2017): 700–718.

enables us to do collectively, not only when we are co-present, but also across vast reaches of time and space. Yet other animals too use signs of various kinds to communicate, whether via sounds, facial expressions, posture, movement, or chemical signals. A growing body of research in the new field of biosemiotics (the study of communication within and among living organisms) indicates that human speech has emerged from and within a panoply of other modes of communication that reach all the way down to single-celled organisms. Furthermore, we too continue to participate in such nonverbal semiotic exchanges, albeit generally below the level of consciousness.[18]

The intimate nature of our interconnections with fellow creatures can be seen in another way as well. A mass of microbiota co-constitute our corporeal frame, including some that protect our skin and hair and others that enable us to digest our food (our weeny "messmates," as Donna Haraway calls them, since they dine with us).[19] The existence of these smallest of our kindred creatures was unknown prior to the invention of the microscope, but they must surely be counted among the "crawling things" of the Sixth Day, whose dwelling place is not only *on* the ground" and within and upon all animal bodies, but also *under* the ground, an integral part of the good soil. These are crucial for plant growth and health, and they help absorb greenhouse gases and degrade pollutants.[20]

---

[18] Jesper Hoffmeyer's book *Biosemiotics: An Examination into the Signs of Life and the Life of Signs* (Scranton, PA: University of Scranton Press, 2008) provides an excellent introduction to this field. On the implications of biosemiotics for repositioning human language and culture, see Wendy Wheeler: *The Whole Creature: Complexity, Biosemiotics, and the Evolution of Culture* (London: Lawrence & Wishart, 2006).

[19] Donna J. Haraway, *When Species Meet* (Minneapolis: Minnesota University Press, 2007).

[20] Didi Pershouse, "Other Species Are Essential Workers in the Earth's

From the microbes that co-constitute our bodies and those that enrich the soil through to the plants and, for most people, the animal parts or products that we eat and the ecological connectivities that facilitate our collective flourishing, humans exist only in and through our interrelations with otherkind. Moreover, in the case of our animal companions, we and they might discover potentials that neither could have realized without the other. Thus it was, for example, with Megan, a golden retriever rescue dog, who took it upon herself to become the invaluable assistant, nurse, and helpmate of her companion, veterinarian Allen Schoen. Megan was forever in attendance with him and quick to identify how she could best contribute, in her own canine way, to his healing labors. Nor was the transformative effect of their companiable collaboration one way. Learning to experience the world through Megan's senses and sensibility, to the limited extent that such is possible for one of another kind, Schoen acquired new organs of perception and greater depths of understanding.[21] If we approach other animals with sufficient attention and empathy, respect and love, then we co-become with them in ways that can transform our lives and theirs.

It strikes me as a profoundly tragic irony that modern science should be catching up with the insights long held by many traditional cultures regarding human kinship with other animals, and disclosing in ever more detail just how extraordinary they really are, right at the moment when our cohabitation of this good Earth with them has been put at risk, not least by the technological civilization enabled by earlier scientific discoveries. At a time of drastically dwindling wildlife populations, accelerating

Economy," in Christina Nellist, ed., *Climate Crisis and Creation Care: Historical Perspectives, Ecological Integrity and Justice* (Cambridge: Cambridge Scholars Press, 2021), 264–85.

[21] Allen M. Schoen, *Kindred Spirits: How the Remarkable Bond between Humans & Animals Can Change the Way We Live* (New York: Broadway Books, 2001).

extinctions, and unraveling ecologies, and of the persistence of older forms of human cruelty toward animals and newer ones that have been established on an industrial scale, we urgently need to reimagine human relations with otherkind. For inheritors of the creation narrative of the six days' work, such reimagining entails fundamentally reevaluating what it might mean to "hold sway" over otherkind.

All of this points to a third possible step to reading the biblical text "with Earth," following its historical contextualization and the reconsideration of earlier commentaries: the concerted effort of reinterpretation that biblical scholars and theologians who have been concerned about human mistreatment of animals and, in the case of free-living species, the destruction of their habitats, have been undertaking for several decades now.[22] This scholarly endeavor was amplified in the public arena by Pope Francis, when he insisted in *Laudato si'*,

> Although it is true that we Christians have at times incorrectly interpreted the Scriptures, nowadays we must forcefully reject the notion that our being created in God's image and given dominion over the earth justifies absolute

---

[22] This call is by no means new. It was made, e.g., by Lynn White Jr. in his influential article "The Historical Roots of Our Ecologic Crisis," *Science* 155, no. 3767 (1967): 1203–7. Jay B. McDaniel's *Of God and Pelicans: A Theology of Reverence for Life* (Louisville, KY: Westminster/John Knox Press, 1989) and Andrew Linzey's *Animal Theology* (Champaign: University of Illinois Press, 1994) were the first major books bringing animal ethics to bear within theology. See also Stephen H. Webb, *On God and Dogs: A Christian Theology of Compassion for Animals* (Oxford: Oxford University Press, 1998); Celia Deane-Drummond and David Clough, eds., *Creaturely Theology: God, Humans, and other Animals* (London: SCM Press, 2009); Bauckham, *Living with other Creatures*, and, with special reference to Genesis, William Greenway, *For the Love of All Creatures: The Story of Grace in Genesis* (Grand Rapids: William B. Eerdmans, 2015).

domination over other creatures. The biblical texts are to be read in their context, with an appropriate hermeneutic, recognizing that they tell us to "till and keep" the garden of the world (cf. Gen 2:15). "Tilling" refers to cultivating, ploughing or working, while "keeping" means caring, protecting, overseeing and preserving.[23]

The most common approach has been to reinterpret "dominion" as "stewardship," frequently referencing other biblical passages in the Hebrew Scriptures that explicitly enjoin considerate treatment of other animals, such as the injunction against muzzling your ox when it is grinding out the grain (Deut. 25:4). This is a clear improvement on discourses of domination, mandating a more just and, potentially, caring relationship with other creatures. Stewardship, however, still places us at a distance, over and above them. To my ears, it conveys a cold and contractual attitude that remains distinctly self-aggrandizing.

As we have already noted in the case of Philo, the Hebrew Scriptures afford an alternative reading, resting on the ancient Jewish concept of kingship as entailing fraternal care and consideration. That notion of rulership was taken up and given a surprising twist in the ministry of Jesus of Nazareth, as was made manifest shortly before the crucifixion when he knelt and washed the feet of the disciples (John 13:2–17), and even more startlingly, in his ultimate self-sacrifice upon the cross. If we were to truly consider ourselves as made in the image and likeness of the creator as incarnate in Jesus Christ, then our "sway" must surely take the form of service: service inspired not by duty, but by unconditional love—and love, moreover, that is no mere passing sentiment, but a resolute commitment to safeguarding and enhancing the others' flourishing that they too might "have life, and have it abundantly" (John 10:10).

---

[23] Pope Francis, *Laudato si'*, para. 67.

At the same time, recalling with Augustine that we are "all animals," we are invited to enter more humbly into fellowship with other creatures, some of whom perform essential services for us, while others might become beloved companions or free-living familiars. Others again, as Job learned the hard way, are best respected at a distance, as fellow singers in the "universal choir of creation," whose lifeways are nonetheless ultimately beyond human ken and control (Job 38–42). Among the latter, of course, are some who would happily have us for supper, or make us very ill, if we gave them half a chance, so it is entirely appropriate that our respect for these creatures, whether great or small, should be modulated by prudent self-protection.

"Holding Sway" in Loving Service
to Kindred Creatures:
Perspectives from the Eastern Orthodox Tradition

It is broadly along these lines that Christina Nellist, animal advocate extraordinaire and cofounder of Pan-Orthodox Concern for Animals (POCA), reinterprets the identity and vocation of humankind as presented in Genesis 1. For Chris, "Dominion is living in the image of an all-loving compassionate God. If that is who you think your God is, that is who you have to be."[24] As she has helped me to appreciate, the Eastern Orthodox tradition, richly informed as it has been by the likes of Basil, Gregory, and Chrysostom, has its own distinct take on this issue.

Chris herself was born to a Jewish mother and Catholic father, and baptized into the Church of England. Her ardent animal advocacy long preceded her conversion to Eastern Orthodoxy, beginning on the streets of London during that high tide of protests in the late

---

[24] Christina Nellist, interviewed on October 30, 2020. All quotes shared here with her kind permission.

1960s with a call to ban the Canadian seal hunt. Her tireless work with a succession of animal protection organizations in numerous countries across five continents carried her advocacy forward to great effect. She persuaded her local English branch of the Royal Society for the Prevention of Cruelty to Animals (RSPCA) to support theologian Andrew Linzey's call for a ban on hunting on church land. She wrote a biodiversity strategy for the SPCA in the Seychelles. She also established a free mobile neutering program there to provide an alternative to the government's poisoning of stray dogs, and during a second residency as British government warden for Inner and Outer Islands, she worked with the chief veterinary officer to update the Seychelles animal welfare laws. She helped establish an animal protection group in Kalimantan, Indonesia. At the Nocosia Dogs' Home in Cyprus, she also ran her own neutering program for stray cats and advised local farmers on neutering their dogs. The Union de Amigos de Animales animal welfare group and sanctuary in Santiago, Chile, invited her to develop an education program on stray dogs for the Public Health Ministry, and her award-winning work there led to the first education program on responsible pet ownership in South America, which was approved by the Metropolitan Environmental Health Service to be adapted for other Latin American countries by the World Society for the Protection of Animals.

Chris's advocacy on behalf of the oppressed has not been restricted to nonhuman others. During her five-year sojourn in Pakistan in the 1990s, she organized an NGO dedicated to preventing the ritual burning of widowed women. In one of her most recent interventions, her compassionate concern for the well-being of both humans and animals led her to successfully lobby the British government to change their quarantine laws to enable animal companions brought to the United Kingdom by Ukrainian refugees to be temporarily held at no cost to their owners and returned to them as soon as they tested negative for communicable diseases, rather than at the end of the mandatory six weeks.[25]

Right from the start, Chris's commitment to animal advocacy was integral to her professional work as a teacher and researcher, and both were intimately connected with her journey of faith. As head of core science teaching at a senior community school in outer London in the 1980s, she incorporated lessons on deforestation and biodiversity loss and educated students about responsible pet ownership. She subsequently volunteered her research skills for various conservation initiatives, working with Birdlife International to research an endangered bird, the white-eye, in the Seychelles. While living in north Queensland in 2003–2004, she worked with other local residents to record nest sites and hatchings along the nearby beach.

When she moved to Cyprus in 2005 Chris experienced a strange sense of homecoming both in the place and in the Eastern Orthodox tradition that she encountered there for the first time. On returning to the Seychelles as a recent convert, she was given the dispensation to found a Christian Orthodox Association there, while also undertaking her own bachelor's and then master's degrees in Eastern Orthodox theology.[26] In the course of her studies, she

---

[25] Christina Nellist, follow-up interview conducted on November 15, 2022. This was not Chris's first intervention regarding quarantine practices, as she had previously challenged the Bahrain Quarantine Facility in 1999 on its "appalling hygiene standards and ineptitude." Nellist, biographical notes on her involvement in animal welfare, personal communication, January 15, 2021.

[26] As Chris told me during the November 15, 2022, follow-up interview, her husband, Simon Peter Nellist, a lapsed Catholic born to Jewish parents, also converted to Orthodox Christianity in the Seychelles, and subsequently became archdeacon of Tanzania and the Seychelles. He is now attached to the Archdiocese in England, and serves as treasurer for POCA, as well as being Orthodox patron for the Animal Interfaith Alliance. See also Pan-Orthodox Concern for Animals, "Who We Are," accessed March 30, 2023, http://panorthodoxconcernforanimals.org.

realized that, although Orthodox theologians like John Chryssavgis and church leaders, above all His Holiness the Ecumenical
Patriarch Bartholomew, had contributed significantly to Christian
ecological thought and advocacy, there had been little focus on
the ethical dimensions of human relations with other animals.[27]
Moreover, where relevant teachings were acknowledged, they were
inadequately followed in practice. Encouraged by Andrew Linzey,
she pursued an ambitious doctoral project at the University of
Winchester intended to bring the ethical treatment of animals into
the mainstream of Orthodox theology, ministry, and daily life.

Successfully completed in 2017, Chris's dissertation was
published the following year under the title *Eastern Orthodox
Christianity and Animal Suffering: Ancient Voices in Modern
Theology*.[28] Here she combines current scientific research on animal
behavior, human psychology, and her own prior sociological
research in Cyprus with biblical exegesis and theological reflection, informed by Orthodox Church documents, the writings of
the Eastern church fathers (including our hexameral commentators Basil, Gregory of Nyssa, and Chrysostom), stories of saints and
sinners, and interviews with contemporary church leaders.

---

[27] The Ecumenical Patriarch Bartholomew is also known as the "Green
Patriarch" for the leading role he has played in putting care for the Earth at the
heart of Christian faith, and vice versa, but it should be noted that his prede-
cessor, Demetrios 1, established September 1 as the day dedicated to protection
of the natural environment. See John Chryssavgis, *On Earth as in Heaven:
Ecological Vision and Initiatives of Ecumenical Patriarch Bartholomew* (New
York: Fordham University Press, 2011). On Orthodox ecotheology, see also
John Chryssavgis and Bruce V. Foltz, eds., *Toward an Ecology of Transfiguration: Orthodox Christian Perspectives on Environment, Nature, and Creation*
(New York: Fordham University Press, 2013), which includes a prefatory letter
by Patriarch Bartholomew.

[28] Christina Nellist, *Eastern Orthodox Christianity and Animal Suffering:
Ancient Voices in Modern Theology* (2018; repr. Cambridge: Cambridge
Scholars Press, 2020).

The epigraph to the book is from Genesis 8:21, which, in the translation given in the *Orthodox Study Bible*, reads, "So the Lord God smelled a sweet aroma. Then the Lord God thought it over and said, 'I will never again curse the earth because of man's works, although the mind of man is diligently involved with evil things from his youth; nor will I again destroy every living thing as I have done.'" This is a key passage for Chris's theological argument, and she believes that it has been disastrously misinterpreted. "The traditional understanding is that because God smelt and liked the sweet aroma of the sacrificed animals, God changed his mind and allowed humans to kill and eat animals," having previously mandated a purely plant-based diet for all land animals, including humans.[29] As she points out, though, God does not comment on the appealing aroma of cooking flesh. Rather, what follows is a reflection on the ineluctability of human sinfulness.

As Chris observers, was it not rather perverse of Noah to turn around and kill several of the creatures whom he had just successfully saved in accordance with his divine mandate? Might this not rather imply that Noah's animal sacrifice was yet further evidence of human erring? This reading certainly seems plausible, and it leads Chris to conclude that the permission subsequently granted to Noah and his descendants to kill and eat animals was neither a right nor a duty, but a concession, or "dispensation," in view of human sinfulness: one qualified, moreover, by the injunction against consuming their "lifeblood" (Gen. 9:4). Chris interprets this injunction as an acknowledgment of the sanctity of all life, enjoining restrictions on how, when, and why animals might be slaughtered (such as are in

---

[29] Nellist, *Eastern Orthodox Christianity*, 53. Nellist notes here that the idea that God would change his mind for this reason was already queried by St. Irenaeus (b. 30 CE), who asserted that "'God does Himself truly want none of these things.'" See also Christina Nellist, "Noah's Failures, God's Dispensations and a Christian Church 'Setting the Scene and Creating the Opportunity' for a World in Peril," in Nellist, *Climate Crisis and Creation Care*, 116–35.

fact laid down in Leviticus). This qualification is combined with the warning that other creatures would henceforth run away in fear from humans, signaling the rupture in human relations with fellow animals, and, as a further indication of God's mercy toward them, making them less easy to hunt down. All this is framed by the reaffirmation of God's love for the entire creation as made manifest in his covenant with "all flesh"—that is, all living beings—to never again bring a deluge to destroy the life of the land.[30]

The Eastern Orthodox tradition understands that, although humans were originally formed in the image of God, an image tarnished by the fall, moving toward God's likeness—which is to say, becoming Christ-like—is a calling rather than a given. Collectively, this calling encompasses the human vocation to "lead every being along the road to transfiguration, to the fullness of life," as Metropolitan Anthony of Sourozh put it.[31]

While all things participate in and are infused with the "energy" of the divine, humans have a special role as "priests of creation." The endeavor to become Christ-like sets the individual on the pathway to life eternal. Since, as Chris demonstrates, that endeavor indubitably

---

[30] For me, this narrative still remains one of those "inconvenient" biblical texts, in view of the insistence that any animal who kills a human must be killed in turn. If some of them can be prey for us, why should we not accept that we too are prey for larger carnivores? The perpetuation of this biblical injunction, for example, in the slaughter of any saltwater crocodiles in northern Australia who treat as legitimate prey anybody stupid (or, commonly, drunk) enough to enter their watery territory, despite ample warning signs, is a cause of deep consternation to local Indigenous people, some of whom claim kinship with the crocodile and consider them fellow members of Country. To kill them for fulfilling their need to eat simply amplifies the harm. Dany Adone, director, Centre for Australian Studies, University of Cologne, personal communication, November 8, 2022.

[31] Quoted in Christina Nellist, "An Eastern Orthodox Perspective on Animal Suffering, Intensive Farming and Climate Change," *International Journal of Orthodox Theology* 9, no. 3 (2019): 153.

entails the cultivation of just and compassionate relations with other creatures, to engage in, be complicit with, or even indifferent to animal cruelty has grave soteriological implications; that is, it is liable to knock you off the path, jeopardizing your chances of salvation. A better appreciation of both the immense harm and suffering that are inflicted upon animals on a daily basis and the damage done to our own souls by our involvement in or tolerance of such evils could provide a powerful motivation for Orthodox Christians to cultivate and advocate for the protection of animals and their environs.

Chris's emphasis on this soteriological dimension of animal cruelty exemplifies the pragmatism that characterizes her book, which is replete with practical recommendations of how the Orthodox Church could embed animal protection in its ministry. The same impetus led her to obtain the blessing of the archbishop of Thyateira, Gregorios, to cofound POCA with Father Andreas Andreopoulos and Bishop Kallistos (Ware), metropolitan of Diokleia. Metropolitan Kallistos Ware had greatly encouraged her in her doctoral studies and became POCA's inaugural patron. POCA's current theological advisers are the eminent Orthodox scholars John Chryssavgis, archdeacon of the Ecumenical Patriarchate and theological adviser to Ecumenical Patriarch Bartholomew, and Archimandrite Jack Khalil, dean of the St. John of Damascus Institute of Theology.

The charity's website contains a wealth of material, including key texts translated into Greek, Russian, and Romanian, to "promote Christ's loving compassionate care for all of His creatures and to advance the Patristic teachings that we as Image are to replicate Christ's love and compassion for all of His created beings."[32] The home page features Aidan Hart's beautiful icon, *Christ Breaking the Bonds of Animal Suffering*, referencing Luke

---

[32] Pan-Orthodox Concern for Animals, "Mission Statement," accessed November 25, 2022, http://panorthodoxconcernforanimals.org.

14:5. Chris commissioned the icon as part of her doctorate, and it graces the cover of her book. In addition to quotes from Orthodox teaching, both ancient and modern, the website has prayers, petitions, short essays, and videos, including a link to an Orthodox film on climate change, *Face of God*, for which Chris was an adviser. Among the educational materials made available is an entire course on creation care that Chris was invited by the Orthodox archbishop of Zimbabwe and Angola to develop for the environmental education of priests. This course has since been adapted for use in the professional development program for faith teachers in South Africa.

Chris's work continues to bear fruit. In 2019 she was invited to speak on behalf of the animal creation at the Halki III Eastern Orthodox Summit in Istanbul, titled Theological Formation and Ecological Awareness: A Conversation on Education and the Environment. At the same time that she is helping to move animal welfare from the margins into the center of Orthodox environmental thought and practice, Chris is also increasingly engaged with ecumenical initiatives of various kinds, including the Animal Interfaith Alliance and a project on the Christian Ethics of Farmed Animals, led by Professor David Clough, cofounder of CreatureKind.[33] Chris's ecumenical engagement extends to her scholarly work, most recently in her transnational two-volume edited collection that brings diverse religious perspectives to bear on the climate crisis. Published on the eve of COP 26, this anthology highlights the interconnections among global heating,

---

[33] CreatureKind is a charity that seeks to "encourage Christians to recognize faith-based reasons for caring about the wellbeing of fellow animal creatures used for food, and to take practical action in response." Chris herself is a vegetarian and ardent advocate of a plant-based, or at least plant-biased diet. However, like Clough, she recognizes that the consumption of animals and their produce is not going to stop anytime soon, so it is imperative that the welfare of farmed animals is improved in the meantime. CreatureKind, "Our Mission," accessed March 30, 2023, www.becreaturekind.org.

biodiversity loss, the emergence and spread of new pathogens, and the mistreatment of animals.[34]

As John Chryssavgis observes in his foreword to the first of these volumes, we find ourselves in a *kairos* moment—"a moment of crisis and consequence"—in which the future of the earthly creation hinges on the "way in which we respond to the unique and universal problems that we have created and face."[35] As I draw toward the end of this long day, I pray that we may face these problems in solidarity with our kindred creatures; that we may rejoice in our shared animality; that we may summon all our not-inconsiderable human capacities in order to act with justice and mercy toward otherkind, as well as one another; and that we may work together in caring for our common home.

⌒

Dogs have loomed large in my meditations on the Sixth Day. Here's one more.

Tucked away in the apocrypha is the remarkable tale of a talking dog. In the Acts of Peter, the evangelist, having been turned away by the human guard, asks the dog chained by the door of the house where the heretic Simon Magus is hiding out to take a message to him, warning him that he will be eternally damned for misleading the faithful. The dog not only does this, he also prophesies to Peter on his return, warning him that he will have a hard fight with Simon but will be rewarded in the end. Evidently overtaxed by his prophetic exertions, the dog then collapses and dies.[36]

---

[34] Nellist, *Climate Crisis and Creation Care*, and Christina Nellist, ed., *Climate Crisis and Sustainable Creaturely Care: Integrated Theology, Governance and Justice* (Cambridge: Cambridge Scholars Publishing, 2021).

[35] John Chryssavgis, "Foreword," in Nellist, *Climate Crisis and Creation Care*, xi.

[36] J. K. Elliott, ed., *The Apocryphal New Testament* (Oxford: Clarendon

Today, too, animals have become prophets, and in huge numbers, the likes of which have never been seen on this planet.

For in their dying, animals are prophesying:

> *With every animal whose life is taken for the sake of human greed, not need;*
> *with every animal whose life is sacrificed in the service of human vanity or entertainment;*
> *with every animal whose future generations are cut off at heedless human hands*
> *... our own future flourishing is forever forfeited.*

In their groans, we stand condemned:

> *With every animal who cries out in agony from a factory farm or a cramped cage,*
> *from a lorry or a laboratory,*
> *from a sea vessel or a wet market,*
> *from a cruel home or a careless zoo*
> *... we will learn that we too are utterly lost and gone astray.*

Time is short, but it is not too late to attend anew to the prophetic calls of otherkind.

So, draw close to your animal companions. Accept the friendship of those who would be your familiars. Stand in awe of those, both great and small, who are strangers to you. Reach out a hand to all in need. Break the chains of animal suffering.

Mark this well: the future of us all depends upon it.

Press, 1999), 408–9. These and many other extraordinary animal stories from Christian texts are discussed in Laura Hobgood-Oster, *Holy Dogs and Asses: Animals in the Christian Tradition* (Urbana: University of Illinois Press, 2008).

Afterword:
The Seventh Day

Then the heavens and the earth were completed, and all their array. And God completed on the seventh day the work He had done, and He ceased on the seventh day from all the work he had done. And God blessed the seventh day and hallowed it, for on it He had ceased from all His work that He had done.

Genesis 2:1–3

Welcome to the Festival!

On the Seventh Day, Elohim fell silent.

Yet this was not the end of the story, not by a long shot.

The significance of the Seventh Day seems to me to have been undervalued in the hexameral tradition. This was, after all, a series of meditations on the "six days' *work*." On the seventh, as we learn at the start of Genesis 2, Elohim laid aside their world-creating labors. Some commentators barely mention this festive final day. "Surely we should now make our contribution of silence," observed Ambrose, for instance, "since God has rested from the work of the world" (AmH, 282). Where the Seventh Day is discussed, it is in a rather narrow sense: namely, as instituting a day of rest for us mere mortals, while reinforcing the point that, although God desisted from creating any new things after the momentous making of Man, he "continued in his unceasing care for us," remaining active in sustaining and governing the world that he had called forth (CHoG, 139).

Failing to talk up what happens when Elohim holds their peace, the hexameral tradition reinforces the idea that the divine creation has what I have called an "anthropic telos." But this is terribly misleading. For a start, it is worth noting that the first half of the opening verse of Genesis 2 actually belongs with the creation story of Genesis 1 in the Hebrew text of this tale. Reading on, moreover, you discover that the culmination of it all is not the making of human beings, but the hallowing of the whole.

Philo totally got what most of his Christian successors forgot: the story of creation reaches its end, which is also a new beginning, only on the Seventh Day, which he extolled as a holy "festival, not of a single city or country, but of the universe" (OC, 73). Pondering the peculiarity of the double completion of creation—if the work of creation was finished on the Sixth Day, why does Genesis 2:2 state that it was brought to completion on the seventh?—later rabbinic commentators came to the conclusion that something new was indeed brought into being in the godly silence of this day. According to the medieval rabbi Rashi, as ecotheologian Norman Wirzba explains,

> What was left unfinished was creation's purpose, which is why on the seventh day God created *menuha*, a term we can translate as the tranquility, serenity, and peace of God. What *menuha* communicates is the happiness and contentment that come from experiencing and knowing that things are as they ought to be, and that they are primordially and constitutively good. What *menuha* teaches is that the point and purpose of creaturely life is for it to be cherished and celebrated.[1]

---

[1] Norman Wirzba, *This Sacred Life: Humanity's Place in a Wounded World* (Cambridge: Cambridge University Press, 2021), 145.

In this Afterword, then, I ponder what follows after the words spoken by Elohim to summon the world into being have done their work with the assistance of Wisdom and the collaboration of sea and land—or at least, since creation is an ongoing adventure rather than a finished artifact, after they have begun to do so. In my reading, we face nothing less than a new summons: one that calls us all into a wider communion of creatures and toward a marvelously multispecies kindom yet to come.

What began in quiet contemplation, illumined by the light that revealed a world-in-the-making, graced by the enduring darkness of unknowing, ends in collective celebration. The celebration is of a radically inclusive eucharistic feast that keeps faith with the continued unfolding of more-than-human life, fanning the vital flames of love, seeding slender shoots of hope . . . even still, even now, when so many more-than-human lives and lifeways are being extinguished, broken, or placed at risk.

"Daily Bread":
Celebrating the Sabbath, Earthing the Eucharist at St. James's, Piccadilly

Rev. Lucy Winkett, rector of St. James's Church, Piccadilly, first impressed upon me that the Seventh Day was a day of rest, yes, but also of rejoicing. The Sabbath, as it became known in Jewish and later Christian tradition, is the true crown of creation.

I met Lucy's canine companion, an ebullient black cocker spaniel, before I met her. Joey bounced up to greet me with ear-flapping, body-wiggling, tail-wagging eagerness when I ventured into the church's award-winning Southwood Garden to interview St. James's sustainability champion and churchwarden, Deborah Colvin, back in August 2020. To be introduced by Joey to the rector was an unanticipated blessing, not least because she, too, has an interest in the hexameral tradition and had recently given a lecture on Thomas Traherne. This visit to St. James's took place right at the start of my own hexameral explorations, and I return back there for inspiration on this Seventh Day.

As Lucy explained to me in a subsequent interview, the Sabbath "isn't about falling asleep on the sofa because you've worked too hard: it's drinking deeply from the well of creation that God is continuing to create and re-create."[2] Lucy is a wonderful singer, having trained to be a professional soprano at the Royal Academy of Music before she was called to the priesthood as one of the first women finally to be ordained in the Church of England. Singing remains very important to her, especially in a liturgical setting. When she chants the opening lines of the Sunday Evensong service—"O Lord, open Thou our lips"—she understands herself to be "joining a note that is already being sung by the whole of creation and will continue to be sung after I've stopped singing." Her words describe a song that is envisioned in Revelation, at the far end of the Christian Bible, as moving toward what Lucy apprehends as an "amazing cacophony of praise and music and eternal dawn-chorus."

This radically inclusive view of the Seventh Day as a "festival of the universe," to recall Philo, is implicit in Jewish teachings surrounding the Sabbath, or *Shabbat*. These teachings recall on

---

[2] Lucy Winkett, interview from October 8, 2020. Quotes from this interview are shared with Lucy's kind permission. Lucy's understanding of the importance of the Sabbath is informed by the theology of Methodist biblical scholar, Margaret Barker, who traces elements within early Christian thought back to the mystical tradition connected to the first temple in ancient Judaism. For an introduction, see Margaret Barker, *Temple Theology: An Introduction* (London: SPCK, 2004). Barker was a participant in Patriarch Bartholomew's symposium on Religion, Science, and the Environment, and he wrote the Foreword to her book, *Creation: A Biblical Vision for the Environment* (London: T&T Clark, 2009). On environmental ethics in the Hebrew Bible, see also Mari Joerstad, *The Hebrew Bible and Environmental Ethics: Humans, Nonhumans, and the Living Landscape* (Cambridge: Cambridge University Press, 2019).

a weekly basis God's resting (*shabath*) and rejoicing in the completion of creation, reaffirming the covenant made between God and "all flesh" in the wake of the flood, and offering a foretaste of the world to come. As we read in the Ten Commandments, this was to be a day of rest for the Hebrew people, and for slaves, strangers, and livestock (Exod. 20:8–11). Every seven years, the land also was to be rested. Land-rest was not for just one day, but for the entire year, with no sowing or reaping, plowing or pruning. Instead, the people, along with their slaves and their livestock, were to gather "what the land yields" and share its natural bounty with "the wild animals" (Lev. 25:1–7). In the fiftieth year, the year of jubilee, *Shabbat* takes an even more radical turn: the people were then "to proclaim liberty throughout the land to all its inhabitants," enabling those who had been enslaved or dispossessed to return to their ancestral lands. No land was to be owned "in perpetuity," we read here, and "Throughout the land you hold, you shall provide for the redemption of the land" (Lev. 25:8–24). Later rabbinic teaching on the Sabbath, as it became known in English, suggests that it was understood as a necessary check on people's propensity to prioritize production, accumulation, and possession over gratitude for the giftedness of their existence and generosity toward other creatures, both human and nonhuman.[3]

Jewish environmental scholars and activists have long recognized the ecological implications and affordances of the Sabbath tradition. Among them is Jonathan Schorsch, professor of Jewish religious and intellectual history at the University of Potsdam and founding director of the Jewish Activism Summer School in Berlin. Jonathan is also the cofounder of the Green Sabbath Project, which reimagines the Sabbath as a "radical ritual" through a multi-faith perspective. This entails actively avoiding "environmental vandalism" so as to "digest anew the biblical prophets' warnings

---

[3] Wirzba, *This Sacred Life*, 148n40.

against the corruption of the rich and powerful, the oppression of the poor, and the self-centered pursuit of short-sighted pleasures, understanding how relevant such warnings are to the ecological devastation wrought by hypercapitalism."[4]

In 2020, as Jonathan observed in his blog post "Sabbath Gone Viral," a kind of "unexpected Sabbath" was forced upon us as a consequence of the COVID-19 pandemic.[5] This was not a happy event; nor, as I write now in late 2022, is it entirely over. Depriving children of each other's company and limiting their learning, leaving the elderly isolated and those at risk of domestic abuse more vulnerable, reducing livelihoods and taking lives—this accidental Sabbath was no cause for celebration. Yet the lockdowns that brought so much industry and travel to a standstill worldwide also gave Earth a temporary breather. More than an accidental Sabbath, this was a quasi-Jubilee. Carbon emissions went down and animals came out, reclaiming the countryside and venturing onto city streets. Disrupting our frenetic busyness, the coronavirus lockdowns afforded opportunities for reflection and reconnection. Freed from the daily commute, we spent more time in parks and gardens, in cooking and conversation. Recalling that others might be coping less well than ourselves, we organized neighborhood support networks. Most of us learned to listen to the science and to revalue our health workers. And, in many countries, we saw what governments could do, once they acknowledged that we were facing a crisis.

Less well recognized was that this crisis was a sentinel event: a warning sign that all was not well in our relations with one another—and especially with our fellow creatures. COVID-19, whatever its precise origins, is one of a series of novel pathogens—

---

[4] Green Sabbath Project "Our Mission and Vision," accessed March 30, 2023, www.greensabbathproject.net.

[5] Jonathan Schorsch, "Sabbath Gone Viral—Green Sabbath and 'Sheltering in Place,'" Green Sabbath Project blog post, March 25, 2020, www.greensabbathproject.net.

including SARS, MERS, and bovine encephalitis (mad cow disease)—that have emerged from the mistreatment of animals within food systems that increase the likelihood of viruses crossing and mutating between species.[6] It will not be the last and is unlikely to be the worst. At the same time, the excessive use of antibiotics that is required to limit disease outbreaks in intensive animal husbandry is producing antimicrobial-resistant bacteria, thereby posing a further threat to world health. The propensity of such pathogens to go global, moreover, arises from the exponential increase in international trade and travel that has hitherto been enabled by the climate-altering combustion of fossil fuels (the profits of which are, at the present moment, also bankrolling President Vladimir Putin's war of aggression in the Ukraine). Having so far failed to heed the warning issued by the coronavirus crisis, it appears that, with its waning, we have lurched back into business as usual.

If this accidental Sabbath was inadequate to the task of transformation, then initiatives such as the Green Sabbath Project, which also includes resources for Christian communities, are all the more important.[7] Reclaiming the Sabbath and proclaiming the jubilee, in a 24/7 world in which, as William Wordsworth foretold over two hundred years ago, "getting and spending, we lay waste our powers," demands dedication and imagination.[8] Let me, then,

---

[6] David Quammen, "Shaking the Viral Tree: An Interview with David Quammen," *Emergence Magazine*, March 25, 2020.

[7] Among the resources for further reading listed on the Green Sabbath website are several from a Christian perspective, including Walter Brueggemann, *Sabbath as Resistance: Saying No to the Culture of Now* (Louisville, KY: Westminster John Knox Press, 2014), and Norman Wirzba, *Living the Sabbath: Discovering the Rhythms of Rest and Delight, The Christian Practice of Everyday Life* (Grand Rapids: Brazos Press, 2006).

[8] William Wordsworth, "The World Is Too Much with Us," in *The Works of William Wordsworth: With an Introduction and Bibliography* (Ware, UK: Wordsworth Poetry Library, 1994), 259.

return to St. James's, Piccadilly, to see how one church in the center of London is doing just that.

At the heart of the Christian celebration of the Sabbath is a ritual that recalls the last supper before Christ's crucifixion, when Jesus, in blessing and sharing the bread and wine in accordance with Jewish practice on Shabbat eve, declared, shockingly, that these were to be his body and blood, "poured out for many for the forgiveness of sins" (Matt. 26:26–28). On October 4, 2020, the Sunday Eucharist service at St. James's was an extra-special occasion. It was the Feast of St. Francis, and, as such, the culmination of the Season of Creation. This season is now celebrated by many churches, and the designated theme for the season that year, as it happened, was Jubilee. Moreover, this was a Harvest Thanksgiving service, in which the church community was able to come together again after months in lockdown to celebrate their very own wheat harvest: a tangible, and indeed edible, outcome of a project that had started in the spring with the blessing and sowing of seeds in planter boxes in the church's courtyard, as well as in the gardens and window boxes of various members of the congregation. A small quantity of the resulting yield was harvested as "First Fruits" for a Lammas (i.e., Loaf Mass) service on August 2. Although the rest of the crop was harvested, threshed, and winnowed in September, continuing pandemic restrictions meant that it had not yet been ground and baked for the Harvest Eucharist, as planned. This service nonetheless afforded a fitting moment to reflect upon the multifaceted yield of this inspired initiative.

Titled "Daily Bread: Grain of Hope, Slice of Heaven," this project resulted from the creative collaboration of three members of St. James's "eco-church" group: Deborah Colvin, church warden and "sustainability champion," who has a background in agricultural science and experience of working in the wheat industry in Australia; poet Diane Pacitti; and artist Sara Mark. At that time,

as I have written elsewhere with respect to another of their proj-
ects, St. James's was one of only a handful of churches in England
to have been granted A Rocha's Gold Eco-Church Award.[9] To
receive this recognition, churches have to demonstrate outstanding
environmental achievement across five aspects of their operation:
incorporating care for the Earth within worship and teaching,
minimizing the carbon footprint and other environmental impacts
of buildings and operations, organizing and participating in
community and global environmental engagement, encouraging a
more sustainable lifestyle, and managing church land for conservation, recreation, and contemplation.

Managing churchyards for biodiversity is now part of the
Church of England's environment program, and it has been
promoted for some years by an interdenominational charity called
Caring for God's Acre. There are over twenty thousand churchyards in England and Wales, and as ever more land is given over to
roads, buildings, and ecologically damaging, high-chemical-input
intensive farming, these burial grounds can become mini wildlife
refuges for birds, insects, small mammals, reptiles, and (if there is
a pond or two) amphibians. Although Southwood Garden is no
longer a burial ground, the church participated in Caring for God's
Acre's Beautiful Burial Grounds citizen science project to chart the
importance of burial grounds across England and Wales for biodiversity. Theirs truly is an oasis of green in the concrete jungle of
Central London, burgeoning with biodiverse life, especially of the
plant and insect variety, and in the microbial-rich soil, to which
their gifted gardener Catherine Tidnam devotes especial care. Her
planting scheme ensures that there is food for an array of pollinators
all year round. There is an assortment of mini habitats—piles of

---

[9] Kate Rigby, "In Praise of Weeds: Sympoiesis at St. James's Piccadilly,"
Arcadia, Spring 2022, no. 1.

leaves, wood stacks, mini bogs—and the garden is frequented by a variety of birds, as well as several species of bat that have been spotted flying through. In 2017 the garden received a Green Flag Award, which has been re-awarded each year, and the church, which sits on a recognized "bee line" for pollinators, contributes to the Wild West End initiative to develop biodiversity corridors through the city.

To reconfigure such sacred spaces as places of welcome to more-than-human others is one very practical way in which to cultivate a wider sense of fellowship within the communion of creatures. At St. James's, this is also an inherently spiritual practice, fostered by a monthly eco-contemplative service held in Southwood Garden. Moreover, this practice stands alongside the welcome also extended by this church to fellow humans who are liable to face exclusion elsewhere: those experiencing homelessness, who are sheltered and fed; refugees and asylum seekers; people who identify as LGBTQI+; and those of all faiths and none.

This interlinkage of conservation and inclusion, ecospirituality and social justice is evident in the Daily Bread project, which also conjoins St. James's dual heritage of scientific enlightenment and Romantic ecopoetics. Designed by Christopher Wren, famed architect of London's St. Paul's Cathedral, and graced by a glorious Grinling Gibbons reredos that frames the altar with a riot of flora and fauna, this airy, neoclassical, light-filled church, consecrated in 1684, is in many ways an architectural embodiment of the natural theology of the emerging Age of Reason. The font, which sits atop a carving of the Tree of Life, is also attributed to Gibbons. As you enter the church, you learn that the Romantic "artist-poet-visionary" William Blake was baptized there on December 11, 1757. Embracing this dual legacy, including Blake's searing social critique, Daily Bread explores both the physiology and life cycle of wheat and the ten-thousand-year-old history of agrarian, and latterly industrial, society's relationship with this plant that provides a staple foodstuff worldwide, with chaff and straw contributing to animal fodder, bedding, and building material.

Alongside the community wheat-growing project that connected city dwellers with food production, re-embedding the liturgical year in the agricultural seasons that underpin its rhythms and imagery, the team created a series of beautiful posters, designed by Sara, integrating visual art, poetry, and science. As recounted in the penultimate poster that takes the guise of an "Agricultural Hexameron," the history they retrace begins early on in the Holocene era with the domestication of this abundantly grain-bearing grass in the Fertile Crescent. Continuing through the rise and fall of empires, entangled with processes of increasing commodification, industrialization, and manipulation, it culminates in the current era controversially dubbed the Anthropocene, the "human-made or human-marred age," as Diane puts it in her poem "The Seventh Day." We read of this era in Deborah's meditation on the Sixth Day:

> The post war "green revolution" powers up intensive agriculture and consequent destruction of ecosystems. The manipulation of genomes races ahead of our ethical and relational understanding. Chemical control of whole environments contaminates our ecosystems, committing us to live with intolerable levels of our own technological excrement. Extinction of species reaches 10,000 times historical rates.[10]

---

[10] Deborah Colvin, Sara Mark, and Diane Pacitti, "Hexameron," Daily Bread: Grain of Hope, Slice of Heaven, St. James's Piccadilly, 2020. All the posters are available to be downloaded from www.sjp.org.uk, which also includes a video of a talk I gave on this project at the University of Freiburg in November 2020.

Moreover, as we learn from the twenty-fifth poster, "Gleaning," the political ecology of global grain production and distribution is highly inequitable. While four wealthy multinationals control 90 percent of the grain trade and a privileged minority throw away and overeat the packaged produce, one billion people still go hungry every night. Wheaten monocultures constitute the largest single crop grown worldwide and are also shot through with vulnerabilities. Although there are now some twenty-five thousand wheat varieties, bred selectively for different conditions, thereby conferring a degree of resilience to this globally dominant starchy staple, wheat is so thoroughly domesticated that its reproduction is dependent upon human inputs and therefore stable social systems. And as global weather systems become destabilized, age-old hazards are exacerbated. The twenty-second poster, "Famine," points out how erratic weather had reduced the wheat harvest in the United Kingdom by 30 percent that year, while locust plagues decimated crops across a swath of Africa, the Middle East, and India.

Daily Bread was inspired by a similar, smaller-scale project that Sara had led as artist-in-residence at All Saints, Dulwich—but this one turned out very differently, not least on account of the pandemic. The very week after the wheat had been blessed and sown in planter boxes in the courtyard of the church, and in some twenty gardens and window boxes across London and beyond, the United Kingdom went into lockdown, leaving the ill-prepared rector, Lucy, to tend the crop on-site under instruction from Deborah. While the crop began to germinate in these separate locations, the project took on a new life online, both through the posters, which acquired a purely virtual existence, and a lively chat group, in which participants shared stories, photos, and videos. Although physically cut off from one another, the church community was held together in their shared care for their vulnerable crop. For those, such as Sara, who found themselves alone, the plants became companions, giving as well as receiving tenderness.[11] And despite all that they were learning about the manufacture of modern wheat varieties and the questionable political ecology of the wheat trade, when the seedlings came up at Easter, it still felt miraculous, recalling, as Diane puts it in her poem "Rising" (fifth poster), the incomprehensible:

> *love-force*
> *That burst out of the Cross, that broke free*
> *From the dragging weight*
>
> *Of the Roman death-machine.*

With the assistance of Deborah's microscope, beholding the "plumule," the first shoot of the embryo plant, they discovered anew what Blake had taught. In Diane's words in "St. James's: 11th December, 1757" (ninth poster):

> *We find a planet in each globular cell.*
> *We learn to see a world in a grain of sand.*

In their effort to tend their vulnerable crop, they encountered a host of other critters for whom, as Diane recalls in "From Mildew to Skylarks" (twentieth poster), it became "home, food, host and hiding-place": grain-pecking pigeons and trampling pets, beetles, spiders, aphids, mildew, and rust—all members of the multispecies community that convened around the crop, with the peskier ones successfully managed, more or less, without resort to toxic weaponry. And as the ambulance sirens that we hear in

---

[11] Sara Mark, follow-up interview with the Daily Bread team, December 5, 2022. The first interview with Sara, Deborah, and Diane took place on November 11, 2020. Quotes from both interviews, as well as from the posters, are shared with their kind permission.

Sara's moving video *Harvest* rang out across the city, while neighbors ventured onto their doorsteps to clap their thanks for those saving lives and comforting the dying in the struggling National Health System, the ripening grain brought a renewal of Eucharistic hope: a hope that is not hitched to belief in an immaterial beyond but directed toward the reign of love, justice, and peace on and with Earth that the faithful are called to co-create, here and now, in a world in which the divine, according to the quote from theologian Barbara Brown Taylor on the fourteenth poster, "Extraordinary," is "revealed in that singular, vast net of relationship that animates everything that is."

When it came to the Harvest Thanksgiving service, the altar was so bountifully bedecked with seasonal produce that Lucy had barely enough room to perform her priestly rites. Alongside the paten laden with loaves of freshly baked bread, in Sara's beautiful arrangement, an ear of wheat recalled its constituents, as did the bunch of grapes nestling up to the jug of wine. The Eastern Cross behind the altar was graced by a wreath woven of straw, and at its base—amid the pumpkins and potatoes, apples and pears, chestnuts and shells, dried flowers and autumn leaves—there were sheaves of wheat and baskets of chaff and straw. In this way, too, the Daily Bread initiative earthed the Eucharist, revealing in the wheaten wafer a glimpse of "the mysterious inter-connectivity of the universe, through a plant whose growth depends on sun-fire and water, air and soil which is an amalgam of minerals from unknown stars and recent deposits."[12]

Partaking bodily of the sacraments of bread and wine, fruit of the earth and work of human hands, we come to know that, though we are many and varied, we come together as participants in a vastly more-than-human, divinely graced, dynamically evolving mesh of interrelationships. Recalling at the same time the

---

[12] St. James's Piccadilly Eco-Church group, "Daily Bread Reflection," Harvest Thanksgiving Service pew sheet, October 4, 2020.

terrible woundedness of the world that we are called to share with our fellow earthlings, human and otherwise, we ready ourselves to respond, always and everywhere, to the lure of love: the self-giving love of resolute kindness and merciful justice, but also the full-blown love of creaturely delight and spellbound wonder. Of this love, Traherne wrote in his *Centuries of Meditations*, "Your enjoyment of the world is never right, till every morning you awake in Heaven; see yourself in your Father's Palace; and look upon the skies, the earth, and the air as Celestial Joys: having such a reverend esteem of all, as if you were among the Angels."[13] In this spirit, Lucy averred in her sermon,

> I truly believe that the only way we have a chance to change our behavior is by falling in love again with the natural world of which we are part. Ceasing to see it as a smorgasbord of plants and animals we can make use of and instead letting our enjoyment, our curiosity, our capacity for delight lead us down the path we see before us.[14]

To lay oneself open to thus falling in love is integral to the restoration of the Sabbath, not only as a one-day-a-week sacred rite, but as a foundational dimension of everyday life. This is how Diane puts it in her poem for the final Daily Bread poster, "Radical Sabbath":

> ***"Restoring Sabbath"***
>
> *a claiming*
> *of stars as our kin, a recognition*
> *of plants and animals as lost family;*

---

[13] Thomas Traherne, "The First Century 28," *Centuries of Meditations*, Christian Classics Ethereal Library, p. 10, www.ccel.org.

[14] Rev. Lucy Winkett, sermon, St. James's Church, Piccadilly, Harvest Thanksgiving Service 2020.

a cell of quiet resistance; a shedding
of the 'advanced' man's burden; a rushing out
to play with the astonished eyes of a child
seeing for the first time;

A sip of water
in our fevered work-desert, a spring
which gathers force to a river irrigating,
restoring the land;

certainly not a Sunday
turned to a duty-day, to an extension
of the week of sober work;

not a six-day making
of a once-and-for-all world
parcelled out
in creation-days, in evolution-stages:

all far too slow
for this seething, collapsing earth, this force field
of interactions

where rotted wheat-stems
feed their own seed-descendants; where hyphae
become the root into which they twist; where sea
travels high in clouds, and suddenly plummets
to earth-shock; and then the floppy drops
capillary through green, thin to ribbed blue
and petal into bells.

a world-being-made
as it dissolves itself, a co-creation
so busily at work that in response
Sabbath must turn to an act of attention
habitual as breath.

Yet sometimes we seem to stand helpless
as if at the helm of a huge tanker, watching
the seep of oil devour the threshing waves,
by the yard, by the mile, and we reach out our arms
to the disappearing blue, out toward bird
and fish and floating green, all being strangled
by glutinous death, and we are left stranded
in the middle of a black wasteland, trapped
inside our own machine.

If we are not to despair,
Sabbath must be marked by a radical sorrow
which impels us to act;

              it must become
an overturning of the brain-eye axis
set at lordly height;

an unleashing
of the imagination, peopling the air
with invisible spores, burrowing
through muck with earthworms, tracing the unseen
networks deep in the soil:

Sabbath must become the realisation
that the earth which we inhabit and destroy
inhabits each of us. The earth is a miracle
in plain sight.[15]

---

[15] With many thanks to Diane for permission to quote this poem in full.

Beginning Anew, Entering the Kindom

On this last day, then, we are returned once more, and every day, to the beginning of it all. We are returned to that big "one day" that held them all, when, with the coming of first light, we beheld creation forever in-the-making and were felled by awe at that primal revelation, paired, at least for we mere mortals, always with the darkness of unknowing and, sometimes also, of despair.

Contemplating the following days of creation from the vantage of our present perilous times, we have been moved to lament the desecration, destruction, and diminishment of the sanctity, diversity, and plenitude of the earth, sea, and sky as beheld by previous commentators on the hexameron from late antiquity to the seventeenth century.

Moving from contemplation through lamentation, we come now, even now, at this late hour, in this crucial moment for the future of our "Sister Mother Earth," and all our kindred creatures, to celebrate with them the miraculous gift of life, and to commit ourselves to its continued unfolding, in faith that creation, in some unfathomable way, is at once primordially good and ultimately pitched toward love incarnate.

For, when Elohim fell silent—awe-struck, perhaps, and clearly pleased with the multitude of creatures who had come forth—they themselves took up the tale.

For far too long, the people of the Book have attended only to the human version, and only to some tellers, a privileged few at that. Unmindful of how their own lives were being spoken into existence by a multitude of unsung others, they have put themselves at risk and extinguished many other kinds.

So, quiet down and listen up, and you, too, might hear what they are saying still, among them trillions not of your kind. Tune in to their lay, and you might learn to augment rather than cut short the tale, lending your voice in newfound harmonious strains to the ancient, endangered, yet enduring chorus of creation.

Holy One,
give us this day and every day

with Brother Sun
and Sister Moon and Stars and Brother Wind
and Sister Water, Brother Fire
and Sister Mother Earth

our daily bread . . .

Your Kindom come,

we pray,

on this good Earth
in which we glimpse
Your Heaven

Index

Abelard, Peter, 30, 57, 60
  on change in creation, 16–17
  on *imago dei* in men, 153
  Islamic science, influenced by, 13
  luminaries, speculating on, 91
  on natural causes *vs.* future
    contingencies, 90
Adani Group, 40, 45, 48
Aelfric, 153
aerial realm, 9, 113, 119
  aerial waters, 30–31, 33
  ecological niche of, 117–18
  flying insects in, 114, 122
  Gondwana, evolution from,
    121–22
  See also wetlands
air pollution, 97–99, 105
Alofa, Pelenise, 41–42
Alter, Robert, 7, 16, 28, 115, 152
Amazonia encyclical, 77
Amazon rain forest
  Brazilian portion of, 71–73,
    75–76
  burning of the forest, 54–55,
    73
  Church in the Amazon, 81–82
  First Peoples of Amazonia,
    73–75, 77, 80, 83
  REPAM efforts in, 77–80
Ambrose, 58, 67, 176
  on astrological fatalism, 90

fleshiness, distaste for, 153–54
honeybees, praise for, 114–15
land animals, on their capacities,
  150
migratory animals, on their
  intelligence, 118
the seas, on the domain of, 30,
  57, 115–16
Anastasios of Sinai, 9, 15, 154
Andreopoulos, Andreas, 172
animals
  animal advocacy, 167–74
  animal cruelty, 164, 172
  animal slaughter restrictions,
    170–71
  biblical narrative as classifying,
    148–49
  classical natural historians on,
    149–50
  humans, distinguishing from,
    151–55, 158–59
  kinship of saints with, 147–48,
    174
  pet ownership, 146, 167, 168
  shared animality, 160–61,
    166, 174
  on the sixth day, 142, 144–46,
    162
Anthony of Sourozh, 171
anthropic telos, 152, 177
Anthropocene era, 35, 186